LAURA ASHLEY
COMPLETE GUIDE TO
HOME DECORATING

LAURA ASHLEY
COMPLETE GUIDE TO
HOME DECORATING

Foreword by NICK ASHLEY

DEBORAH EVANS

CAROLYN CHAPMAN
LINDA GRAY
CELIA RUFEY

Edited by CHARYN JONES

Weidenfeld & Nicolson, London

CONTENTS

GENERAL EDITOR
Charyn Jones

CONTRIBUTORS
Deborah Evans
Carolyn Chapman
Linda Gray
Celia Rufey

ART DIRECTION AND DESIGN
Bob Gordon

COLOUR ILLUSTRATIONS
Tig Sutton

PICTURE RESEARCH
Shona Wood

Phototypeset by Keyspools Ltd,
Golborne, Lancashire
Colour separations by Newsele Litho Ltd
Printed in Italy by Printers Srl, Trento
Bound in Italy by L.E.G.O., Vicenza

SOFT FURNISHINGS 127

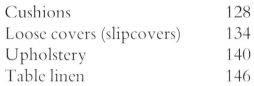

BEDS & BEDLINEN 151

ACCESSORIES 175

FOREWORD BY NICK ASHLEY

We are living in an age of revived interest in decorating the home. During the eighteen years that Laura Ashley has been producing fabrics and wallpaper there has never been so much interest. As a consequence of this huge demand the whole industry has responded and blossomed, there are more books and magazines on the subject, a greater choice of furnishings, and more specialists to help obtain that professional finish.

What we have aimed to do with this book is to provide you with a framework to which your own ideas can be added. There is usually some sort of restriction attached to decorating a room; whether this is structural or financial, it should be looked at in a very positive way, as a disadvantage can often turn out to be an advantage. When my family first moved into a little farmhouse in Wales, we spent so much money buying slates for the roof that the curtains had to be made single-width so that they were completely ungathered when closed. The effect they created was actually much nicer than full curtains as the windows were very small and the walls surrounding them were of rough stone.

Another way to plan your decoration is to concentrate all your efforts on one area at a time rather than 'spreading it thin' across the whole home. We used this plan on our house in France, which we wanted to restore to the eighteenth-century style with very opulent curtains and furniture. There was no way that we could have restored the whole house at one time, so the first room to be decorated was the large kitchen in the *commun*, complete with dining table, sofas and a log fire. Meanwhile, the rest of the rooms on the ground floor were furnished one by one, then the first floor and finally (but never quite) the top floor. The whole process took about five years but we achieved an end result that could not have been done in one go. So be patient and remember, 'where there's a will there's a way'. (We all used to cram into the kitchen anyway!)

Laura Ashley has built up a reputation around the 'Period Look' for interiors. This is not to be confused with a 'Perfect Period Restoration'; rather we prefer to recreate the 'spirit of the age'. For example, if we were to revive a pure Regency room the cost of the furniture would be prohibitive – if it could be found in the first place. So we would just use the Regency theme: the Prince Regent believed in the use of bold dramatic schemes using larger-than-life scale, so we could interpret that in a humble room by bold use of colour and fewer pieces of furniture along with brave applications such as brightly coloured lining on the curtains.

You will notice throughout this book how we have used a particular period as an influence for a room while maintaining a contemporary furniture layout and adding useful modern innovations such as electricity and central heating! After all, a room that looks like a million dollars is worth nothing if it is not comfortable.

Be bold.

Nick Ashley.

STRUCTURE & STYLE

UNDERSTANDING YOUR *HOME*

Living spaces today are more diverse than ever, ranging from large houses subdivided into apartments to industrial structures and warehouses, ecclesiastical and farm buildings, all of which are being requisitioned as exciting environments in which to live. The possibilities now open to the home decorator are limitless, but whatever your personal environment, it should complement your particular lifestyle. Take into consideration at the outset any special needs and the activities that each room will have to accommodate. Does the layout work or could it be better organized? This may be a simple matter of re-arranging the furniture, or a more substantial structural alteration such as lowering a ceiling, closing off unnecessary doorways, opening up two small rooms into one, or converting loft space into an extra room. Decide which rooms should be in close proximity – a kitchen and dining room, for example – and which rooms should be kept apart, such as a children's room and a study.

Apart from answering your own needs, a room should be decorated sympathetically to reveal its true character, with an interior that complements the exterior of the house. Assess the potential of a room before you start planning a decorative scheme: are there special features, such as architectural details, which might be highlighted, or problem areas like radiators which need to be disguised? Are the size and proportions of a room aesthetically pleasing? Is it flooded with natural light or does it have a darker aspect? Having established the character of a home and what changes need to be made, you can now start to look at the solutions to the problems.

The framework

Windows, doors, moldings and fireplaces are all a part of the architectural framework of a room and when in proportion with each other, and with the walls, they help to create a sense of order and balance. Shallow skirting looks mean with high

LEFT *A bedroom lacking in architectural detail has been given a simple treatment, introducing features in the form of cupboards with fine moldings and a symmetrical arrangement of pictures and accessories. Subtle stencilling below the cornice and fabric ties behind the pictures are less intrusive than elaborate panels or friezes and this minimal scheme enhances what space there is in a small room.*

RIGHT *A compact, split-level studio has realized maximum potential from one large room with a high ceiling. A bedroom has been constructed on a platform above the dining area, thus releasing space on the ground floor. The end wall is made up of the same open bannisters as those used for the new stairway, thus avoiding the intrusive look of a solid partition and consequent loss of light.*

LEFT *This nineteenth-century warehouse, recently converted into open-plan apartments, has a decidedly modern appearance with its emphasis on the structural framework. Yet the eclectic mix of furnishings gives it a comfortable air – large armchairs in a Victorian-style floral chintz, generous full-length curtains and a combination of ancient and modern furniture and accessories. Rugs help to define different areas of activity.*

ceilings, which may look all the higher in the absence of a deep cornice or picture rail. An open-tread staircase or picture window looks out of place in a home with intricate cornices and ceiling centres. Conversely, elaborate panelling and a picture rail are inappropriate in a cottage where a plain skirting and colourwashed wainscot with a plate rail will be more in keeping with its rustic idiom. In a modern apartment, ornate details are equally incompatible; keep to clean, classical lines and wide expanses of sheet glass or maximize the architectural bones of a room by emphasizing natural materials such as brickwork and wood.

Change of use

There is no rule which says that the living room should be downstairs or beneath the bedroom. Indeed, in a tall terraced house the first-floor rooms are often brighter and have a better view than those on the ground floor. If ground-floor rooms are gloomy, keep them for evening occupation – as a study or dining room, perhaps – or for use as a guest bedroom, which will not be in constant use (ground-floor rooms are particularly beneficial where visitors are likely to be elderly).

LEFT *Opening up one small room into another is a relatively easy way of increasing a sense of space and also light. This curved arch links a living room to a smaller dining room; extending the decorative scheme through both rooms creates unity.*

RIGHT *Conservatory-style rooms can be built on to the exterior of a house to provide extra space with a garden atmosphere. The brickwork has been disguised with white paint and hung with paintings and prints. The glass roof is shaded by expanses of cream muslin to give privacy at night and shade by day.*

BELOW LEFT *Adjoining rooms provide the potential for one large living area. But this may not always be required. A pale yellow sitting room is separated from its adjacent room by a folding screen, thus providing a more comfortable space for everyday use. Where a partition would slice a window, or a delicate molding, in two, screens provide a flexible alternative.*

FAR LEFT *The structure of this single storey extension is evident in the framework of original beams, white-painted brickwork and warm brick floor. White woodwork and natural linen upholstery, with simple shutters, emphasize the structural elements. The furniture is focused on the fireplace, leaving a clear route through to adjacent rooms.*

Kitchens and bathrooms often require restructuring. A small scullery can be amalgamated with a small kitchen to create a kitchen/dining area, while a box or dressing room can be opened up to enlarge a tiny bathroom. But think carefully before you tamper with the original layout of a house. It may seem a good idea to knock two rooms into one to provide more light and space but remember that a heavy joist will almost inevitably be needed to support the ceiling, and as front rooms were often built to a different scale and style to those at the back, you may be left with a room that has different ceiling heights, or two disparate styles. If there are two fireplaces, you will either have two focal points or, should you remove one, a fireplace at the extreme end of the room.

Alternatively, in open-plan homes you may want to make sub-divisions that will create more personal spaces, or that relate to particular functions. Perhaps an extension is the answer to your problems rather than structural alterations. This needs sympathetic handling, using materials appropriate to the overall style and design of the house and should not overwhelm the original layout.

On the following 12 pages, there are many examples of ways to restore, renovate and create structural and architectural details in the home. In some cases, you may decide to disguise them and reduce their significance in the decorative scheme of things. In other cases, the fireplace, window or staircase, for example, might become a focal point.

*C*EILINGS are all too often disregarded and yet they are one of the largest surfaces in a room and therefore cannot be ignored. There are many ways to reduce or increase their height visually – either structurally or by careful choice of colour, for example. Many ceilings have a wealth of decorative detail in the cornice and ceiling roses, or in the rich texture of exposed ancient beams.

LEFT *A series of wooden moldings, picked out in striking colours, emphasizes in truly eye-catching fashion the contours of a room. Further definition is given by the border beneath, based on an Owen Jones motif.*

ABOVE *The original beam in this kitchen has been painted white to reduce the effect of the low ceiling height. The beam over the fireplace however, has been left unpainted in keeping with the rustic idiom of the room.*

RIGHT *A magnificent deep cornice was often a standard feature in houses in the past. This molded plasterwork cornice extends down to the picture rail in its detail. In the absence of the original cornice, try to maintain the dimensions of the room in correct proportion with a frieze or wallpaper border.*

RIGHT *The traditionally cosy, comfortable feeling of the garret has been emphasized with an extensive use of borders and stencilled patterns. The designs have been planned to centre on the sloping ceilings on either side of the dormer window. The borders frame each area neatly.*

LEFT *The concave dome in this ceiling houses a porthole-shaped roof light. The rest of the ceiling has been lowered to bring a more intimate feel to a dining room and study. The book-lined wall and vibrant floor carpet and chair covers draw the eye to the hearth.*

ABOVE *This elaborate cornice of vine leaves is accentuated by a band of stylized ornament on the ceiling, intended to make the cornice look wider. Traditionally, these two elements are painted to match. Attention is drawn to the ceiling with a fabric sock for the chandelier.*

*W*INDOWS let in light and are usually a prominent focal point in any room. They are also seen from the outside and so, whether covered with fabric or not, they are just as important to the exterior design of a house as the interior.

ABOVE *The traditional shutters are still in place at this window. They fold back into the alcove during the day and shut out the darkness at night. The Roman blind affords privacy and screens the sunlight.*

RIGHT *Attic and dormer windows are usually a challenging shape for the home decorator. Privacy may not be a problem at the top of a house as in this attic bathroom, but in cold weather, some form of insulation may be necessary. The hexagonal shape of this deep recess has been accentuated by a wallpaper border and the fixed curtains are held back at the sides with tie-backs.*

ABOVE *Bathrooms need light but they should also be private places. This is a clever way of achieving both. Stained glass, once an ecclesiastical domain, has since the last century been extended to ordinary houses in door panels and windows such as this bobbled, Art Nouveau design.*

LEFT *Internal windows were originally designed to allow light to penetrate basement rooms. This window adorns a pretty corner of what is still the kitchen. The view through it shows the living room, but for the purposes of privacy, curtains have been hung to close off the scene when pots and pans are inappropriate.*

ABOVE *Windows don't have to have curtains. These louvred shutters are the ideal solution, particularly in tropical climates where the sunlight has to be screened whilst allowing air to circulate.*

LEFT *The symmetry of the windows is a large part of the success of this room, overlooking rolling countryside. Rather than hide them, the draped curtain and pelmet (valance) frame the windows and do not destroy the look of the elegant sashes on either side of the glazed doors with the fanlight above.*

*W*OODEN PANELLING AND ARCHITRAVES are an integral part of some period homes. Today, if plasterwork is uneven or you prefer the panelled warmth of a wood wall, tongue and groove boards can be used to cover a ceiling, the wall below the dado rail or the entire room. When restoring or adding architraves, remember to take into consideration the dimensions of the room. Unadorned walls look appropriate and suitably stark in modern open-plan rooms, but try to replace missing architraves and panels in older houses with the correct patterns.

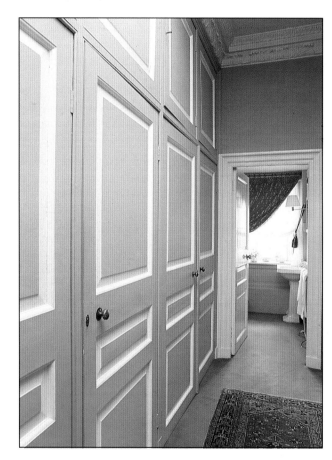

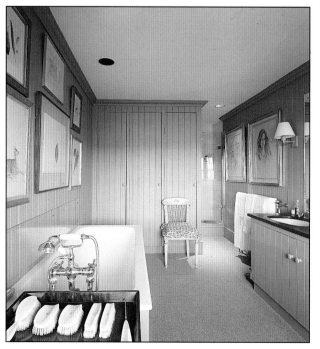

ABOVE *A decorative framework in beech outlines the structural elements of the partition walls in this wood-framed room. 'Panels' of wallpaper create the same effect as wood with less expense – a tonal print lends a warmer look than plain paint.*

ABOVE *This run of cupboards along a landing has been matched to the doors of the adjacent room by the detail in the molding* and panels. *The panelling becomes even more of a feature on the cupboard doors when it is picked out in contrasting colours.*

LEFT *Tongue and groove panelling is a useful device for covering poorly plastered walls, and in this bathroom it has been designed to match the doors of built-in cupboards.*

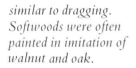

ABOVE *This Victorian panelled door has been painted with a wood grain effect, using a technique* similar to dragging. *Softwoods were often painted in imitation of walnut and oak.*

LEFT *The panelled corner wall and window recesses in this country bedroom, tucked in under a lofty gable end, have been painted a flat white to contrast with the coloured walls. The high panelled ceiling is washed with thinned white paint which lets the wood grain show through and adds to the light, airy atmosphere.*

BELOW *Unusually wide boards, fitted horizontally, have been stained and polished to match the cupboards that have been custom-built for this small kitchen. The cleaned bricks and glazed tiles are in keeping with the rustic look.*

ABOVE *A panelled dado is a practical choice for a nursery. Painted with an oil-based paint, it will* withstand the onslaught of *sticky fingers, dolls' prams, tricycles and would-be mural artists.*

FIREPLACES have once again become the focus of attention in period homes and modern apartments alike with the use of gas-fired imitation coal fires.

ABOVE LEFT *The two main elements of most eighteenth- and nineteenth-century fireplaces are the surround, usually of wood, marble or cast-iron, and the insert with its cast-iron grate or firebasket. To create a focal point this rustic wooden surround has been combined with a painted iron insert. There is no hearth, and the fireplace is not intended to be functional.*

LEFT *Inside an extravagant carved and gilded continental frame, hand-painted Delft tiles imitate original designs, an idea that can be added to as time allows.*

LEFT *A natural stone hearth and chimney breast, with built in wood store, would originally have been the hub of family life. The fire itself is set on a raised platform, and a kettle and spit are reminders of the earlier function of the hearth as the place where all the cooking was done.*

RIGHT *This cast-iron Art Nouveau-style fireplace has been sand blasted and polished up into sparkling condition. The tiled surround is a common feature of many small Victorian fireplaces. The alcoves to either side of the chimney breast are fitted with display shelves for collections of paintings, ceramics and silver.*

LEFT *A simple, symmetrical arrangement of accessories enhances the clean, classical lines of this Georgian marble fire surround. The striped wallpaper reflects the vertical fluting of the columns, and the urn echoes the classical theme.*

RIGHT *A completely mirrored wall surrounds the fireplace in this vibrant dining room. The fireplace is the focal point, its presence doubled by its mirror image and given added emphasis by the painting hung above it. The mantelpiece is used to display flowers and glass candle holders.*

STAIRCASES denote entrances and exits and by their very nature are dramatic, whether leading to a grand hall and reception room or to a tiny passageway to a cellar or attic. Although there are traditional ways of decorating staircases, you need not feel limited when planning what to do with them. Stencilling the treads of wooden stairs, using highly polished brass rods to hold the carpet in place, painting the wooden spindles with a paint effect and faking a dado rail to give a symmetry to the staircase: decorative devices offer endless possibilities.

ABOVE *The sweep of this elegant, cantilevered staircase has been skilfully matched by the curving dado rail along the facing wall. Stairwells often need added artificial light. Here, picture lights add to the natural light source above.*

RIGHT *This open stairway in a Spanish villa with its curved, wrought-iron balustrade, is flanked by a handrail of thick tasselled rope, knotted through bronze rings decorated with lions' masques.*

ABOVE *The practical coconut matting on the stairs is perfectly in keeping with this heavy carved oak staircase, tiled floor and whitewashed walls. A collection of wicker baskets, some filled with dried flowers, are used as decorative accessories.*

RIGHT *A colour scheme in shades of white reflects the maximum amount of light down this narrow staircase. The subtle grey tones of the trompe l'oeil dado rail and skirting detail lend an extra elegance. A stairwell links rooms, so colour schemes must be complementary.*

FAR RIGHT *The stairs running down from this landing are wide enough to accommodate extra shelving for the overspill from the kitchen below. The upward flight, with a green 'runner' carpet fitted with brass stair rods, anticipates the elegance of the reception rooms above.*

LEFT *The idea of an en suite bathroom takes on a new dimension when the two rooms are connected by a spiral staircase. This example is particularly slim and space saving, but would not be a practical link between family living spaces.*

ABOVE *The staircase of this American Federal-style house with its New World simplicity is perfectly in keeping. Decoration is minimal, almost naive, with wooden spindles painted white, and treads of unstained, natural wood.*

STORAGE is a problem every home decorator has to consider. Whether you like to display your clutter or hide it away, there is no disguising the fact that today we all have more household items and personal possessions than our predecessors. Displaying cherished possessions and beautiful objects is a clever way of accessorizing a room, but invariably there is a vast amount of material that has to be stored out of sight.

ABOVE *In a bathroom created from a larger room, cupboards made from seasoned softwood provide ample storage for towels* *and toiletries along one wall. The space at the end of the cupboard has been designed as a convenient recess for a shower.*

ABOVE *Open shelves in this bright country kitchen are both practical and decorative, topped by a solid pine work surface. The plate shelf above is reminiscent of the interiors of Carl Larsson. The collection of bread boards forms an attractive frieze while cooking utensils and herbs hang from butcher's hooks below.*

LEFT *Wardrobes are essential in every home. Custom-built, they make maximum use of space, but need not be bland. Glass doors, lined with gathered, cased curtains, give a soft look to these cupboards.*

LEFT *Corners are often wasted spaces but a simple corner cupboard like this can provide storage without encroaching on the room.*

RIGHT *The recess of a blocked-up doorway provides display and storage space, with open shelves and a cupboard below. The architrave on the original door surround has been retained as a frame to this arrangement. Adapt the idea for alcoves beside a fireplace.*

LEFT *In a small bathroom, make maximum use of space by setting the basin over a custom-built storage unit. The cream painted doors match the bath panel, and the elements of the room are further linked by the marble splashback.*

ABOVE *The whole wall at the end of this study becomes an elegant storage unit for books. The arched top and false panels turn the bookcase into an architectural feature and provide space for recessed spotlights.*

ORGANIZING SPACE

Re-arranging the layout of a room is a good way of exploring its possibilities. A large-scale plan drawing on graph paper with scaled cut-outs to represent the furniture shows immediately if the door will open fully when the sofa is against a certain wall, or whether a cabinet will mask an electrical socket. Keep a colour board with your plan as a record of samples of furnishings you have or intend to buy. Take these with you when you shop so that you can establish whether a piece of furniture will fit or whether a certain fabric is right for your room.

The way furniture is used and arranged today differs dramatically from what was customary two or three hundred years ago. But whilst the twentieth century has invented its own designs, such as the coffee table and the kitchen unit, it can also draw on a wealth of traditional styles. Adaptations of many furniture and fabric designs of the past are now being re-created or re-interpreted for today's market. Furnishings from any one of these periods will evoke a very distinctive style. So, too, will contemporary designs with their sinuous lines fashioned in wrought-iron and sleek glass that play off one texture or medium against another.

Although furniture arrangement is now fairly informal (a notable exception is the dining room), convention still dictates that most of the furniture is placed against the walls, even when rooms are large. Yet seating can make a strong impact when placed centrally in a room, with an occasional table decorated with one or two favourite possessions to form a focal point. More usual focal points include the fireplace, which can be filled with green plants or flowers out of season; paintings grouped on a wall; or the window, especially if this has a striking view. Decorative pieces of furniture also make effective features and have a practical use too. A chest placed between facing sofas or at the foot of a bed can serve as an occasional table and storage unit while a chaise longue provides extra seating as well as looking

decorative. Freestanding wardrobes, perhaps handpainted with stencils or given a paint finish, can make a decorative contribution to a bed-room as well as storing clothes, and a console table can double as a serving table in a dining room.

Storage
Modern families have more possessions than most homes in the past and this wealth may mean that existing storage is inadequate. Many period homes have alcoves and recesses which can be converted to take shelves or cupboards. Decorative pieces, china and books, for example, can be displayed effectively on open shelves or in cabinets built each side of a chimneypiece.

BELOW The space under these stairs has been drawn into use by careful positioning of a sofa, occasional chairs and storage boxes which double as a table. In a smaller home, consider opening up the cupboard under the stairs to make room for a hall table and telephone, or reorganize cupboard doors to provide better access for storage.

Supplement them with freestanding furniture in the form of tall bookcases, corner cupboards or glass-fronted cabinets for china, and tallboys or chests on chests for linen – all traditional designs that are equally elegant and practical today. Dressers can be used for storage and display and provide a useful work surface while chests will hide blankets, toys or books and newspapers from view. Clothing can be hung in pine or mahogany wardrobes, or in cupboards fitted along the wall of a bedroom. Cull storage space from a corner of a landing, attic or hall and paint the shelves to blend with the walls.

Preserve that traditional delight, the walk-in larder, which will take all your provisions and often a fridge or freezer too. Seek out space beneath the stairs, in cellars and under the eaves of the house for long-term storage needs.

BELOW *A solidly built sideboard provides ample storage for china while more attractive dining room items are displayed on open shelves nearby. Window seats, given a hinged lid, can also store items not in constant use.*

RIGHT *A bed can be an unwelcome intrusion in a studio room, or in a study which has to double as a guest bedroom. This arrangement, which has its origins in history when beds were enclosed for warmth and privacy, screens the bed and provides welcome extra storage space in cupboards and drawers beneath the raised platform.*

RIGHT *In a large bedroom, you can make extravagant use of space with a casual chaise longue and occasional table. An attractively painted free-standing wardrobe accommodates clothes without dominating the room, and the top of the cupboard has been put to good use with a pair of old-fashioned suitcases, which can be used to store away clothes which are out of season.*

LEFT *The space relinquished by unused fireplaces can be put to good use. In this kitchen, the hob has been installed in place of the original fireplace. It may be necessary to have units custom-built to take full advantage of awkward spaces.*

WAYS TO DISGUISE

Not all home comforts are pleasing to the eye, so decide what can be discreetly hidden and choose good contemporary designs for pieces which cannot. Radiators, for example, can be painted to match the walls (try a sponged or dragged finish), or boxed in behind mesh, sheet cane, or fretwork panels. Classic designs work well in most settings: Raeburn and Aga cookers, deep Belfast and London china sinks, bath tubs with Edwardian-style taps and shower cradles all look attractive in the traditional home. What should be avoided is the temptation to put modern conveniences in period dress.

Colour

Colour can play an important part in disguising or enhancing the proportions of a room. You can make the room feel spacious with pale, cool colours, or draw the surfaces inwards with warmer tones and darker colours. Look at the proportions of a room. High ceilings may make the room appear cavernous so dark colours or patterned finishes will reduce that feeling and help the room feel and look cosier.

Relieve the claustrophic effects of low-ceilinged cottages and modern houses with pale colours on the ceilings. Paint effects applied to doors and

BELOW Murals can provide the perfect disguise for a dreary perspective, poor plaster on the walls or sparse furnishings. This fanciful parkland setting creates a magical backdrop for a dining room – an immediate conversation point.

ABOVE A blocked-up doorway has been turned into an open display area with shelves that house a fine collection of china.

The dado rail continues across the opening, and a trellis screens the radiator behind.

windows, for example, help to diminish their importance so they are not so noticeable. Other visual colour techniques are vertical stripes to give the impression of height, and dominant all-over patterns to unify a large space by making the walls appear to advance.

Picture rails and dado rails, dividing the room into bands of colour can also help to reduce the apparent height of a room, but avoid too many divisions if ceilings are low.

On reflection

Mirrors are invaluable because they increase both light and space and add to the decoration of a room – as well as serving as a looking glass. Mirror can be fitted behind shelves to increase the impact of plants or ornaments. Placed next to a window, in traditional pier-glass style, it will increase the availability of light, while an overmantel mirror balances and increases the impact of a fireplace.

LEFT *Stretch space with inventive use of mirrors. The far wall of this dressing room, glimpsed from the adjoining bedroom, is opened up by placing a large sheet of plain mirror behind the wash basin, which also reflects light into this small space. A feeling of unity is created by linking the decorative scheme from one room to the other with blue walls echoed in curtain fabric.*

LIGHTING

The aspect of a room regulates more than the quality of the light. It also determines when the room will be sunniest and this may help to decide its function. Dual aspect rooms which face north–south or east–west have the advantage of receiving light throughout the day but most homes are designed with rooms which face one way. In the northern hemisphere an east-facing room may make an undesirable bedroom for all except early risers but could become a delightful breakfast room which will be filled with sunshine at the start of the day. It may be less suitable for a sitting room where you relax in the evenings unless it is used by the family throughout the day. A west or south-westerly aspect is ideal here. A south-facing room will make a better living room than a kitchen, screened with a protective awning to prevent it becoming uncomfortably hot, while north-facing rooms receive a cold, clear light which artists and many students prefer. Geography is important too. Towards the tropics the fierce sun may dictate a cool or dark colour scheme, while in temperate countries pale, light-reflecting colours will be a more popular choice.

Artificial light

Lighting in the home must do more than dispel the darkness. It should highlight the features of a room, give general background illumination or direct light for working, or create atmosphere with soft pools of light. Candlelight for special occasions creates a sense of theatre all its own, but for everyday use most settings need at least two types of lighting, and busy rooms, such as family living rooms, require all four.

Bright ideas

Decorative light fittings include chandeliers and candelabra, pendant lights and ceiling fittings, wall lights and table lamps. All of these are meant to be seen and their style is as important as the light they produce. In comparison, other types of lights, such as recessed downlighters, are built-in

and their purpose is mainly functional.

Most homes benefit from a combination of functional and decorative lights, relying on the former to set the scene and the latter to add interest. In a living room, recessed ceiling lights or unobtrusive wall lights will give general lighting, supplemented by spotlights or uplighters for emphasis and individual downlights for atmosphere. Table lamps or pendant shades can be added to create further pools of low light while a traditional ceiling fitting complements an elaborate ceiling centre. Picture lights will cast a soft glow over paintings and spotlights can focus on other possessions but their direct glare creates too strong a contrast with the darkness to depend on for general lighting. Recessed downlights can be used successfully to give general light in a kitchen together with wall or ceiling spotlights or strip lights, shaded by baffles and mounted

RIGHT *In hot climates, natural light has to be filtered to create a cool sitting area, particularly in the afternoon when the sun is lower in the sky. On this verandah, louvred blinds screen strong light by day.*

LEFT *A modern, matt black counterbalanced light can be angled to provide task lighting for study work. The halogen bulb casts a strong, white light which brings out the true colours of the crisp grey and white décor.*

beneath high cupboards, to provide efficient working light without glare. Combine this with softer mood lighting if the kitchen doubles as a dining room.

Halls and landings should be well-lit for safety, illuminating stairways and changes of level, so use wall lights or recessed downlighters. Bedrooms can be equipped with pendant or wall lights for soft background lighting supplemented by bedside lamps and concealed strip lighting at a dressing table—mirrors should be flanked by lights which illuminate your face but not the glass. Study bedrooms need more directional light. Only in the dining room is the conventional central pendant an appropriate choice, hanging low over the table (add a rise-and-fall attachment to raise it after the meal) and partnered by recessed or wall lights.

Warm and cool

Conventional tungsten filament bulbs have a warmth which flatters most homes and accentuates tones of pink, peach and yellow. Silvered tungsten bulbs are used in spotlights where they reflect the light and cast a wide or narrow beam, depending on where they are sited. Fluorescent fittings emit a cool blue light which may be too harsh for the home, so they are often tinted warm white for domestic use. Brightest of all is the strong white light of halogen tungsten lamps which require special fittings. Often used for directional lights, these are especially effective when used to bounce light on to a wall or ceiling which returns it to the room as soft, indirect light – but for obvious reasons, these should only be fitted where the plaster is in good repair.

ABOVE *Tiers of candles on the display cabinet add their flickering light to the array of candles grouped on the table – a theatrical setting for a formal dinner party.*

RIGHT *A pair of symmetrically positioned table lamps provide a focal point on this console table. Warm light from the tungsten bulbs illuminates ornaments and pictures.*

RIGHT *Unobtrusive, recessed downlighters throw gentle background light from a high ceiling, while table lights with soft pleated fabric shades form bright pools of light in the corners of the room. Dark lacquer shades, reflecting light downwards, provide directional lighting for specific activities.*

THE DECORATOR'S PALETTE

Colour, pattern and texture are the principle ingredients of any decorative scheme. Colour is the decorator's most powerful ally. Its chameleon quality plays tricks with proportion and perspective, moderates warmth and light and acts, quite literally, on our hearts and minds: red may raise the blood pressure while blue will cool you down. Texture adds a subtle tactile quality, playing off light against shade in a variety of media from paint to fabric, while character and vitality can be created through use of pattern – either as a dramatic focal point or as a muted backdrop. These three components, used in harmony with one another, are the touchstones that will bring a room to life.

Colour and mood

Use colour to invoke the mood you wish a room to convey. Understated tints of ivory, taupe and pale jade partnered with grey-blue tones or soft pink and gold create an elegant, country-house interior where the faded colours complement the patina of antique furniture. Cottage-garden colours of crimson, jade and forget-me-not blue, offset by white, have a vivacity which brightens up a dark kitchen or bedroom. For a more delicate effect, choose sweet pea tints of rose and lilac. Dark, rich shades of burgundy and midnight blue create a formal setting. Entwined with silver or gold the effect is one of magnificence: add sand or forest green for a more intimate appeal.

RIGHT *This formal, Victorian bedroom has a dramatically dark colour scheme in keeping with the period. Deep pink is counterbalanced with midnight blue accessories and furnishings. Splashes of white add a crisp finish to the scheme.*

BELOW *Yellow walls and sapphire blue furnishings bring light and a cheerful aspect to this small morning room whatever the weather.*

ABOVE *When choosing furnishing fabrics, the style of the furniture itself can help with the decision. Bold, strong patterns in glowing colours of red, blue and gold recall the richness of tapestry and lend a quiet grandeur to the solid oak chair.*

Sources of inspiration

The natural forces of fire, sky and sun are represented by the primary colours of red, blue and yellow from which all others are formed. Landscapes inspire more subtle schemes from the greys and blues of a heather-clad moor to the brilliant blues and yellows of Van Gogh's Provence. Paintings can be a rich source of inspiration: look at the rich crimson, blue and gold of the Renaissance, the shadowy blue-grey tones of Dutch domestic interiors and the exuberant splashes of colour which distinguish the Impressionists. The styles of the last century, preserved in period homes or re-interpreted in opera and theatre sets, give an insight into the traditional use of colour. The greens and terracottas of Federal America, the dusty blues of Gustavian Sweden and the mahogany browns and plums of Victorian England can supply a range of colour scheme ideas for today's interiors.

Using colour

As fashions change, the colours which are deemed acceptable alter, but the way colour is used remains constant. All schemes fall into one of three main types. Rooms decorated in tones of a single colour are chic and simple to create.

Accentuated by a bold splash of contrasting colour or with a range of textures to add variety, these can be among the most eye-catching settings. Families of near colours such as green and blue, sand and ivory, create delicate blends of colour, while complementary or contrasting colours, whether bright or muted, have a vital, painterly style.

The effect of colour is magnified or reduced by texture. Smooth, shiny surfaces like silk, lacquer or ceramic enhance the effect while matt textures such as wool and wood soften its impact. This is modified further by choosing colours from the warm or cool side of the spectrum. Warm colours like red and orange bring objects into focus while cool blues and lavender make them recede. Adding white or black to a tone to reflect or absorb more light allows us to fine tune the effect: pink (derived from red plus white) will warm a dark room and a greyed beige (a variation of orange plus black) will tone down a south-facing sitting room. Neutral tones of grey, sand, ivory, and taupe provide tranquillity and act as a frame for more vivid colours. As a soothing background used on walls to offset paintings, or on flooring to highlight rugs and furniture, they have an invaluable role to play.

RIGHT *Soft sweet-pea colours are offset by the cream tones of the painted wooden furniture and vinyl flooring. The fresh colour scheme reflects light into the room and brings the garden indoors.*

BELOW *A white ceiling, delicate chinoiserie-patterned wallpaper and ivory upholstery provide a foil for the strong stripes of the blinds and table cloths. The yellow painted dado anchors the scheme and, together with the natural wood floor, brings a sunny warmth to the room.*

ABOVE *The carefully balanced colour scheme of taupe with cool smoke blue and touches of coral gives this formal drawing room its sense of sophistication.*

TEXTURE

The grain of a timber door or window frame, the sheen of paintwork and the sparkle of glass are a few examples of the textures which contribute to the look of every room. By modifying colour and reinforcing pattern, texture adds an extra dimension to the home. Without this variety, a setting may seem dull, however carefully co-ordinated it may be.

A soft touch

The contrast between marble and wool shows how texture can vary the effect even where the colour is constant. Matt textures absorb light and convey an impression of warmth, particularly welcome when using cool colours in a temperate climate. Blue takes on a warm tinge when rubbed into wood to reveal the grain, while silvery scoured floorboards look softer than polished oak. The warmth is more than just apparent. While the mellow brick walls of Britain absorb sunlight and retain much-needed warmth, the white painted surfaces of many continental homes reflect the sun and dispel unwanted heat. Raised textures emphasize warmth (though remember that they may also reduce the sense of space) and have an informal effect which suits contemporary or cottage interiors. Loop or long pile carpet, rattan or wood furniture, tweed upholstery and slub weave curtains give an instant impression of warmth and comfort.

Sheen finish

There is an inherent formality in smooth textures like marble, chintz and ceramic tiles which makes them the perfect choice for many traditional homes. Mirror and glass are important because they add brilliance to a room, whether in the form of overmantel mirrors and pier glasses which reflect the light or cut-glass goblets and chandeliers which refract it. It is not always necessary to choose materials with a natural sheen, for even matt textures can be treated so that they become smooth and reflective. Wooden floors can

be polished to a high shine which rivals that of ceramic tiles, and cotton can be glazed to create chintz or calendered to produce a soft sheen. Close woven fabrics and velvet pile carpets have a smoothness which complements reflective materials and there is a wealth of oil-based paint finishes which add distinction to walls, ranging from the soft sheen of eggshell to the translucence of scumble glaze. Dark or warm colours are often used to offset a high shine: look at the crimson of lacquer work and the black of a town house front door. Remember that it is important to offset smooth and shiny finishes with warm textures for the best results. The traditional combinations of an iron gate in a brick wall, rush matting and quarry tiles and fringed rugs and polished floorboards show that there is an instinctive awareness of the need to balance warm and cold elements.

ABOVE *Flat painted wood, damask cushion covers and herringbone-weave upholstery fabric are perfect foils to the sheen of the wooden side table and the polished silver.*

FAR LEFT *Texture, rather than colour provides the decorative interest on these kitchen shelves: the polished copper, shiny glass and rich sheen of earthenware contrast with the mellow wood of the dresser. Even the garlic and sausages are part of the textural scheme.*

LEFT *The crisp lines of the unbleached wooden shutters, the polished floor and the tapered bedposts make the plump, feather-filled eiderdown look all the more inviting. Natural textures have become a substitute for elaborate decoration in this bedroom.*

PATTERN

Pattern adds life and rhythm to interiors, blending or contrasting colours in figurative or abstract shapes. It also creates a sense of order, through the regular repetition of motifs, whether these are geometric, figurative or floral.

Sources

Many modern prints take their inspiration from historic styles. When Laura Ashley first started designing fabrics and wallpapers, she developed many prints from the decorations used in Victorian homes. These were simple patterns used in small country houses and cottages and in turn reflected earlier eighteenth-century designs. They are ideal for small rooms and those with awkward proportions, which are best camouflaged by an all-over pattern. The more elaborate prints of the period, popular among the urban middle classes, are equally suitable for larger modern homes, and are often recoloured to suit current tastes with

BELOW A pretty chinoiserie-patterned wallpaper with luxurious ivory bed drapery and full-length curtains at the windows act as a foil to the rich pattern and colour of the oriental floor carpet. The vivid blue tone is picked out in the tie-backs, curtain rod and cushions.

brighter tints of blue, sage green or plum replacing sombre Victorian shades.

An earlier source of inspiration was the east, which provided the paisley, floral chintz and distinctive chinoiserie designs first popular in the eighteenth and nineteenth centuries. Abstract patterns have been borrowed from Moorish and Turkish designs which reflect the rules of Islam, which forbade the representation of living forms. The stencils and patchwork of early American styles and the folk patterns of Eastern Europe also influence modern styles while the rich damasks, blocked in gold, that evoke Venetian and Renaissance interiors and the splashy exuberance of the Bloomsbury prints of the Thirties have been adapted to suit current fashion.

Using pattern

The choice of an appropriate pattern always helps if you wish to create a period atmosphere. A Morris wallpaper, for example, immediately evokes the enthusiasm of the Arts and Crafts movement while an eighteenth-century damask recalls the grace of Georgian times. The scale of the pattern can play an important part in creating the right mood, though it should always be in

keeping with the size of the room. A large-scale design in traditional powder blue and gold can add grandeur, while a small single colour design conveys a cottage-style charm.

Trellis, sprig and stripe designs provide a transition between figurative pattern and plains. They are invaluable for wallpaper and upholstery as they add interest without conflicting with patterns used elsewhere. Flamboyant patterns are more successfully used for curtains, where texture and drape add softness, than for walls, where simpler motifs which relate to the master design look effective. Both designs can then be repeated by a border or frieze, cushions, bedcovers, table linen or rugs, building layers of pattern and colour to make a rich feast for the eyes. Remember that it can be equally effective to use a single area of pattern – a sofa or a rug – to create a focal point in a room where plain surfaces predominate.

BELOW The use of pattern upon pattern is a concept much loved by the Victorians. Simple designs based on sprig and trellis patterns are a happy combination. The pattern on the floor is a large-scale version of the wallpaper.

BELOW LEFT These five patterned fabrics are designed to co-ordinate with each other, and the combination is a formula for success. The balance of colour and pattern varies from one fabric to another, and the two styles, floral sprigs and stripes, are offset by the trellis of the wallpaper.

DECORATING

WALLPAPERS & BORDERS

Lift a corner of wallpaper in many homes and a decorative history unfolds, layer upon layer. Adding pattern to plain walls is a decorative device that has an age-old pedigree. Wallpaper was first introduced as a substitute for tapestry wall hangings. Later it was used to compensate for the lack of architectural features such as a cornice or frieze, and eventually columns and garlands mingled in designs which made wallpaper a unique decorative link between textiles and architecture.

Nowhere is wallpaper's role as a substitute more valuable than in the hallways and workrooms of a house. Tile-patterned wallpaper suitable for kitchens dates from the eighteenth-century when it was used as a replacement for Delft tiles – the real thing. Architectural borders have a similar pedigree and are invaluable today when so many homes have been stripped of ornament. Carefully shaded to create perspective, egg and dart, dentilled or Greek key borders will compensate for a missing cornice, while deep borders or friezes, purpose-made or cut from lengths of random-design wallpaper, fill the gap between cornice and picture rail. And lower down, wallpapers or high-relief panels provide a practical dado. For a decorative effect, use garlands and ribbon design borders to surround a mirror or window, to define a skirting board or to accentuate a picture rail.

LEFT *Who accepts that blue is cold? Powder blue, cream and gold add warmth and richness to this dining room, complementing the glow of the solid oak furniture. Colour is concentrated on the walls for effect, where the wallpaper's delicate gold leaf motif is amplified by a co-ordinating gold and white border which accentuates the cornice. Textiles play a supporting role, confined to softly swagged blinds at the window and cushions tied to the upright chairs.*

Choice of paper

As walls present the largest area in a room, it is wise to choose wallpaper with care. Subtle designs are often best for living rooms, where the impact of a distinctive design may soon wane. Damask effects in rich colours suit a traditional sitting room with more formal furnishings. For a lighter look, consider a sprig or abstract design taken from the background of a fabric print. The soft, overall pattern creates a hazy, broken-colour effect on the walls and can co-ordinate with curtains where it is given emphasis by the addition of a more dominant motif.

Stripes are always elegant in a living room setting. You may need to break the rules when hanging striped and geometric designs. They should be hung to appear straight to the eye, not the plumb line, and any discrepancies can usually be tucked out of sight in an alcove or by a door. If the walls are obviously out of true, add a picture or dado rail to provide a practical frame.

Rich hues like jade green or plum on a paler ground create a soothing backdrop, while ivory and cream let in the light and are more subtle than white. As you search for compatible colours and styles, look to the past for inspiration. Remember that time has bleached period furnishings and affected our perception of earlier styles. Before they faded, many wallpapers were surprisingly bright. The eighteenth century had a penchant for yellow, chocolate brown and verditure (blue-grey) wallpapers as well as the soft sage green

BELOW *Bring the freshness of a cottage garden indoors with a floral stripe wallpaper on a white background which adds a sense of spaciousness to the room. This cottage bedroom lacks architectural details like a cornice or picture rail so a sweet pea border gives a perfect finishing touch, drawing attention to the exposed beams which are painted soft white.*

often associated with the period. Horace Walpole's house at Strawberry Hill featured no fewer than seven designs of wallpaper and border, all in different colours, and 'the room where we always live' was decorated with a 'blue and white paper adorned with festoons . . . and luxurious settees covered with linen of the same pattern' – an early example of co-ordinated furnishings.

Victorian wallpapers were darker, densely patterned with trefoil or paisley shapes in deep burgundy and forest green, which suited the heavier style of decoration and, more practically, disguised the results of pollution caused by smoke and smog.

A sense of occasion

Rooms in less frequent use may benefit from a more dramatic treatment. A dining room will glow in Renaissance gold against cream, offset by midnight blue or Turkey red, or gracefully echo eighteenth-century chinoiserie with a design of exotic birds, flowers and fruit. The sinuous quality of Art Nouveau or the organic vigour of a Morris print are styles to consider where a rich, all-embracing design is required. Don't be afraid of the dark, especially if the room is reserved for evening use, where pools of light can be used to enhance the scheme.

An original effect can be created with paper panels edged by borders to enclose areas of pattern or to correct the proportions of a room. Vertical panels add height while horizontal ones give width and it is possible to widen a narrow ceiling by dividing it into square panels, each with a central motif. An attractive variation is the idea of an eighteenth-century print room where the walls are clad in black and white reproduction engravings, perhaps aged by a wash of cold tea, framed by wallpaper borders. The borders are characteristically monochromatic and classical in style, featuring acanthus or oak leaves, for example, and the background wallpaper traditionally would be grey or yellow.

Bed and bath

From sprig to spray, floral patterns in a bouquet of colours like lilac, rose pink, duck-egg blue, cowslip yellow and sage are the chosen favourites for bedrooms. Wallpapers, borders and ceiling papers can be used pattern upon pattern to give a sumptuous air while simple one-colour designs such as those once reserved for attic bedrooms can be used in smaller settings to create a cottage look. Wallpaper in related patterns can successfully be used above tiles in well-ventilated bathrooms. Choose vinyl for extra protection from condensation, or varnish the wallpaper to create a practical surface with a traditional glaze.

LEFT *Borders at ceiling height help to reduce the effect of high ceilings. Placed at the junction of wall and ceiling, a border can compensate for a missing cornice as well as providing a neat finish.*

BELOW *This border uses a larger version of the wallpaper design to magnify its effect. Pattern is confined to the upper part of the walls and is curtailed by a dado rail which defines the scale of the room. The stylized design provides a fine background for prints.*

RIGHT *A rope and ribbon design border in rich colours reinforces the effect of the damask seat cushion beneath and creates an air of formality which suits its style. The dado rail provides a natural route for the border to follow but there is vertical emphasis from the panel above, finished with exuberant bows which define the corners.*

ABOVE *The large-scale wallpaper design is confined to a simple panel, outlined with moldings painted sage green to blend with the painted walls. It provides a perfect frame for the eye-catching arrangement above this mantelpiece and effectively repudiates the idea that paintings are best hung on plain walls.*

LEFT *A floral border used to outline the architrave adds prettiness to this traditional nursery where it repeats the pattern of the frilled curtains and co-ordinating rug. Elsewhere the emphasis is on painted surfaces including robust freestanding furniture and a practical dado.*

WALLPAPERING

If rooms were perfectly regular, with straight walls and true corners, wallpapering would be easy. To ensure that the paper hangs straight, even if the walls are not, it is important to use a plumbline to get the first drop straight and to correct any errors that creep in when you take the paper around corners.

Normally, start hanging wallpaper near the door, or any full-height obstruction, so that when you get back to the starting point, any mismatch will be less obvious. With bold patterns, hang the first drop so that it is centred on the focal point of the room, such as the chimney breast.

You will need a plumbline (or weight tied to a piece of string), chalk, a bucket and wide pasting brush, a pasting table or suitable surface at least 55 cm (21 in) wide and 1.5 m (5 ft) long, a wallpaper smoothing brush, a pair of long-bladed scissors, a smaller pair of scissors, a trimming knife and a seam roller.

Wallpaper comes in standard-sized rolls, 53 cm (21 in) by 10 m (11 yd). To work out how much you need see page 212.

Wallpaper paste is available in powder form or ready mixed. The powder form is more economical, easier to use, and provides a good bond for normal papers and vinyl wallcoverings. Always choose a paste containing a fungicide when hanging vinyls.

1 Mix the paste, following the instructions on the packet. Measure up and cut the first drop, allowing at least 10 cm (4 in) extra for trimming. Cover the plumbline with chalk, hang it at your starting point and hold the weight in place while you snap the chalked line against the wall.

2 Lay the paper on the pasting table, wrong side up, with one edge of the paper aligned with the edge of the table and the top aligned with one end of the table. This prevents paste getting on the table and spreading on the right side of the wallpaper. Apply the paste, working towards the matched edge

down the length of the table. Then shift the paper so the other edge matches the other edge of the table, and apply the paste working out the other way.

3 Ensure the whole strip is evenly covered. When you need to move the paper down the table, fold over the pasted end in an S shape. Apply paste to the other end of the drop in the same way, then fold up the lower end of the paper. Leave the paper to rest according to the manufacturer's instructions so the paste soaks in.

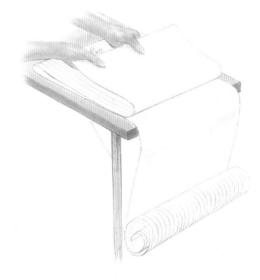

4 Carry the pasted paper to the wall, draped over your arm. Hold it up to the wall so that the top is 5 cm (2 in) above the edge of the cornice or picture rail and one edge matches the plumbed line. Gradually unfold the paper, smoothing it down with a smoothing brush as you go. Do not apply too much pressure as this might stretch the paper. Avoid getting any paste on the right side of the paper.

If bubbles and wrinkles appear, lift the paper away from the wall beyond the fault, and smooth down again. Apply extra paste to the wall if necessary. Try not to stretch the paper as you lift and re-position it.

5 When the whole drop is in place, mark the cutting line at the top by drawing the back of the scissors along the angle between the cornice or picture rail and the wall. Peel the paper back from the wall slightly and trim along the marked line, or trim with a sharp trimming knife while it is still in position. Repeat at the skirting.

6 Cut subsequent drops, allowing extra for pattern matching if necessary. Always start to paste at the top of the drop, and hang from the top, aligning the pattern carefully. This will be easier if you identify bold elements of the pattern which fall at the seam line before you start. Run the seam roller down the seams to ensure they are well stuck down.

7 At internal corners, cut down the length of the drop to make a strip 2.5 cm (1 in) wider than the distance to the corner. Hang this strip, wrapping it around the corner and cutting into the overlap if necessary to accommodate any bulges. Then mark a new vertical around the corner, and paste and hang the strip you cut off the drop, overlapping the latter slightly. Use the same technique to wrap paper around external corners.

8 When wallpapering around an obstacle, paper up to it, then cut into the paper to release it, clipping diagonally to any angles or radially around circular obstructions. Turn the power off at the mains before papering around electric switches and fittings. Then you can trim the paper roughly to fit, unscrew the fitting slightly and tuck the edges under the faceplate. When fitting paper around large obstacles such as doors or windows, cut away waste paper to make it easier to handle.

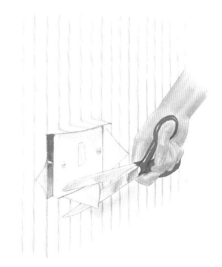

9 If there are air bubbles behind the paper which you have missed, use a sharp trimming knife to cut a cross into the bubble. Peel the four triangular flaps back from the wall and apply more paste to the wall. Smooth the flaps back in place, wiping off excess glue and running over the cuts with a seam roller.

The paper will take a day or so to dry out – longer if it has a vinyl surface. Do not worry about patchiness when you first hang the paper: this is caused by the paste, and should disappear as the paper dries out.

Borders & Ceilings

If you decide to paper the ceiling, you might also consider using a border to disguise the join where the ceiling meets the wall. This may be the best solution if there is no cornice or picture rail.

Hanging Borders

Borders can be used to break up large wall surfaces above skirting boards, at dado level (approximately 90 cm/36 in from the floor), or at cornice height, or used in panels.

Plan the position of borders carefully before you start. Use a long batten or rule to establish a horizontal line. If you are not sure of the effect, stick lengths in place with Blu-Tac before making a final decision. Mark the positions of borders very lightly in pencil if they run across an expanse of plain wall. On a papered wall, follow the pattern when aligning the border.

Wallpaper borders are available in various widths, but most rolls are 10 m (11 yd) long. They may be made of paper or vinyl, and some are self-adhesive, which saves pasting.

1 If you are sticking borders to a vinyl surface, use a specially formulated overlap and repair adhesive. Lay the wallpaper border wrong side up on the table, and paste down the length. Wipe the table after pasting each length to keep it clean. Fold the pasted border up into a concertina that you can hold comfortably in your hand. Start to smooth the paper in place, using a sponge or a wallpaper smoothing brush, and align it carefully with any guidelines you have marked. Wipe off any paste which oozes out from under the border.

2 At corners, such as around a door frame or when pasting the border to form panels on a wall, you should either buy a special decorative corner piece to cover the joins or mitre the corners.

It is worth doing a couple of practice mitres to ensure that you can match the pattern around a corner. Paste one strip of paper in place, leaving an overlap of about 15 cm (6 in) beyond the corner. Cut the second strip of paper, again allowing a 15 cm (6 in) overlap and paste it in place. Before the paper dries, lift the ends of the strips at the corner and slip a piece of card or hardboard beneath. Lay the paper in position over the protective backing, draw a diagonal line with a ruler and pencil and cut through both layers of paper. Remove the backing and offcuts of paper and smooth the border back in place on the wall.

1

2

PAPERING CEILINGS

Ceilings, like walls, have a much softer feeling if you hang lining paper before you paint them. If you want to cover a ceiling with patterned paper, choose pale colours (unless the ceiling is very high) and patterns which do not have an obvious 'right way up'.

Ensure that you are standing steadily at a comfortable height to reach the ceiling with your head just below ceiling level, using scaffolding planks with ladders.

Decide which way you want to hang the paper. Patterned paper is hung with the pattern running down the length of the room. With plain or broken colour paper, the job may be easier if you hang shorter strips across the room.

1 Mark a straight line across the ceiling, 53 cm (21 in) from the wall with which you want to align the paper. Measure out from the wall at each end, and join the two points with a length of chalk-covered string, pinned in position. Snap it to leave a mark on the ceiling as a guide for the first strip of paper.

2 Paste the paper as for wallpaper, making neat, concertina-style folds so that you can control the paper more easily. The folds should be about 50 cm (20 in) apart, and arranged so that the pasted side is sandwiched to the pasted side of the next fold.

3 Lift the folded wallpaper to the ceiling, beside the marked line. Unwrap the first fold, sticking it in place so it is in line with the mark. Allow a few centimetres to overlap the cornice or wall at the end. Work down the length of the paper, unfolding and smoothing as you go. Trim ends by marking with the back of the scissors as before.

Repeat for subsequent strips, butting the edges carefully and rolling seams with a seam roller.

4 If there is a ceiling rose, cut a hole to ease the light fitting through the paper. Turn off the power at the mains, then snip into the paper around the rose. Trim away the paper to leave a couple of millimetres overlap, unscrew the rose slightly and tuck the edge of the paper under the rose as you tighten it up again.

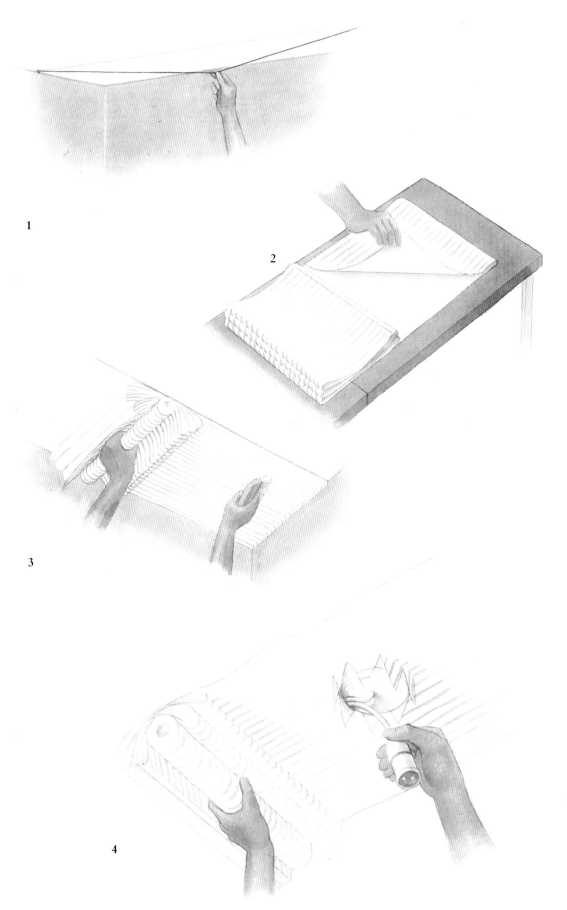

1

2

3

4

PAINTWORK

All the colours of the spectrum – and over 1000 variations – are available as paint. This vast range of hues means you can choose precise tints and shades to get the effect you want whatever the general colour scheme.

Natural colour

Compare this wealth of colour with the restricted palette available to early decorators. It is a common misconception that historic homes were decorated in pastel tones. The colours contained natural dyes which faded fast. Buff, sky blue and brown were among the first commercially produced paint colours and a favourite Georgian colour scheme was sage green woodwork teamed with chocolate coloured walls – an adventurous and effective combination. Strong colours of equal value like these underline the beauty of perfect proportions but altering their relative depth can help to improve the perspective where necessary. A dark colour appears to lower a high ceiling, while muted, matching tones allow unsightly features like radiators and pipes to pale into insignificance.

The nineteenth century saw the development of synthetic dyes, progressing from the crude brilliance of mauve, magenta (named after a battle) and Prussian blue, to delicate shell pinks, creams and celadons used in elaborate paint effects at the turn of the century. These were oil-based paints like modern eggshell finish, whose sheen suits both walls and woodwork, increasing the impression of space and giving a soft, subtle look.

The chalky colours of distemper had been used in unpretentious cottage settings but urban living demanded dark colours which did not show the dirt. Until well into the twentieth century, pastels were the preserve of the rich who did not have to concern themselves with cleaning. Pure white paint became available in the 1920s, and contributed to the widely held image of the homes of movie stars in the 1920s and 30s, made famous by interior decorator Syrie Maugham.

LEFT Small rooms need a spacious treatment, which is why this bedroom has been painted ivory. The same finish is used on ceiling, walls and woodwork, including the panels and fireplace, to create a sense of space.

BELOW Related tones of terracotta and gold create a rich and dramatic colour scheme. Woodwork in both rooms is painted to blend with the walls to add interest without any break in colour. The exception is the doorway, painted white for emphasis.

Modern times

Pale colours have proved highly desirable because they reflect light and increase the impression of space. Soft matt emulsions give the effect of traditional distemper without its drawbacks while undercoat, sealed by varnish, has an attractive velvety appearance for those who want an alternative to gloss. Paint can also be applied over textured wallpapers.

ABOVE *Tea rose and cream give warmth to this Victorian living room without destroying its period atmosphere. Pale colours are useful where natural light is limited but cool tones would have been inappropriate here. Cream was chosen in place of brilliant white to pick out the details of the high relief frieze and filigree window screen – a perfect partner for the rose-beige walls.*

RIGHT & ABOVE *Break with convention and paint woodwork and ceilings a deep, dramatic shade using a mid-sheen finish which is suitable for both walls and woodwork. Choose a single colour for all paintwork in a busy room where furniture, books and paintings add immediate decorative interest. In both examples here green has been used. Vary the tones for a less formal scheme.*

Painting Walls & Woodwork

The better the surface, the easier it will be to get a good finish when painting walls, ceilings and woodwork. Prepare the surface well for the best results (pages 208–211). If you are using a paint roller, paint the ceiling, then the walls before painting woodwork, as the roller tends to create a fine spray of paint which covers adjacent surfaces. With a paint pad or brush, paint the ceiling first, then the woodwork and finally the walls.

Work in a clean, dust-free room, preferably in daylight. Start with the highest point and work downwards. When painting an absorbent surface, such as bare plaster or lining paper, thin the first coat of paint as directed by the manufacturer to get an even undercoat. Open paint tins carefully so that dust from the lid does not get into the tin.

Always check the manufacturer's instructions before buying paint: with water-based paints you can wash your brushes out in water, while oil-based paints have to be washed out with white spirit or brush cleaner. Large areas can be painted with a paint roller or paint pad, although many decorators prefer to use a wide paint brush. You will need a smaller brush or paint pad to get an even finish at the edges of walls and in corners. Arrange plenty of plastic sheets or dust covers over floors and fixtures.

Ceilings & Walls

1 When painting ceilings and high rooms, arrange two sturdy stepladders with a stout plank between, or use a solid box or milk crate, at a convenient height.

2 Start by cutting in around the edge of the ceiling or wall using a 5 cm (2 in) wide paint brush. Paint a band about 5 cm (2 in) wide down the corners and up to any obstructions such as doorways, windows, light switches and fireplaces. Do not overload the brush: wipe any excess on a string tied across the top of the paint can. Use a light touch, working the paint in all directions so that the brushstrokes do not show.

Fill in the rest of the area working in blocks

1

about 2 m (2 yd) square. When using a brush, apply the paint with horizontal strokes first, then work vertically over the same area, finishing with upward strokes.

With a roller, dip the roller in the paint tray and squeeze out excess paint by rolling it over the ribbed part of the tray. Then apply the paint with criss-cross strokes for an even finish. If you prefer a paint pad, apply the paint with vertical strokes, finishing with horizontal or diagonal strokes if necessary. The aim is to cover the area evenly without any strokes showing.

2

Continue to the next 'block', working the paint into the wet edge so that it doesn't show. Work so that the edges of one block do not dry out before you start on the adjacent block.

WOODWORK

Generally woodwork requires tough paints or polyurethane varnish, particularly if it is likely to be knocked – at skirting boards or doorways. If you want to create a decorative colour effect (pages 62–65), use the required paint.

Woodwork must be prepared even more carefully than walls (page 208). If it is not in bad condition to start with, wash it, and rub it down lightly with fine glasspaper before applying the new top coats. It is worth using good-quality brushes that do not shed bristles when applying oil-based paints.

Clean brushes thoroughly after use in white spirit, concentrated washing-up liquid or brush cleaner, according to the paint maker's recommendations. If you want to stop painting for a short break, wrap the brush in tin foil to keep the bristles moist and to prevent the paint hardening. Always replace the lid of the paint tin firmly after use.

1 Start by applying the paint along the grain of the wood: the area you cover depends on the surface you are painting. Cover an area about 30 cm (12 in) square, or a strip of skirting about 60 cm (24 in) long that you can reach easily.

Apply the paint along the grain without re-loading the brush, then dip the brush in the paint again, and apply a little more paint with crossways strokes.

Finish by stroking the paint along the grain, working only with upward strokes if the grain runs vertically. This is known as laying off the paint.

2 When painting windows, you should allow the paint to creep over the putty and a couple of millimetres on to the glass to seal the surface of the frame properly. If you don't have a steady hand and a good eye, you can use a paint shield – a triangular metal plate with a handle. Hold it against the glass as you paint the glazing bars. Use a paint shield when doing the skirting board too.

Alternatively, use masking tape to give a crisp edge to the paintwork. Peel off the tape when the paint is touch dry but not hard.

3 By painting the different elements of a window in the right order you will avoid touching any wet paint.

With sash windows, start with the window open, so that the upper, outer sash comes down below the lower, inner sash. Paint the lower edge of the upper sash before sliding the sashes back to the slightly open position. Then paint the upper sash, the lower sash, and finally the window surround and sill. Don't paint the sash cords.

4 When painting casements, paint any glazing bars first, then paint the casement, and finish with the frame and the sill.

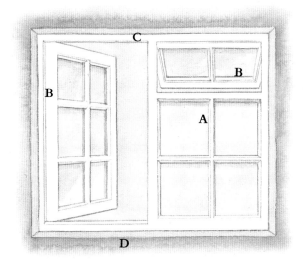

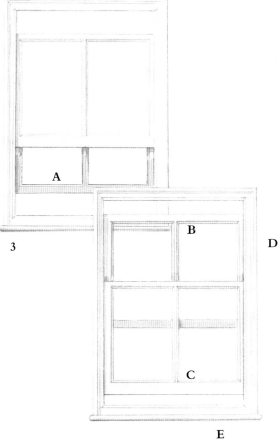

2

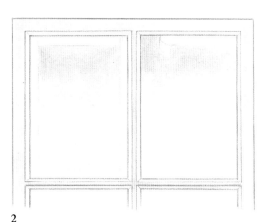

1

3

4

PAINT EFFECTS

Paint effects introduce pattern to paint – the perfect medium if you are tired of plain walls but are not prepared to paper. Crafts such as dragging, stencilling and *trompe l'oeil* have been part of the professional decorator's repertoire for centuries and now it is possible for amateurs to achieve the same effects, using traditional scumble glaze or paint alone.

Selecting a style

There is a paint effect to suit every setting. The lustre of dragged walls and the watered silk appearance of rag-rolling have a formality which flatters traditional furnishings and provides a rich background for paintings and *objets d'art*. Sponging, stippling and ragging have a random broken colour effect which gives depth to walls and suits a cottage or smaller home. It is also a means of combining colours in a subtle way. More overtly decorative is stencilling, which was particularly popular in eighteenth-century America where a shortage of wood pulp limited the supply of wallpaper. Used as a border in place of architectural features like a cornice or dado rail, in regular designs to resemble wallpaper, or in single motifs to decorate furniture, stencilling never fails to charm whether the style is simple and reminiscent of folk art, or an elaborate botanical or architectural design.

Other paint effects were originally designed to imitate scarce or expensive natural materials. Marbling is perhaps the best known but malachite and tortoiseshell finish, bamboo and wood graining are all examples of this decorative sleight of hand. As they need a fair degree of time and skill, these techniques are best reserved for decorative areas like table tops and chimney pieces. More elaborate still is *trompe l'oeil* whose convincing vistas and architectural effects are purely illusory. Still widely practised in northern Italy where painted cornerstones, shutters and pediments adorn the simplest terraced house, this exuberant technique has become an art form.

LEFT *Using samples of marble rock as a guide, it is possible to trace the veins and natural variations in colour to produce a marbled effect which looks disconcertingly real. Choose black or white marbling for a convincing effect, deep colours for richness.*

LEFT *Ragging is one of the simplest paint effects and needs only emulsion paint and a lint-free cloth. Experiment with different types such as cheesecloth, stockinet or mutton cloth, and with colours, ragging dark colours over light or vice versa, or using two related colours on a contrasting background.*

RIGHT *Marbling has an abstract quality which suits contemporary furnishings as well as period styles. Here it is used as a fantasy finish which does not pretend to deceive the eye. Panels, cornice and dado rail are all marbled to complete the effect.*

BELOW *Broken colour finishes such as ragging and sponging add interest and depth to painted walls and provide a perfect background for stencilling. Here a single motif, which is quick and easy to stencil, has been repeated to create a border to define the dado and windows, thus emphasizing the room's symmetry.*

RIGHT *Stencilling is more than a stand-in for wallpaper, it can also substitute for art and certainly adds interest. Small, self-contained areas are easiest to treat, which is why stencils are often used as borders or to decorate furniture. They are equally effective used in place of paintings or as* trompe l'oeil *ornaments.*

Applying Paint Effects

Before applying a paint finish, prepare the surface and give it a suitable undercoat (page 210). Then apply the base coat. The decorative effect is then built up by adding one or more shades of top coat in either emulsion or oil-based paint. It is normally necessary to thin the top coats, and you may need to add an oil-based scumble glaze (rather like paint without any pigment – available from specialist stores) to make the top coats workable and translucent. The glaze doesn't dry as quickly as ordinary oil-based paints, giving you more time to move the paint around.

Mixing top coats enables you to create your own tones and shades of colour – the colour may come from household paint or you can add extra pigment. Add powder colour or artist's acrylic paints to water-based paints, and artist's oil colours to oil-based paints.

Always experiment with the paint to try out the effect and test it before you start. The brand of paint you use, the porosity of the surface, even the weather can affect the result, so there are no hard and fast rules for the proportion of paint.

You will need special tools for some of the effects shown on pages 62–65. For example, natural sea sponges are essential for applying a sponged finish, and you can experiment with rag, paper or even plastic bags for a ragged or rag-rolled effect.

For the *trompe l'oeil* effects which imitate natural materials such as marble or tortoiseshell, you will need a selection of soft artist's brushes, and there are special comb-like graining tools for creating wood effects. Have a selection of old jam jars and paint kettles or clean tins to mix the various stages. Always mix sufficient glaze to cover the whole of the area to be painted.

Described below are some of the most frequently used techniques for decorative paint effects.

Mixing a Glaze

Suggested proportions for a mixed glaze are: 1–2 parts eggshell paint, tinted with artist's oil colour if necessary, mixed with 5 parts oil-based glaze, thinned with 3–4 parts white spirit or turpentine.

First prepare a tint by blending artist's oil colour into white or coloured oil-based eggshell paint. If you need several batches of glaze in graduated tones, mix all the tints at the same time to ensure evenly graded colours.

Add the transparent, oil-based glaze, stirring in just a little to start with, then adding more. A large metal spoon is useful for ladling out the glaze. You will need at least twice as much glaze as paint. Finally thin the paint with white spirit, adding it gradually and testing the consistency until you get a creamy texture.

Sponging

This effect is quick and easy to create using ordinary emulsion paint. Choose closely related colours for a subtle effect, or contrasting colours for a more mottled look. Try out several combinations, mixing small quantities of colour to start with, until you are happy with the balance of colours.

Prepare the wall in the usual way (page 209) and apply a base coat of matt or silk-finish emulsion with a brush, roller or pad. Choose a pale colour for the base coat, and do not be too meticulous in getting an even finish. A slightly uneven base will not show once the final finish is applied. Leave the wall to dry completely.

Take the first of your chosen top coat colours and thin with a little water. A paint roller tray makes an ideal paint kettle for mixing and holding the paint while you work. Dip the flattest side of a damp, natural sponge in the paint and dab it on the ribbed part of the paint tray to remove excess paint. Then dab the sponge lightly over a test surface (lining paper is ideal for this). This takes any heavy drops of paint off the sponge, and gives you a chance to test the amount of pressure you need to apply.

Apply the paint to the wall, dabbing it on with the sponge until the effect starts to fade. Use a slightly rolling motion each time you dab on the paint and twist your hand to a different angle each time you lift the sponge. This gives an all-over effect without any obvious pattern from the shape of the sponge. Don't twist the sponge while it is in contact with the surface of the wall, as this will give smears and swirls.

Cover the whole wall with the first colour, then repeat the process with a second colour. On a reasonably large wall, you will find that the first colour is dry by the time you get back to the starting point. If required, apply further coats, either of the first colour or of other colours, until the wall is evenly covered.

COLOUR WASHING

Paint a base coat of matt or silk emulsion. Allow to dry. Using the same colour, or a slightly different tone, mix a wash of emulsion and water in equal parts. Then gradually increase the water to make a thin colour which will not fall in heavy droplets down the wall but which allows the base colour to show through when it is applied to the wall. Test the wash, then apply it using a wide brush, with long, sweeping strokes. Further coats can be applied in toning colours.

For a more durable finish, try using a subtly tinted, thinned glaze as a wash over the surface.

RAGGING

Apply a base coat of oil-based eggshell in a medium to pale tone. Leave until completely dry. Prepare a large batch of tinted and thinned glaze in a darker colour. Have several white lint-free cloths ready to work with. Cut them from the same piece of fabric, making each one about 40 cm (15 in) square so they are easy to handle. Ragging may also be worked in emulsion using the same base coat and top coat as for sponging.

Scrunch up a piece of cloth. Dip the cloth in the paint and remove excess paint by padding it on a piece of paper or the ribbed part of a roller tray if you are using that as a paint kettle. Then dab the rag over the surface of the wall, applying even pressure and re-charging the rag when necessary. If the rag becomes clogged with paint, either re-fold and use a cleaner part of the rag, or use a clean rag.

You can experiment with substitutes for the rag, such as screwed up lining paper or even a plastic bag. Make sure that you can achieve the same effect all over the surface: if the paper becomes clogged with paint, you must have more of the same quality to continue over the surface.

DISTRESSED EFFECT

Apply a base coat of matt, gloss or eggshell oil-based paint and allow to dry. Mix a batch of glaze in a deeper tone, or in a similar or contrasting shade. Prepare some squares of lint-free rag and moisten the first with white spirit. Don't soak all the rags at once – the white spirit evaporates quickly, and they are a fire risk.

Apply the glaze quickly, ensuring you work it into the recesses of the surface you are painting. Cover an area a couple of metres (yards) square, or a length of skirting or architrave a couple of metres (yards) long. Wipe the glaze off the raised part of the surface with the moistened cloth. Leave to dry.

For a graded effect, repeat the process, using a darker batch of glaze and wiping off slightly more to reveal the first colour beneath.

RAG-ROLLING

Apply a base coat of oil-based emulsion paint in a mid to pale tone. Leave it to dry. Mix a large batch of glaze in a darker tone, and prepare plenty of rags about 30 cm (12 in) square.

Paint the glaze onto the wall, covering an area of a couple of square metres. Twist a rag into a sausage shape and roll it up the wall, lifting off the paint as you go. Work in overlapping bands, so that you do not leave any streaks of 'un-rolled' glaze.

Move quickly to the next area, applying and rolling the glaze before the first area you covered is dry. This way you will be able to merge the pattern, and will not get a hard line where glaze has dried. The whole process is easier if you work with a partner, one applying the glaze and the other rolling it off. But don't swap tasks half-way through the job: different people apply different pressure and movement as they roll the rags.

DIRECTORY OF PAINT EFFECTS

Mainly for walls

Sponging is one of the quickest and easiest ways to achieve a broken colour effect on walls and ceilings.

BASE COAT Emulsion in a pale colour (pale grey *right* and white *far right*)

TOP COAT Slightly thinned emulsion in one or more darker shades. The top coats here are a darker grey with coral to liven up the effect (*right*) and pale plum and taupe (*far right*). Use similar tones of the same shade for a subtle effect.

SPECIAL TOOLS Natural sea sponge to apply the top coat(s).

Colour washing produces a subtle variation in tone, giving a comfortable faded appeal to walls.

BASE COAT Pale emulsion (cream), thinned with water in the ratio of 10 parts paint to one part water.

TOP COAT This effect can be achieved in two ways. Use two or more washes of emulsion in slightly darker tones thinned in the ratio of 5 parts paint to one part water (or add more water). Or, as here, use one top coat of glaze in yellow to give a more lustrous effect.

SPECIAL TOOLS Apply the top coats with a 10 cm (4 in) wide decorator's paint brush.

Ragging produces a more obvious colour effect. Oil-based paints give a richer finish than emulsion.

BASE COAT Oil-based eggshell paint, or emulsion (pale duck-egg blue).

TOP COAT Oil-based eggshell thinned with white spirit or turpentine, and possibly mixed with an oil-based scumble glaze, or thinned emulsion. Here, pale taupe and pale smoke have been used.

SPECIAL TOOLS Apply the top coat with a pad of lint-free rag, or an improvised tool, such as paper or a scrunched-up plastic bag.

Ragging off involves applying a glaze top coat which is lifted off by dabbing with a rag.

Rag-rolling is similar to ragging, but the top coat is applied with a brush and then lifted off the surface by rolling a rag over it.

BASE COAT Oil-based eggshell paint (cream).

TOP COAT Tinted, thinned glaze, usually in a darker tone than the base coat (in this case, sapphire blue).

SPECIAL TOOLS Lint-free rag.

Rag-rolling on involves applying the paint by rolling a rag dipped in tinted glaze over the surface.

Distressing is a technique which can only be used on relief surfaces: heavily textured or relief pattern wallpapers (as shown here), wooden moldings, such as those on panelled doors or architraves and skirtings, and traditional Victorian or Edwardian cast-iron fireplaces are all suitable surfaces.

BASE COAT Oil-based eggshell paint in a pale colour (grey).

TOP COAT Tinted and thinned glaze, in a deeper tone or contrasting shade (jade green).

SPECIAL TOOLS Lint-free rag to wipe off the glaze.

Mainly for woodwork

Dragging is a softly striped effect which is often used on woodwork, and may also be used on walls. When used on woodwork, the technique can be developed to create a woodgrain effect, using natural tones and varying the brush marks to imitate knots and other characteristics of wood.
BASE COAT Oil-based eggshell in a pale colour (rose *right* and ivory *far right*).
TOP COAT Thinned eggshell or tinted and thinned oil-based glaze (burgundy glaze *right* and grey-green glaze *far right*).
SPECIAL TOOLS Wide, stiff brush to run through the top coat to create the dragged effect. Artist's brushes for adding wood grain.

Marbling imitates the effect of real marble, and should be confined to surfaces which could be made of such a heavy material: skirtings, fire surrounds, floors and dados take the treatment well. The two examples here reproduce the effect of Siena (*right*) and Breccia marble (*far right*).
BASE COAT Eggshell finish, oil-based paint, in cream or white for pale marble, or very dark grey/black, deep rose pink or earthy tones, depending on the type of marble you want to imitate.
TOP COAT Thinned and tinted glaze in two or three shades according to the type of marble. Here, tones of sienna and grey have been used. The glaze is interwoven with veins of undiluted artist's oil paint (Siena) and diluted raw umber and black (Breccia).
SPECIAL TOOLS Fine artist's brushes and feathers to apply the veins and soften the effect.

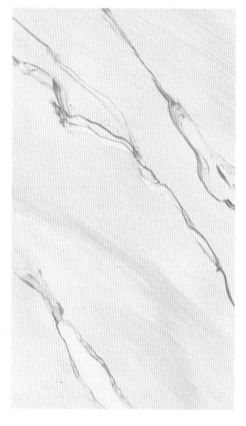

Tortoiseshelling gives a rich, warm texture to woodwork and ornaments such as wooden boxes and frames. Imitate the real thing, or create fantasy effects with rich sea-greens and warm reds and pinks.

BASE COAT For traditional tortoiseshell, chrome or bright yellow gloss paint.

TOP COAT Three glazes were used here: raw sienna, burnt sienna and burnt umber. After the glazes have been softened with a broad, clean, soft brush, small areas are spattered with white spirit and burnt umber.

SPECIAL TOOLS Clean, dust-free decorator's brushes to apply varnish and soft artist's brushes for the mottling.

Malachite (*right*) is a fantasy finish, not a direct copy, which imitates the effect of this vivid green mineral.

BASE COAT Pale eggshell (white).

TOP COAT Eggshell (jade green) slightly diluted with white spirit.

SPECIAL TOOLS The effect is obtained by dragging a piece of torn cardboard through the top coat. The areas in between are then stippled using a small artist's brush.

Walnut (*far right*) is a way of imitating in paint the beautiful grain of this costly wood.

BASE COAT Eggshell in a very pale colour (pale yellow/off white).

TOP COAT A glaze of raw umber and burnt sienna is applied in irregular patches and then wiped with the firm edge of a folded cloth. The cloth is moved to make ribbon shapes. The knots are obtained by twisting a small stubby brush and the areas in between the knots and swirls are stippled with a small brush.

SPECIAL TOOLS Cloth, small brushes including a stubby, stencil-type brush.

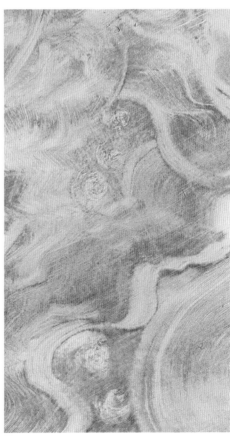

Stencilling

Traditionally stencils were cut from waxed card, brass or other metals; now they are also available in acetate sheets. Plastic is easy to clean after use and, being transparent, it is easy to align. Plastic and card stencils are available pre-cut, in sets, one sheet for each colour in the pattern. Metal stencils are also available, but they are usually sold individually rather than in sets. These are long lasting, and there is less danger of damaging the stencil.

Printed stencils, which you cut yourself, are also available. If you have a steady hand, and an artistic streak, you can design and cut your own stencils from acetate or waxed card. A sharp stencil knife, a rubber 'self-healing' cutting mat and metal straightedge are essential tools.

You can get a good effect by applying the same paints with a stubby stencil brush or sponge using ordinary emulsion or oil-based paint. Mix the paint to a creamy consistency so that it will not clog the brush or sponge, but not so thin that it will run down behind the stencil. Tint water-based emulsion with artist's acrylic paints, and oil-based paint with artist's oils to achieve the required colour.

If you are painting woodwork, water-based paints will have to be protected with polyurethane varnish (matt or satin finish are best as the low level of reflection enhances the handywork). If you have to mix colours to get the tones you want, mix enough for the whole room; it is difficult to repeat a colour exactly. There are also specially formulated quick-dry stencilling paints and crayons for use with acetate sheets.

1 Paint the surface in the normal way before stencilling. Use a plumbline and spirit level to mark the position of the decoration, marking horizontal or vertical base lines for border patterns.

2 Using the stencil as a template, mark the position of each corner along the length of the border, or around the position of each central motif. These are known as registration marks and are vital to the planning and correct

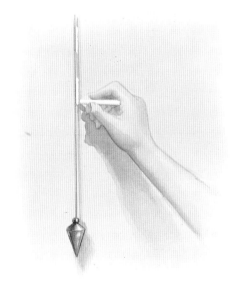

1

2

alignment of borders. Use blackboard chalk which will wipe off easily when you have finished.

3 Attach the stencil to the surface with masking tape, aligning it with the chalk marks. If you want to use the stencil to apply more than one colour, use tape to mask the areas where the next colour is to be applied.

4 Dip the stencil brush or sponge in the paint; hardly any paint is necessary – it should be almost dry. When you are happy with the consistency, dab the paint on, working outwards from the middle of each cut-out. Don't feel that you have to make a solid block of colour: part of the charm of stencils is the gentle, textured effect and variation in density of colour from one motif to the next.

5 When the paint is dry to the touch, move the stencil on to the next marked position. Wipe the paint from the stencil if necessary, and clean the brush or sponge if it is getting clogged with paint. If you find that the stencil overlaps the work you have just done, move on to the next but one position, and fill in the gaps once the paint has dried. When you have completed one colour, you will find that the first motifs you applied are dry and you can start on the second colour. Clean the stencil and brush thoroughly, then proceed in the same way.

3

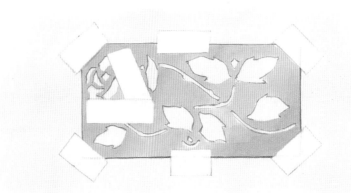

4

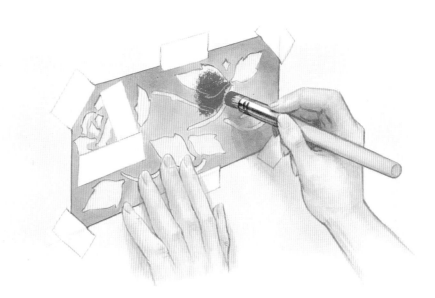

5

TILES

The beauty of ceramic tiles does not diminish with the years. Tiles that were once used for Roman pavements, Dutch living rooms or Victorian fireplaces still glow with rich colour, sealed beneath an impermeable glaze. Because this is one of the most durable and lasting surfaces in the home, it is important to make a considered choice. Choose a colour or design that relates to the existing scheme but is sufficiently adaptable to blend with a variety of others. Trellis or border design tiles have this chameleon quality, and narrow border tiles can be used above plain tiles to co-ordinate with patterns and provide the perfect finishing touch.

Alternatively, make the tiles the focal point of a room. A small bathroom looks impressive with walls, floor and bath panel tiled in a single colour design, while more elaborate patterns can be used above a basin in a bedroom or on a window ledge or table to co-ordinate with curtains and wallpaper. Patterned, multi-coloured tiles, reminiscent of the Mediterranean, also have their place in a tropical scheme.

On the surface

Be imaginative in your use of tiles. Patterned tiles do not have to be used *en masse* but can be laid to form a panel or in horizontal bands to stretch space and probably your budget. Take inspiration from the past by setting a line of tiles above the skirting where they will protect the wall, or co-ordinate with the floor and echo the horizontal emphasis of a cornice or picture rail. Because of their ability to resist both heat and water, tiles can add decorative emphasis in areas unsuitable for wallpaper or paint. What can be more eye-catching than decorative tiles flanking the grate in a Victorian chimney piece or patterned tiles used to clad a table top or line a window sill? A collection of antique tiles can be set into shelves or a window reveal and even shards of broken tiles can be used to create a mosaic design incorporated into a wall of plain tiling.

ABOVE *Tiles are ideally suited to kitchens and bathrooms for their durability and water resistance. For large areas, choose a timeless design like this delicate trellis in charcoal on cream.*

LEFT *Here, tiles used in a chequerboard pattern create a border which improves the room's proportions by reducing its apparent height. Most of the tiles are green, but blue and white tiles are used above the window to echo the effect of the breeze-block style glass panes.*

RIGHT *Border tiles provide a neat finish for partly tiled walls. This distinctive sapphire and white design combines with trellis pattern tiles on the worktop and splashback, candy stripe wallpaper and plain woodwork to create a fresh and attractive co-ordinated kitchen scheme.*

BELOW *Tiles with matching fabric or wallcovering provide instant co-ordination. Here the walls are clad in tiles with a simple geometric motif; a floral design is used above the basin and at intervals along the lower courses. These patterns set the style for the rest of the room.*

TILING WALLS

When starting on a tiling project, plan the work carefully so that you can calculate the exact number of tiles you need and, more important, ensure that you cut as few tiles as possible to give a neat finish and so make the task easier. It is worth drawing up a plan of the wall on graph paper, marking out the area to be tiled. Always plan to position the finished edges of tiles along the exposed edge of the tiled area to give a neat finish.

Tiles are fixed in place with tiling adhesive, available ready-mixed; use waterproof adhesives for splashbacks. An adhesive spreader is usually included. For cutting tiles, you will need a tile cutter (usually sold complete with cutting guide), and a tile snapper to break the tile along the line scored with the cutter. If you are cutting thick tiles, buy or hire a heavy-duty tile cutter. After fixing the tiles, they have to be grouted – the spaces between the tiles are finished with a cement-based, acrylic or epoxy filler to give an even surface.

The surface to be tiled must be suitable for tiling and properly prepared. Bare plaster walls give a perfect surface, but you can also tile over existing tiles. Firmly fixed wood and exterior grade plywood are also suitable but avoid using chipboard as a surface for tiling: the tiles are rarely entirely waterproof and chipboard will swell and 'blow' if it gets wet.

When the tiling is completed, fill the angle at the bottom of the splashback with silicone or acrylic sealant to give a flexible joint. (When applying sealant, always push the nozzle of the tube away from you, rather than dragging it.)

TILING A SMALL AREA

1 Plan the tiling so that cut edges are not obvious. Where the tiles are over a basin, for example, try to use only whole tiles. If the width of the basin does not coincide with the width of the tiles, position cut tiles down the centre of the tiled area. If the height of the tiled area is not an exact number of tiles, cut the bottom row of tiles. When tiling to the corner of a room, behind a bath or kitchen work surface for example, position the cut tiles in the corner.

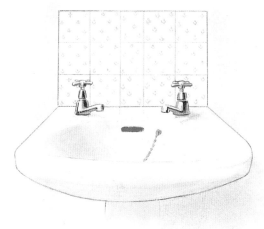

2 Apply the adhesive to the wall, covering an area about the size of six tiles. (You may be able to work in larger areas once you have had some practice.)

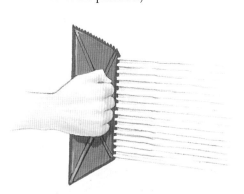

3 Position the tiles along the level edge. If the tiles have bevelled edges, butt them together neatly. If they have straight edges, the job is easier if you use tile spacers; position one at each corner of each tile. Spacers ensure even gaps between the tiles giving a neat finish. Continue, until all the whole tiles are in position.

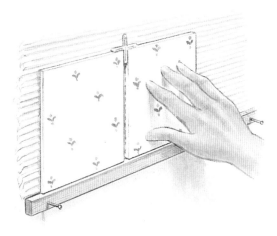

4 To cut a thin tile, determine the cutting line (page 82) and score the glazed surface of the tile using a jig. Place the tile over a slim pencil and press down firmly to snap the tile along the scored line.

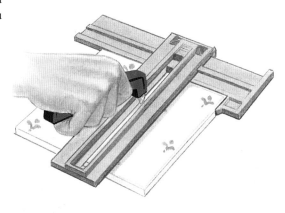

5 To cut a thicker tile, score the cutting line and position the jaws of the snapping tool on either side of the marked line and squeeze to make a clean break. Use a tile sanding block to smooth the cut edges.

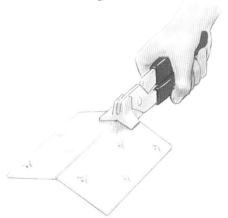

6 To cut tiles to fit around awkward shapes, nibble at the area to be cut away with a pair of pincers after you have cut a template from paper and traced it on to the tile.

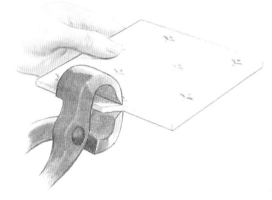

7 When the whole area is tiled, leave the adhesive to set – normally at least 12 hours. Then spread tile grout over the surface, paying particular attention to the gaps between the tiles. Immediately clean the grout off the face of the tiles with a sponge, rinsing it out frequently.

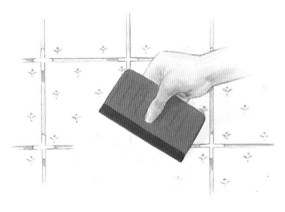

1

TILING LARGE AREAS

1 Plan the work carefully, so that you do not have to cut tiles at external corners or along the top of half-tiled walls. You must start from a level line at a height to suit the overall plan of the tiles, such as skirting board. However, most skirtings are not level and you may want to finish the wall with a new skirting over the bottom edge of the tile.

You may also have problems tiling above windows and doors. The solution is to fix a temporary batten to the wall to support the first row of tiles you lay. Decide on a suitable starting point, an exact number of tiles from the top of a half-tiled wall, or in line with existing tiles over a window or doorway, and fix the batten in place with masonry nails. Check that it is exactly level with a spirit level.

Spread adhesive and lay tiles as before, working upwards from the batten. Some ranges of tiles include special fittings, such as soap-dishes and towel rail fittings. If you are using these accessories, they may be a little heavy, so hold them in place with sticky tape until the tile adhesive is dry. Finally, fill in

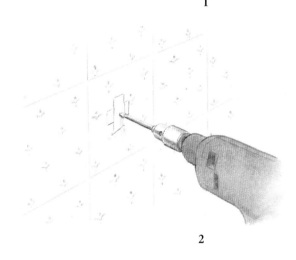

2

around the lower part of the wall, or neaten the area around the top of the window or door with part tiles. When dry, apply grout and polish up the tiles.

2 If you have to drill into tiles to make fixings after they are laid, use a slow drill speed and choose round or dome-headed, non-rust screws. Place a piece of adhesive tape over the tile to prevent the drill slipping while you work.

FABRIC-LINED ROOMS

Fabric can transform a dull room into a romantic pavilion complete with fabric-lined walls and tented ceiling – a look which is particularly impressive in a dining room but which also adds a touch of the Arabian Nights to a nondescript bedroom. Square, regular rooms are natural candidates for this treatment as the fabric can be fastened in the centre of the ceiling and allowed to billow softly to the sides. In a rectangular or less symmetrical room, you will need to plan the ceiling panels more carefully.

Fabric options

Use fabric lavishly to achieve the sumptuous draping on which this look depends. Not that you need luxury materials to create an opulent effect – light cotton will drape well and you can work wonders with generous use of cheesecloth and muslin to create a cloudy, diaphanous look which is all the more striking when hung against richly painted walls. Consider wide-width sheeting in plain colours or fine stripes, decorated at intervals with ribbons or rosettes, or choose cotton sateen lining in glowing colours to catch the light, finished with rich fringes and tassels. Watered silk adds elegance without encroaching on space but if the room is large, pattern can be used upon pattern, with garlands on the ceiling and a floral stripe on the walls, or intricately twined trellis matched with a single leaf design.

A sense of proportion

Choose materials and patterns which flatter the proportions of the room. Gauzy materials over a low ceiling or fine candy stripes on the walls will add height while a richly figured fabric for the tented roof with a deep plain one on the walls will create a more intimate setting. Opt for a tented ceiling alone to disguise an unusually high ceiling, concealing the edge beneath braid or a cornice. If the ceiling is richly decorated, concentrate fabric in pleats or panels on the walls, draping doors with *portière* curtains and windows with full-length drapes which will not interrupt the look.

RIGHT *Sumptuous yet practical, this tented ceiling adds drama to a conservatory dining room while shielding the occupants from the glare of the sun. Yards of cotton voile have been draped from the ceiling's centre and arranged in generous pleats while swags of the voile are caught up with ribbon rosettes and finished with a lace trim to decorate the windows.*

RIGHT *Walls blend with windows in this bedroom, where the wall at the head of the bed is covered with a curtain which echoes the style of the full-length drapes. The curtaining is creamy voile to match the walls and it is defined by swags of striped cotton which match both curtains and bedspread. Wooden columns mark the extent of the fabric-covered walls.*

COVERING *UP* WITH *FABRIC*

FABRIC WALLS

Measure up the area to be covered, and check the width of the fabric you intend to use. Calculate the total width of the area to be covered. For fabric gathered on to curtain wires, you will need at least 1½ times this width; for stretched and stapled fabric you will need to add an allowance for joining widths plus about 10 cm (4 in) for turning down the sides of the area to be covered, and for a pleated and stapled finish you will need to allow 2–3 times the width of the area, plus side turnings. Divide the total width of fabric required by the width of the fabric you plan to use to give the total number of drops of fabric.

Each drop of fabric has to be the height of the wall to be covered, plus 10 cm (4 in) top and bottom for making a casing or turning and stapling – make allowances for any pattern repeats. Multiply the length of each drop by the number of drops to give the total amount of fabric required.

1 Battens have to be fixed all around the room to carry the stapled fabric or the curtain hooks (page 211). The battens can be nailed in place with masonry nails, screwed, or glued with a strong building adhesive.

2 The fabric lies away from the wall, so you will have to adjust the positions of light switches, fittings and sockets, raising them away from the wall and edging them with battens so that you can fix the fabric around them. Always turn off electricity at the mains before doing this; if you do not feel confident about working with electrics, ask an electrician to do this for you. If you want to hang pictures afterwards, remember to position battens in suitable places.

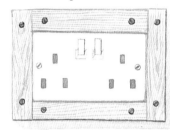

3 For gathered fabric, string curtain wires around the room along the battens. Fit extra wires above and below sockets and switches, above doors and above and below windows. Make up panels of fabric for the major areas to be covered, turning under a narrow hem down each side. Form casings top and bottom by turning under a double 5 cm (2 in) hem and making two rows of stitching 2.5 cm (1 in) apart, 2.5 cm (1 in) from the finished edge of the panel. Thread the wires through the casing and hang in place, adjusting fullness across the wall.

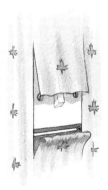

Mark the position of electrical sockets on the fabric curtain. Take down the fabric, cut an H shape and turn hems to make casings above and below the area removed for the sockets. Neaten the sides of the opening with zig-zag stitch before re-hanging.

4 For stapled fabric place extra battens vertically down the corners of the room and around doors and windows. Join widths to make up panels of fabric for each area to be covered and press under 10 cm (4 in) turnings all around. Staple one side edge of the first panel to a vertical batten at the end, working from the wrong side of the fabric with the panel of fabric turned to face the adjacent wall. Work across the wall, stapling the top edge of the fabric to the horizontal batten. Stretch the fabric, then staple the bottom edge in place. (This may be easier with two people, one working at the ceiling and the other working along the skirting.)

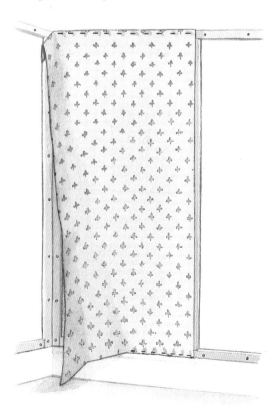

5 For pleated and stapled fabric, make up the panels, then press the pleats in position. Staple the fabric, first fixing one side, then stapling each pleat top and bottom.

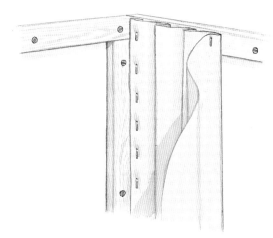

6 Finish around light switches by clipping diagonally to the corners, then turn under edges and staple in place. Cover lines of staples around the panels of fabric with strips of bias-cut fabric or lengths of woven braid.

TENTED CEILINGS

If you plan to line the walls, fit the ceiling fabric first, then fix more battens to carry the fabric on the walls. Remove any central light and check for live wiring before fixing battens to the ceiling.

1 Fix battens around the top of the room either at the top of the walls or 30–40 cm (12–15 in) down the wall for a more tented appearance or to lower the ceiling.

2 Make a scale pattern of the tent by measuring the total length of the wall and by calculating the distance from the centre point of the ceiling to each corner of the room. This will give you the measurements of the sides of the four triangles that will go to make the fabric pieces of the tent. Add an allowance for gathering, if required, and for turning under each edge and for joining any widths of fabric. Divide by the width of the fabric you plan to use to give the total amount of fabric required, allowing for any pattern repeats.

With measurements for the four triangular segments, make up the panels of fabric, hemming all sides and adding extra fullness along the base edge (the edge that is attached to the batten) if you want to pleat the fabric.

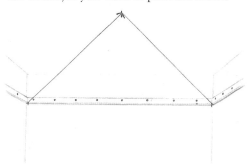

3 You can make a simple ceiling boss to provide a support for the fabric on the ceiling. Find the position of a suitable ceiling joist in the centre of the room by drilling into the ceiling every couple of centimetres until you find you are drilling into wood. You may be able to judge the position of the joists by tapping the ceiling (page 121). Alternatively, you can screw a strong hook into the joist and attach the fabric triangles to that.

Cut a block of wood about 5 cm (2 in) square and 4 cm (1½ in) thick. Then cut out a

circle of chipboard or plywood about 20 cm (8 in) in diameter.

Cover the plywood with fabric, stretching it over the front and stapling or glueing it in place on the back. Drill through the square block of wood and screw it to the joist.

4 Screw or nail the fabric-covered plywood to the wooden block. Gather each fabric piece up and staple to the underside of the batten along the top of the wall.

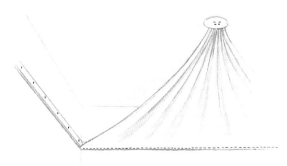

5 Gather up the centre of each piece of fabric, either with running stitches or by making a casing and drawing a cord through it. Tie it around the neck of the ceiling boss or staple in place.

Glue a decorative rosette over the raw edges of fabric. Trim with matching fabric and finish with braid or tassels as required.

HARD FLOORS

The gleam of richly waxed floorboards, the cool beauty of ceramic tiles and the warmth of cork and vinyl all demonstrate the wealth of materials available for floors. Equally extensive is the range of effects created by materials which mimic each other, where ingenuity and the need for economy combine to create floorboards stencilled to resemble a rug, ceramic tiles laid to look like marble and vinyl printed in classic tile designs.

The appeal of wood

Wood has a warmth and traditional appeal which makes it a natural choice for the home. Cherish broad oak planks with regular applications of wax polish to produce a dark glow, or follow the eighteenth-century practice of scouring with wet sand to bleach them to an attractive silvery grey. Softwood boards may have a gingery hue, so consider treating them with a translucent colour wash in grey or blue, or a creamy glaze or peach colour wood stain rubbed along the grain to reduce their brightness. This also creates the perfect background for stencils, arranged to form a border, a marble-effect chequerboard, or even a *trompe l'oeil* rug, which can be protected beneath a coat of varnish.

If the floorboards are too thin or splintery to warrant special treatment, the best solution may be to replace them with sealed softwood strips which need no further polishing, or parquet, laid in traditional herringbone or brick-bond designs, wax polished and buffed to a shine.

RIGHT *Broad, wax-polished boards form a flooring that is unrivalled for comfort and good looks. Don't aim for a varnish-like shine which looks unnaturally bright; conserve your energy by confining polish to the perimeter of the floor, adding a runner or rug to take the brunt of the wear and give extra warmth.*

LEFT *The creamy pallor of these colour-rubbed floorboards recalls the traditional look of eighteenth-century floors, which were scrubbed with sand and bleached to a silvery sheen. This treatment is achieved with eggshell paint rubbed well into the grain to provide a soft background which complements the wallpaper and furnishings.*

RIGHT *Heavy stone flags have been used for centuries in farmhouses and country homes. They need the minimum of care – simply sweep and wash – because sealing and polishing can impair their function and appearance. Here they are left to speak for themselves, but for comfort, an Indian carpet or an oriental rug suits a traditional style.*

ABOVE *What look like classic marble tiles are actually prosaic floorboards, stained and sealed for a realistic effect. The technique is relatively simple but careful planning is essential for success. Marbling has been chosen to mirror the marbled walls and dado in this setting but combed or spattered finishes can look equally attractive.*

Hard natural materials

Tiles intended for floors are thicker and less glossy than the more delicate wall tiles and are often textured for safety. Designs too are stronger, ranging from exuberant Iberian motifs to modern screen prints and facsimile Victorian designs. Plain tiles abound, in hexagonal and Provençal shapes as well as rectangles and squares, and can be interspersed with traditional diamond pieces to imitate a marble floor, or defined by a decorated border. A patterned tiled floor will become the focal point of any room so choose a design and colour which will neither date nor limit your choice of future schemes – Gothic green for a conservatory to complement plants and rattan furniture, Delft blue for a kitchen, or classic black and white for a hallway, for example.

Unglazed tiles have an unpretentious charm. Lay Mediterranean clay tiles in a hall or lobby, traditional terracotta quarry tiles in a kitchen or create a Victorian-style chequered step for an impressive entrance.

Brick and stone floors are an integral part of the fabric of a house. Like quarry tiles, they are often laid because they can cope with a degree of damp and need only minimal care. Sealing and polishing are unnecessary and may be harmful, for these floors are best swept and washed in the time-honoured manner.

Manufactured flooring

Cork, vinyl and linoleum combine the practical benefits of a smooth floor with a warmth which is welcome in cold climates. Waxed cork has a soft sheen which looks attractive in bedrooms but as cork, like wood, swells in the damp, it should be sealed for use in kitchens and bathrooms. Vinyl's resistance to water makes it an obvious choice here. There is a design to suit every taste, from travertine or tile effects for a classical floor to dazzling solid colours or three-dimensional designs which create an optical illusion. Choose a simple tile or speckle design to form an unobtrusive background for furnishings, a stronger pattern to add decorative emphasis; select vinyl tiles to make light work of awkward and irregular spaces, wide-width vinyl for fast coverage of large areas.

As an alternative, consider linoleum, made from natural materials in a range of rich, usually mottled, colours, and one of the most durable forms of flexible flooring.

RIGHT *Play tricks with perspective with a* trompe l'oeil *design like the three-dimensional block vinyl flooring shown here. A favourite with textile designers, it translates equally well onto floors.*

BELOW *Vinyl flooring is economical and easy to clean and it has a warmth and resilience which many smooth floors lack. Seamless vinyl sheeting is simple to lay and is ideal for bathrooms where flooring may get wet.*

ABOVE *Ceramic tiles lend elegance to any setting. Here black and white tiles have been laid to look like* a marbled floor. The flooring design is echoed by the border of small diamond shapes.

Finishes for Floors

Renovating Floorboards

Wooden floorboards must be thoroughly prepared to give a smooth, evenly coloured surface before you can apply a new protective finish of polyurethane varnish or floor seal. This job is too much for the average power sander, and impossible to do by hand, so you will need to hire a floor sander – which looks like a cross between a lawn mower and an upright vacuum cleaner. A large roller carries the sandpaper and the sawdust is sucked into a bag on the side. You must wear protective clothing – particularly a face mask with a replaceable muslin filter, available from the hire shop or good DIY stores. You will also need a smaller belt sander to finish around the edges and these are also available for hire. Finally, you also need several sheets of rough and smooth glasspaper, according to the condition of the boards.

1 Clear the room completely if possible and open the windows. Block the cracks around the door by stuffing paper into them. If the floor was previously covered with tacked-down lino, carpet or hardboard, lift as many nails as possible. Ensure any remaining nails and the floorboard nails are knocked well in.

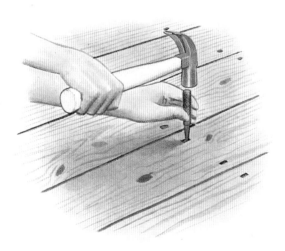

2 With a rough grade of sandpaper on the machine, start to work diagonally across the floor, first in one direction, then in the other. When you have covered as much of the floor as possible, change to a finer grade of glasspaper and work up and down the length of the boards, sanding with the grain. Finally, use the belt sander around the edge of the room, again working with the grain.

Vacuum the room thoroughly, then wipe up any remaining dust with a tack rag – a piece of lint-free rag soaked in white spirit. Avoid dampening the wood and don't walk on the surface more than you have to.

Finishes for Floorboards

Because wood is porous, it is necessary to seal the surface of the boards to prevent dirt getting ground in and water soaking in and staining. To colour boards, you can bleach them using a commercial two-part bleach, or apply a wood dye to make them darker.

To bleach the boards, apply the first part of the bleach – this will darken the wood slightly. Apply the second part of the bleach and leave according to the manufacturer's instructions. Neutralize the bleach by washing it off. This will raise the grain of the wood slightly, so sand it down lightly before sealing.

If you are staining the wood, use a purpose-made spirit-based stain, which will not raise the grain of the wood like a water-based stain. Apply evenly with a cloth, following the manufacturer's instructions.

To finish the floor, seal it using what is known as a two-part, cold cure lacquer. This has to be mixed in a china or glass (not plastic) bowl and brushed on to the floorboards. Ensure the room is clean and free from dust before you start. Work in a well-ventilated room and do not allow young children or people with weak chests to come near. The lacquer dries quickly and you should apply two or three coats. Do not rub down between coats unless there are obvious blemishes.

To bring a high gloss to the surface, use a special burnishing cream sold for the purpose. If you prefer a more natural sheen, abrade the surface by rubbing it over with fine wire wool dipped in wax polish as a lubricant to make the work easier.

If you choose to use polyurethane, thin the first coat with white spirit – ten parts polyurethane to one part white spirit. Apply two more coats of gloss polyurethane, and either finish with satin or matt polyurethane, or rub with wire wool dipped in wax for a sheen finish.

To make the polyurethane look less synthetic and to prevent it from yellowing the boards, you can mix in a little white eggshell (oil-based) paint to give it a milky colouring.

LAYING SHEET VINYL

Vinyl is available in sheet or tile form, often imitating other types of flooring such as brick, tile, wood or cork.

Start by measuring up the room (page 212) and choose an appropriate width. Aim to lay the flooring with a minimum of seams. If you are laying the vinyl over old floorboards, prepare the floor by covering it with sheets of hardboard nailed down every 15 cm (6 in). Unroll the vinyl as much as possible and leave it in a warm room for 24 hours.

Most types of sheet vinyl need no fixing, but thinner types can be anchored with a double-sided flooring tape.

1 Decide which way the vinyl should be laid in the room, and unroll it so that one straight edge is aligned with one wall of the room. If the wall is straight, you can butt it up straight away; if it is irregular, keep the edge of the vinyl a couple of centimetres from the skirting.

Fit the first edge by scribing the vinyl. The simplest way to do this is to take an offcut of wood about 10 cm (4 in) long. Hold a pencil against one end and run the opposite end of the piece of wood along the skirting, so that the pencil marks the vinyl, and reproduces the irregularities along the wall.

Use a sharp craft knife to cut the vinyl along the marked line. If one of the adjacent walls has minor irregularities, repeat the process and scribe the adjacent edge. Larger irregularities, such as chimney breasts and window bays, have to be treated differently (see 3).

2 Butt the trimmed edge to the skirting, and flatten out the vinyl as much as possible. The next step is to make 'freeing cuts' at the corners of the room, cutting into the waste part of the sheet. Cut diagonally across the corner: trim a little at a time and test the fit, so that you do not cut too far into the sheet.

At external corners, cut diagonally towards the point of the corner. Handle carefully, particularly with lightweight flooring, to prevent tearing.

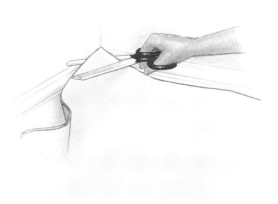

3 As you make each freeing cut, the waste will lap up the skirting. Trim the waste to about 10 cm (4 in) to make the vinyl easier to handle.

With the vinyl lying flat, crease it into the angle of the skirting. Use a sharp trimming knife to trim away the final strip of waste, following the skirting as accurately as possible. Trim neatly around pipes.

Around larger obstacles, such as WCs and basin pedestals, the trimming will be easier if you cut a paper template. Adjust the template for a perfect fit, then transfer the outline to the vinyl and trim with a sharp knife.

4 If you have to make a seam in the vinyl, try to use the machined edges to ensure a good join. Lay one portion of the vinyl, then stick a strip of double-sided tape under the straight edge of the next strip to be laid. Butt this strip up to the first so that the pattern matches and press both edges together, sticking them to the tape.

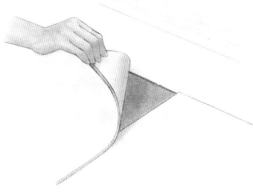

5 If the seam is not along the machined edge of the vinyl, overlap the two edges to be joined, arranging the upper sheet so that the pattern matches down the free edge. Use a straightedge and trimming knife to cut through both layers of vinyl at once. Peel away the waste from the top layer, then lift it up and pull out the waste from the bottom layer. Finally, position a strip of double-sided tape along the seamline and stick the edges to make a perfect butt joint (see 4).

With square or rectangular tile patterns, try to arrange the seam along the line of the pattern.

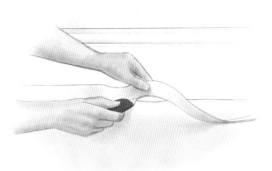

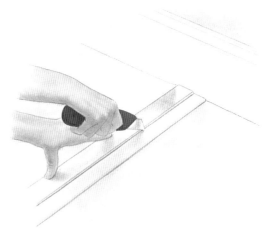

LAYING VINYL & CORK TILES

Tiles are available in many sizes, shapes and materials. Planning is important to avoid having to cut awkward amounts off the tiles around the edge of the room. To make the job easier, start from the centre of the room.

Some tiles are self-adhesive, others have to be stuck in place with special tile adhesive. Vinyl tiles, for example, may have a self-adhesive backing, or may be laid with suitable flooring adhesive. Special adhesives, which do not soak into the tile, are available for cork tiles. Like vinyl sheets, tiles should be laid on to a hardboard or playwood subfloor (page 210). Look at the backs of the tiles; some are marked with an arrow to show which way they should be laid.

1 Find the centre of the room by marking the mid point of each wall, and joining the points with straight lines. Check that the lines join at right angles. Lay a dry run of tiles, so that you can check how they will fit: the aim is to arrange the tiles so that a manageable amount, a third to two thirds of a tile, has to be trimmed around the edge of the room. This makes trimming easier, and builds in an allowance for slightly angled walls; no room has truly square walls. Adjust the position of the central tile until the tiles fit well.

2 If you are using an adhesive, spread a thin layer over an area about a metre (3 ft) square, starting from the guidelines in the angle furthest from the door.

3 Position the first tile, then butt the adjacent tiles to it. Fill in the first square, then spread adhesive over the next area, working towards the wall. Use a soft cloth to wipe off any adhesive which oozes out between the tiles. Lay all the uncut tiles, finishing with the quarter of the room closest to the door. Leave the adhesive to set on these tiles for about 24 hours; don't walk on them. With self-adhesive tiles, simply peel off the backing and stick them in place in the same order.

4 To fit the edge tiles, lay the tile to be cut over the last complete tile. Take a spare whole tile and butt it to the skirting board. Mark the tile to be cut along the outer edge of the spare tile.

5 Cut along the marked line and fit the trimmed tiles into the spaces around the edge of the room.

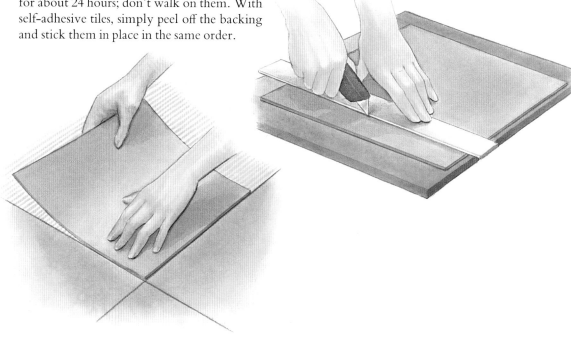

6 At internal corners, cut a paper template to fit the space and use it to mark the tile to be cut. At external corners, mark as for straight edge tiles, adjusting the position of the tile to mark each angle of the corner.

7 At doorways, use a scribing tool to transfer the shape of the molding to the tile. Allow the adhesive to dry for at least 24 hours or according to the manufacturer's instructions.

Seal cork tiles with three coats of varnish, following the instructions for sealing floorboards.

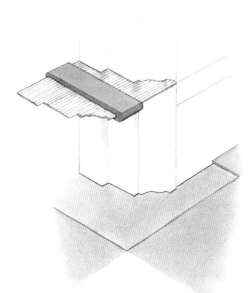

LAYING CERAMIC TILES

Ceramic tiles are laid on a thin layer of ceramic floor tile adhesive, and quarry tiles are laid on a bed of mortar. Both types have to be grouted – use a thin mortar mix for quarry tiles.

For best results, ceramic tiles should be laid on a solid subfloor, and if the tiles you choose are not glazed, they should be sealed to prevent them soaking up water and grease in kitchens and bathrooms.

1 Plan the position in the same way as for vinyl and cork tiles. Use spacers to make even gaps between the tiles for grouting. Spread adhesive and lay about four tiles at a time, using a spirit level to check they are flat.

Work out from the centre of the room and lay all the complete tiles, finishing at the door, as for vinyl and cork tiles. Leave the adhesive to set for 24 hours, then fit the edge tiles. Use a tile cutting machine to cut the tiles (page 71), and apply the adhesive to the trimmed tile rather than to the subfloor.

2 Grout the tiles, using a rubber window-cleaning blade to smooth it into the cracks. Smooth the grout by running a piece of dowel or the adhesive spreader along the joints. Wipe all the surplus grout off the surface of the tiles. If you have laid quarry tiles, they may have to be sealed.

Carpets & Rugs

Originally carpets were precious items, draped over furniture or proudly displayed on walls but never laid on the floor, where rush matting sufficed. Although we now take soft flooring for granted, it can have great impact on any scheme, both aesthetically and practically, whether you use wall-to-wall carpeting or a variety of rugs. Laid over waxed wood, ceramic tiles or even plain wall-to-wall carpets, oriental carpets or densely woven Brussels weave rugs (a wool weave with tight uncut loop pile) give a layered look to soft furnishings and a sense of opulence. A similar effect can be achieved with simple rag rugs or painted floor cloths set over bleached or colourwashed floorboards in a bedroom, or sisal matting on quarry tiles in a country kitchen. But there is no need to confine rugs and squares to the floor: they look equally splendid hung from stretchers on the walls or cast over sofas and beds in the traditional manner.

Fitted carpet

Wall-to-wall carpet is warm, luxurious and comes in a range of colours and patterns. It should add to the decoration of a room without overwhelming it. Plain carpets are usually preferable because they give an impression of space, and soft or neutral tones are favourites because they blend with a variety of furnishings. When choosing a colour, it is important to realize that dark carpets absorb light. If it is impractical to lay pale carpet in a dark room to reflect more light, consider a soft tone like apricot, gold or pale jade, with bordered rugs placed strategically in front of the sofa and fireplace to take the wear. Pure wool weave is the classic, if expensive, choice for fitted carpet but a pile which includes a percentage of synthetic fibres can look equally acceptable and is more hardwearing.

For well used halls and stairways, look for carpets with tiny flecks of colour which disguise wear or opt for a carpet with a stylized design like a *fleur-de-lys* motif or a trellis pattern.

ABOVE *Layered treatments give a sumptuous effect, even when the materials are as economical as the sisal matting here. The matting looks surprisingly effective teamed with a blue carpeted border. The colours are chosen to repeat the gold and midnight blue of the wallpaper and soft furnishings.*

LEFT *Traditional woven carpet squares are natural companions for elegant furniture. The design on this midnight blue carpet adds decorative interest at floor level, picking up the geometric pattern of the sofa cushions.*

RIGHT *Rugs have a warmth which is always welcome underfoot in bathrooms. Their texture also conveys a visual warmth which offsets the cool gleam of impervious flooring, such as these ceramic tiles. Even small rugs should contribute to the décor, so choose colours and designs that emphasize those used elsewhere or that blend with the overall scheme.*

Rugs

Rugs in geometric or floral patterns, bordered designs or antique kelims, or textured rugs in neutral shades can be used to define areas in a room. Choose one large rug rather than several small ones. Underlay helps to prevent slipping on a polished floor, and reduces wear.

Pattern or plain

Some collections of carpets include both patterns and plains in a palette of co-ordinating colours. Borders can be fitted to plain carpets to emphasize the shape of a room, or when used throughout the house to link rooms with one another. Bear in mind the pattern or colour combinations that occur where rooms meet. Where two patterned carpets run together, try to ensure they are harmonious in design or linked by common colours. In smaller homes it is wise to choose a single style of carpet throughout to increase the

LEFT *Revive the Victorian floorcloth with a printed design which can be put to a variety of decorative and protective purposes. Although it is cheap to buy, you can create a unique design by painting or stencilling a pattern onto sturdy cotton yourself.*

feeling of space and to provide a neutral background for furnishings. Consider plain carpet in one colour but two grades, for heavy and medium wear, or a hardwearing and unpretentious floorcovering such as cord. With the addition of carefully chosen rugs, this economical scheme can look most luxurious.

Making Floor Cloths & Rugs

There are a number of ways to use fabric for floor coverings. Rag rugs are a traditional way of covering floors with fabric, whether plaited or tufted. To make a patterned floor cloth, choose tightly woven canvas, available from artist's suppliers in a good range of widths if you can't find suitable canvas in the furnishing fabric department. Deckchair canvas is a good choice, but because it is usually narrow it is really only suitable for 'runners' in hallways, for example. You can stencil the fabric first, or do your own freehand design with fabric paints, or you can leave the cloth plain. Always wash fabric before stencilling to remove the dressing, and dye it with a cold water dye if necessary to give a good background colour.

If the floor covering is laid on floorboards, you can prevent it from slipping by laying rubber mesh beneath it.

Stencilling Fabric

Prepare a padded surface – an old blanket and white sheet stretched over a table is ideal. Press the fabric to be stencilled, and pin it over the padded surface.

Use dressmaker's chalk to mark guidelines for the stencil – a border pattern, a series of motifs spaced evenly or irregularly across the fabric, for example – and decide which colours to use for which element of the stencil. Position the stencil, fixing it in place with masking tape to hold it steady.

1 Tip a little fabric paint into a saucer and use a stencil brush or sponge to dab the paint on. Apply very little at a time, gradually building up the colour. Err on the side of too little: if you apply too much it will seep under the stencil and take a long time to dry, or soak into the fabric and run. If necessary, you can always repeat the process to strengthen the colour once the first coat has dried.

2 Work around the area to be stencilled, applying the first colour. When dry, press the fabric to set the colour, then repeat the process for subsequent colours.

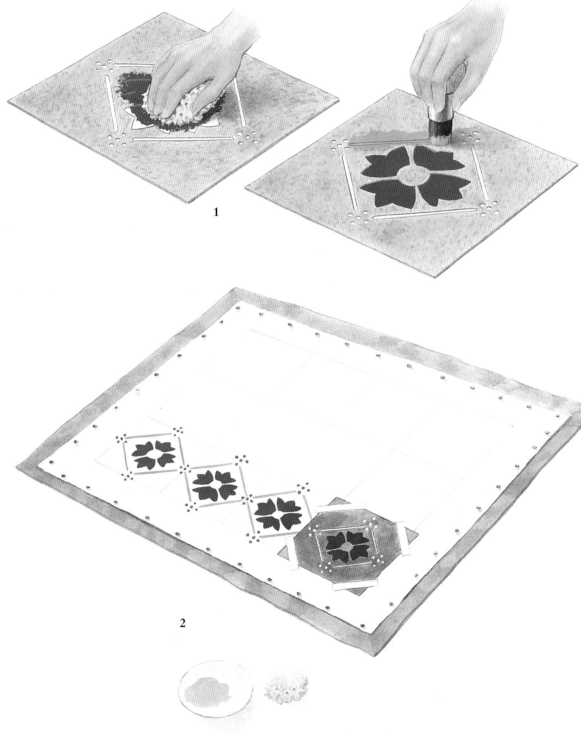

1

2

MAKING A FLOOR CLOTH

Cut the fabric, allowing a substantial seam and trimming allowance along the edge of the canvas. Wash the fabric, and press while still damp to ensure a completely flat panel.

To give a protective finish and to prevent the fabric from curling up at the corners, use fabric stiffener or a PVA adhesive mixed with water in the ratio 1:5. Spray or dip the canvas; for a large panel, lay it out flat and paint on the solution. If the canvas is slightly damp, it will soak up the stiffener more easily.

Hang the fabric up to dry, keeping most of the panel as flat and smooth as possible.

Prepare a hessian backing and a 10–15 cm (4–6 in) wide strip of canvas binding, cut on the straight grain, stiffening it in the same way. When dry, lay the fabric on top of the hessian (*right*). Trim edges to match, then pin and stitch together around the edges. Fold and finger press the binding strip, and use it to finish the raw edges (page 200).

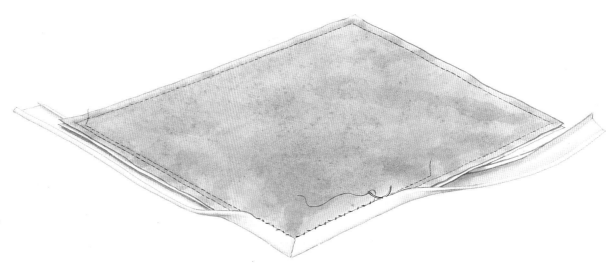

PLAITED RAG RUG

A plaited rag rug can be made from remnants of fabric, but because it takes a surprising amount of material, you may have to buy some of your needs. Choose colours and weights to suit the situation. For example, towelling would be appropriate for a bathroom, and remnants of chintz in deep colours would be a good choice for disguising wear and tear in a child's room.

Cut the fabric into strips, about 15 cm (6 in) wide. Press in the raw edges by about 6 mm ($\frac{1}{4}$ in) and then press the strip in half along the length so that only the right side of the fabric shows and the raw edges are enclosed. Prepare plenty of strips in this way.

To begin the plait, you need to stitch three strips together at one end. Plaiting is easier if someone holds the end of the plait; otherwise anchor the end by pinning it to an old table or chair. Plait the strips, taking care to keep your tension even. When you reach the end of one strip, simply stitch the beginning of the next to it and continue plaiting. Coil up the plait as you work. Try not to join all three strips in the same place; bumps will appear in the finished plait.

When you have plaited several metres, start to stitch the plait to form a coiled rug: for an oval rug, start with a straight strip of plait and double the plait back on itself, slipstitching the sides of the plait together. Work round and round the central strip, until you have reached the desired size. Trim and turn in the raw edges at the end of the plait and stitch firmly to the side of the rug.

The rug can be backed with stiffened cotton or canvas. Cut a backing the same size as the finished rug, turn under a 12–15 mm ($\frac{1}{2}$–$\frac{5}{8}$ in) hem all around and lockstitch the lining to the back of the rug. Slipstitch the folded edge of the backing to the inner edge of the outer plait.

Doors

Doors set the style of the entrance to a house and every room within it. The front door is all important because it combines with the windows to define the character of a house. Interior doors should relate to each other and to the house so that whatever the individual treatment, a sense of unity prevails.

A sense of style

The right door is not necessarily one which catches the eye. It may be a simple ledge and brace cottage door or a classic panelled design, lacquered in black or white for an elegant entrance or waxed or matt painted to blend with interior walls. Examine flush doors to see if they are unexpectedly thick as frequently the panel can be prised off to reveal an original door beneath.

The treatment depends on the condition of the door as well as the style of the room. Many old doors have been patched and filled over the years and look best covered with paint rather than unforgiving varnish; a dragged finish looks particularly elegant. Panelled doors offer the most scope as the panels can be papered to match the walls (particularly pretty in bedrooms and bathrooms), sponged or marbled to contrast with the surround, or the moldings can be highlighted for emphasis. A flush door can substitute for a panelled door with the addition of beading to create false panels. Etched or bevelled glass fanlights above a door (never within it) let light into a room while preserving privacy.

The finishing touch

Choose door furniture which is in keeping with the style of both door and house – brass or china for a nineteenth-century home, a black iron latch for a traditional cottage. Though it should be similar in style there is no need for all door furniture to match. Keep to one material, with plain china on kitchen doors, simple geometric designs for living rooms and delicately painted floral or fruit designs for bedrooms.

ABOVE *An attractive arched larder door provides an unusual alternative to the ledge and brace doors commonly found in cottages and farmhouses. This modern version is designed with slats for ventilation.*

RIGHT *'Losing' wardrobe doors by decorating them in the same way as the surrounding walls helps to create an impression of space and prevents the doors from interrupting the contrived décor. Paint treatment can be continued over the doors and frame, as well as other obstacles like pipes and radiators, for an all-embracing effect.*

ABOVE *Reverse the decorative conventions of coloured walls and white woodwork by selecting a deep colour for doors and skirting. Here the soft blue of the wallpaper is picked up by the paintwork which offsets the rich tones of the solid oak dresser and cabinets and links the kitchen to the lobby beyond.*

RIGHT *Graceful doors are enhanced by a treatment which shows off their elegant proportions. A traditional nineteenth-century four-panelled door can be decorated in a number of ways – painted a single colour, given contrasting moldings or decorated with a painted surround and panels papered to match the walls. Here the first option has been chosen, leaving nothing to distract the eye.*

ABOVE *Carefully distressed to simulate the patina that comes with age, this painted wardrobe has an understated charm which adds to its period setting. The line decoration is drawn to resemble panels and to give an effect of symmetry. This is a technique to copy on doors that are in poor condition, where patched or filled areas make stripping or varnishing impractical.*

DECORATING DOORS

The most popular finish for doors is gloss paint, although an eggshell finish produces a softer effect. Other paint finishes (pages 62–65) should be given protective coats of varnish. Doors can also be decorated by applying beading to reproduce panelling.

RENOVATING A DOOR

1 Whatever finish you choose, first prepare the woodwork thoroughly. Remove the door handle by unscrewing the grub screw on the side of the handle and slipping the handle off, then removing the faceplate. If the door was covered with hardboard, remove tacks and fill any holes with wood filler. Strip the door back to the bare wood. Rub down with medium and then fine grade glasspaper.

For a traditional waxed finish, apply good-quality beeswax polish, with wire wool, working in a little at a time. Apply the polish along the grain, rubbing up with a circular motion. Stand the polish near a radiator to help it flow if it is very hard.

For a natural, more hardwearing finish, apply a first coat of thinned polyurethane gloss varnish, then a coat of full strength gloss. Work with the grain of the wood. Then apply further coats of gloss, silk or matt finish.

For a painted finish, apply a coat of primer if necessary (page 208), and then an undercoat. Apply at least two top coats. For flush doors, divide the door into six imaginary panels. Apply paint to each in turn, first laying the paint on with two or three vertical brush strokes (page 57). Work the paint in horizontally, then 'lay off' the paint with upward, vertical strokes.

2 On panelled doors work in panels, following the numbered sequence for applying the paint and finishing with the grain of the wood.

3 If the door and frame are painted a different colour on each side, paint the hinge edge the same colour as the visible side of the door and the lock edge the colour of the side that opens into the room.

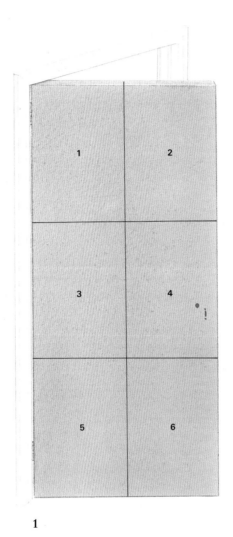

1

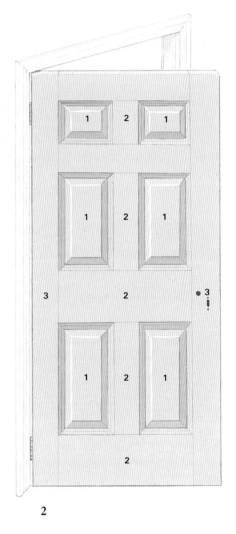

2

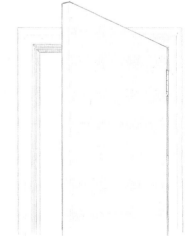

3

DRAGGING THE PANELS

For a dragged finish, apply a base coat of eggshell, then mix the glaze (page 60). Apply the glaze, following the same order as for painting the door. Run a dry, wide brush or dragging brush through the wet glaze to give a gently striped effect.

When dragging the outer frame of the door, use a piece of card or a strip of metal to mask each section of the door as you apply the glaze and drag the strips which run at right angles. Combine two effects, for example, distressing the molding and dragging the flat panels of the door to give extra emphasis. You could also choose marbling as a decorative finish for a door and architrave.

REPLACING DOOR FURNITURE

To replace door furniture, slip the square spindle through the catch mechanism and position the plates, which fit around the neck of the handle, flush against the door. Fit the handles on to each side, inserting packing blocks if necessary. (These should be supplied with the door handles. They prevent the handle from rattling.) Screw the handle in place with the grub screw in the neck. Add keyholes and covers (escutcheons), if they are not included in the faceplates.

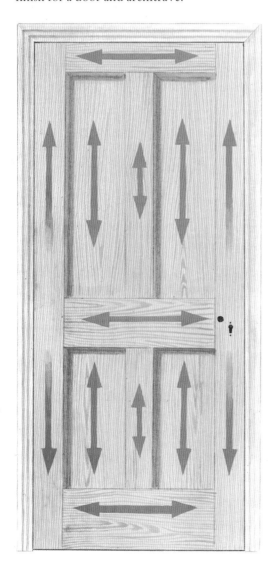

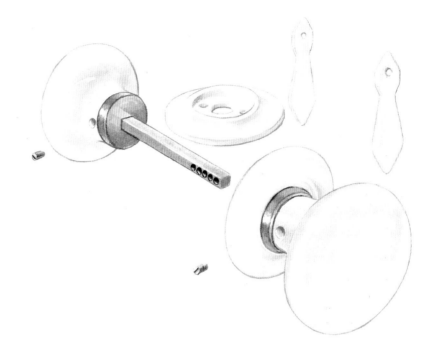

WINDOW DRESSING

DECIDING THE STYLE

Decorative window treatments can lend style to rooms that have no distinct character of their own, or emphasize architectural details that already exist. Be adventurous in your choice of window treatment but make sure that it works with the scale and style of the room. A simple Roman blind or muslin drape may not seem the obvious choice for a tall sash window but it can underline the serene proportions and architectural detail of a large, airy room.

The spare lines of a small modern interior can look more expansive when windows are distinguished by neatly scaled pelmets (valances) that conceal the gap between the top of the frame and the uncorniced ceiling; full curtains held with tie-backs will also soften the hard angles of wide rectangular windows. In a rustic cottage-style interior, opt for a decorative treatment in keeping with its robust simplicity. You may decide against having curtains at all. Or try gathered curtains without frill or trimming in natural linen or simple stripes and checks, fitted to a plain brass rod, or screen windows with discreet blinds.

Shutters, either in cold climates or full sun, are a screen to the outside world, while in many European homes, curtains are never drawn, allowing passers-by the view of a beautifully lit room by night.

The window shape
For ideas and inspiration look at magazines and design catalogues but consider first the size and shape of your windows. Depending on the age of a house, the windows usually cannot be changed without affecting the character of the house. Sash and casement windows take most window treatments; emphasize the elegance of sash windows with curtains that draw right back in the daytime. Horizontal windows and bay windows should be treated as a single unit. If the sill is not wide, floor-length curtains are best and they help to give a sense of proportion depending on where the pole or track is positioned. Experiment to get

ABOVE *Where privacy exists in the location, and the window itself is appealing, there is advocacy enough for neither curtain nor blind. A hand-carved Gothic arch within each window frame requires no dressing beyond the blue and white china and country flowers on the deep sill.*

LEFT *A window cut awkwardly into the line of a sloping ceiling would defeat any standard style of curtaining. A gathered drape fixed along the top of the window and part way down the slope is lifted back along its edge and hooked on to the ceiling.*

the best effect and be generous with the fabric. Horizontal windows can be kept simple with wide roller blinds in a plain colour to correspond to the colour of the surrounds.

Large picture windows, depending on the climate, can be left without window dressing, or install an awning to keep out strong sunlight. If insulation is necessary, hang full-length lined and interlined curtains across the expanse of glass.

Shaped windows often benefit from no window dressing at all. Arched and porthole windows will lose their appeal if they have traditional curtains. An individual approach is better; fit fixed curtains with tie-backs, or an extra long track so that the fabric hangs well away from the window by day. Fixed curtains on curtain wire or rods with cased headings top and bottom are ideal for French windows, skylights and pivoting windows where the fabric would get in the way if it was not secured.

Style and fabric

Simple window dressing in which the pattern and texture of the fabric have greatest emphasis can still make effective use of detailing. Try using a lining in a contrasting colour. A simple gathered pelmet (valance) or shaped tie-back can be neatly trimmed in a contrasting binding, while the graphic lines of a Roman blind can be defined with a plain border, or edged with gimp.

LEFT *Full Austrian blinds pulled up high at the side windows partner door curtains which are tied back to outline a triangular fanlight and then fall clear of the swing of the door. With both blind and curtain headings fixed at the cornice and cruciform bows adding detail, unity is settled upon the architectural pattern of the windows and door.*

ABOVE *Shutters are not an original feature of this room but they have been used well to provide privacy and let in light. The top half has been lifted clear of the window in this narrow bathroom by means of a hydraulic system.*

The length of a curtain treatment will also have a bearing on the overall effect. Full-length curtains can hang to the floor, skimming the carpet or floorboards, or they can create a luxurious pool of fabric. For small windows that require a less ornate treatment, try hanging short curtains high above the top of the window frame and instead of the traditional sill length, let them fall the same distance below for a more sophisticated look. If there is a radiator beneath the window, team full-length dress curtains with a Roman, Austrian or roller blind.

The choice of fabric for curtains is almost unlimited. Only the heaviest tapestries and weaves are unsuitable because of their weight and bulk. But every fabric has a distinctive draping quality which can be used to advantage. Visualize the impact of a festooned heading in damask, and then in glazed chintz. The damask will exude richness and weight by the way it folds; the chintz will crumple with a light, crisp vitality. Some fabrics, such as soft cotton satins, have an almost liquid quality. This is the type of fabric to use in a single dramatic length, looped round a heavy pole and falling to the floor. If it is a tailored look of weight and substance that is required, then nothing will equal a pelmet (valance) of box pleats in a fine linen that will press knife-sharp.

Some of the most humble fabrics, such as undyed calico and muslin, are inexpensive but do not look cheap. The simple propriety of unbleached linen, neutral woven cottons and ticking stripes can be fashioned into a grand statement or one that has simple, classic lines.

The scale of a pattern must also suit the context and the proportions in which it is to be seen. Use designs that are imposing in scale and colour for special effects. Small prints lose their definition over a large area and tend to look fussy. Keep them for neat windows where the detail of the design will not be lost. Discreet tone on tone prints, however, will add depth of colour and surface texture.

Pelmets (valances) and tie-backs

Stiffened pelmets (valances) give structure to a window. They can be draped and partly concealed with swags and festoons of fabric that loop or overlap across a wide window, or they

can be a feature in themselves, perhaps stencilled or painted with *trompe l'oeil*.

Some pelmets (valances) have a softer face, overhanging the heading of the curtains beneath and sometimes shaped for a more decorative outline. Any of the usual heading styles can be used, from soft gathers to more formal pleats.

Crisp pleated pelmets (valances) suit small formal rooms, gathered ones suggest artless prettiness. But for the bravura performance, they can hang deep, subtly shaped and lavishly trimmed. Or they can be cut into elaborate shapes and underpinned with festoons; they can grow into lambrequins that extend well down each side of the window, or they can be shaped with an easy elegance of line and given added definition with a plain contrast edging.

Tie-backs are another decorative detail for window dressing. They can be utilitarian or purely decorative, plain and shaped or braided and finished with a rosette. Choose a contrasting fabric or use the main curtain fabric with a contrasting trim.

ABOVE *Windows that lie side by side on the same wall should be considered as a unit. These casement windows are covered with a series of single scoop festoon blinds in a lightly patterned chintz. Where privacy is not a main concern, as on a landing, the blinds can be drawn up permanently to provide a fabric pelmet (valance). The window dressing unifies the room décor by linking all three windows and co-ordinating with wallpaper, border and floor covering.*

LEFT *The gathered pelmet (valance) is naturally predisposed to express prettiness, not high grandeur. However, when it is made in a heavier cloth, such as printed linen, and trimmed with a fringe, the extra weight and substance provide added dignity for a formal bay window treatment, while concealing the curtain track.*

RIGHT *An eye-catching shaped pelmet (valance) emphasizes the proportions of this bedroom window. Curtains are abbreviated to half drops of voile, casually tied in loose knots; there is the suggestion rather than the substance of privacy in a location that does not demand a screen for light or view.*

ABOVE *A deep fabric border intended to work with a companion print makes a distinctive impact when used to make up a pelmet (valance). Tie-backs cut and shaped from a section of the border print capitalise on the co-ordinated range.*

ABOVE *Cord and tassel tie-backs have an elegance of style that particularly suits the period interior, adding a touch of formality. Pick out a contrast or toning tassel and cord. Cord tie-backs are traditionally positioned just above dado rail height.*

ABOVE *Crescent-shaped tie-backs are deepest at their centre, and cut into the leading edge of the curtain. These wide tie-backs also influence the appearance of the curtains at the hemline, creating a descending tail from the leading to the outer edge.*

CURTAIN *EQUIPMENT*

The way your curtains hang is affected by two things: the type of track you use, and the type of heading you make at the top of the curtains. The heading gathers the fabric, an important element in the style of the curtain, as well as providing a means to hang it from the track. Hooks fitted to the heading link into runners or rings, normally supplied with the track. There are one or two variations on this arrangement. Some tracks have runners with hooks built into them, so you do not need separate curtain hooks; and cased headings slot directly onto a rod or pole, so there are no runners or tracks. There are special fixings for panels of lace and shower curtains.

Choosing tracks, rods and poles

For most purposes, a plain metal or plastic track is suitable. Some tracks are on show when the curtains are open, others are intended to be covered by a pelmet (valance) or swags and tails.

More decorative effects can be achieved with wooden or brass poles above the window, and for lighter curtains there are slim brass rods or stretch curtain wires for use with a cased heading.

When buying tracks, check that the track is suitable for the weight of curtains you plan to make, and that it can be fixed to the wall or frame above the window (face fixed), ceiling mounted or fitted within a recess, according to your needs.

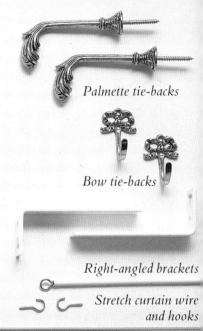

Palmette tie-backs

Bow tie-backs

Right-angled brackets

Stretch curtain wire and hooks

Café curtain rod

Corded brass pole with rings

Wooden pole with rings

If the window has angles or curves, as with bay or bow windows, check that the track can go around the bend. For medium- and heavy-weight drapes, and pale-coloured curtain fabric, it is worth using a cording set so that you can draw the curtains without putting unnecessary strain on the leading edge of the curtains – this helps to prolong wear and reduces the need for cleaning.

Heading tapes

Heading tapes either have drawstrings running through them which pull up to form a gathered or pleated heading plus woven loops to fit the hooks into or they have woven slots into which pronged curtain hooks are fitted to form pleats across the top of the curtain. Many heading tapes have the effect of stiffening a few centimetres across the top of the curtain, which gives a crisp finish and helps heavy curtains to hang well. The manufacturer will indicate how much fullness is required in the curtain for the different sorts of heading tape.

Roman blinds and Austrian blinds have special tapes with rings sewn to them at regular intervals to carry the cords for pulling the blind. Cased headings involve making two lines of stitching across the top hem of the curtain so they can be slotted onto a pole, rod or wire.

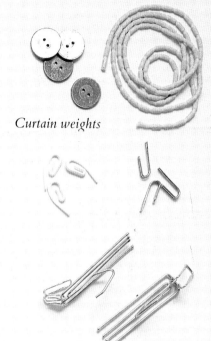
Curtain weights

Standard tape

Lining tape

Regular and pronged hooks

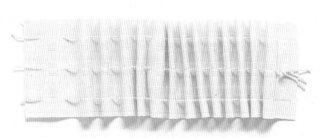
Pencil pleat tape

Triple or pinch pleat tape

Interfacing

Plastic track with cording set

Regular plastic track

MAKING HEADED CURTAINS

Heading tapes enable you to finish the top of the curtain and draw up the fullness with the minimum of trouble. They may be used on lined or unlined curtains. To simplify the instructions here, a standard 2.5 cm (1 in) wide gathered heading tape is shown on unlined curtains, and a 8 cm (3 in) wide pencil- or pinch-pleated heading tape on lined curtains. You can use whatever combination you need, and other widths and styles of tape are available. Adjust dimensions and turnings accordingly.

Before buying fabric, fit the curtain track or pole and measure up (page 204). Decide on a suitable fabric, noting the width, and check how much fullness you will need for the heading tape you have chosen. This will help you to calculate the amount of fabric.

Curtains do not take heavy wear but they do suffer from the fading effects of sunlight. Some colours, such as deep blues and apricots, are especially susceptible and, although not all curtains need to be lined, this is one good reason for doing so. Lining, and interlining with bump or domette, also improves the fall of curtains and controls heat loss through the windows. Sateen lining fabrics are tightly woven in cotton or blended fibres, in white, cream and other colours. Match the lining fabric to the ground colour of a patterned curtain. Brightly coloured linings are best kept for deep toned curtains where the colour of the lining will not show through. Co-ordinated furnishing prints or patterned linings are another alternative to plain sateens and follow the nineteenth-century practice of making the exterior view of the windows both consistent and attractive.

For standard, unlined curtains, allow $1\frac{1}{2}$–2 times the fullness. Divide the total width required for each finished (ungathered) curtain by the width of the fabric, rounding up to the nearest half width for each of the pair of curtains. Check that this gives you enough for 4 cm ($1\frac{1}{2}$ in) hems down each side edge. Each curtain is made up from one or more drops of fabric, full or half-width. The total length of each drop is the finished length of the curtains,

plus 2 cm ($\frac{3}{4}$ in) turning at the top and 10 cm (4 in) for the hem. Include an allowance (the length of the pattern repeat) for pattern matching. Multiply by the number of drops of fabric required.

For lined curtains, allow fullness according to the type of tape you are using. Allow 4 cm ($1\frac{1}{2}$ in) side hems when calculating the number of drops of fabric. Include a turning allowance of 8 cm (3 in) – the depth of the heading tape – and a hem allowance of 10 cm (4 in). Include any allowance for pattern matching.

Since lining fabric is generally slightly narrower than curtain fabric, it is usually fairly simple to calculate the amount needed. Allow the same amount of fullness for the total width of the curtain, but there is no need to include an allowance for side turnings. No allowance is needed at the top of the curtain, and only 6 cm ($2\frac{1}{2}$ in) for hems.

The amount of curtain tape for each curtain is the same as the finished (ungathered or unpleated) width, plus a few centimetres for turning under at each end.

JOINING FABRIC WIDTHS

The first step in making curtains is to join fabric widths. Use only full and half widths of fabric. Always make sure that the pattern matches across the complete set of curtains. Slip-tacking (page 196) is useful for patterns which are difficult to match. Position half widths (if required) at the outer edge of each curtain. Use flat seams for curtain fabric and lining, and clip into selvedges to prevent the seams from puckering.

MAKING UNLINED CURTAINS

1 After joining fabric widths with flat fell seams (page 198), turn under 2 cm ($\frac{3}{4}$ in) wide double hems down each outer edge of the panel of fabric for each curtain. Topstitch or hem in place.

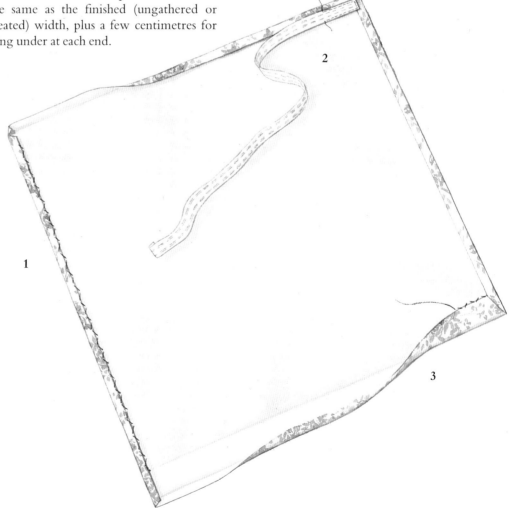

2 At the top, make sure that the fabric edge is straight (page 197), turn over a 2 cm (¾ in) wide turning, mitring corners (page 200) and trimming away excess fabric if necessary. Cut heading tape to length, turning under 1 cm (⅜ in) at each end, and pin it in place across the top of the curtain 1 cm (⅜ in) from the top fold, so the raw edge is covered. Pin, then topstitch, making extra lines of stitching across the tape ends to hold the drawstrings firmly.

3 Turn up 2 cm (1 in), then 8 cm (3 in) across the lower edge of the curtain and slipstitch in place, or use a machine hemming stitch. Use drawstrings to gather the curtains, tying the cords firmly near the centre of the curtain. Fit hooks into the woven loops and hang the curtains.

If the curtains are to fit inside a window recess, the length has to be precise, therefore gather and hang the curtains before hemming. This is also advisable with loosely woven fabrics which may 'drop' – leave them for at least 24 hours before hemming.

Unlined curtains can be backed if you make up separate lining and fit a special lining tape. This requires no extra allowance along the top edge of the lining. The lining fabric slips between the two layers of tape and is machined in place. This method will not however, improve the hang of the curtain. It will provide extra insulation and protect the curtain fabric from strong sunlight and fading, as well as making it easier to wash. The curtain hooks are inserted through the lining tape and then into the curtain heading tape before hanging. The lining and curtain can then be hand-sewn together at intervals down the edges, if necessary.

LINED CURTAINS WITH HEADING TAPES

It is not essential to line curtains but linings do make them more efficient, keeping out the light on bright summer days and keeping in the heat on cold winter evenings. Purpose-designed lining fabrics are available in tightly woven cotton or blended fibres, in a range of colours to suit most needs. You can use co-ordinating furnishing fabrics for curtain linings, plain glazed cotton with floral prints, formal satin stripes with rich velvet or combinations of printed fabric of the same weight.

Always check the effect of the fabric and lining together before buying by draping a length of both fabrics together while they are still on the roll. Ensure that they hang well and that no colour or pattern shows through the main fabric.

To make curtains even more effective, both in the way they insulate the window and in the way they drape, interlining can be used between the curtain fabric and the lining. Thick, soft fabric (usually bump or domette) is held against the curtain fabric with tiny, loose stitches (page 196).

1 Join fabric widths for curtain and lining, so that the lining panel is 8 cm (3 in) narrower and up to 15 cm (6 in) shorter than the main fabric. Turn under a 4 cm (1½ in) double hem across the lower edge of lining. Lay out the fabric, right side up, and position the lining on top of it, so that the raw edge at the top of the lining is 10 cm (4 in) below the raw edge at the top of the curtain. Adjust fabric so that you can pin the side edges of the curtain and lining together. Stitch together, taking 2 cm (¾ in) wide seams. Press seam allowances towards lining.

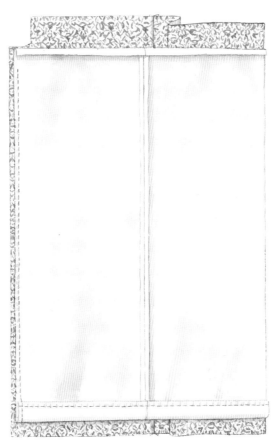

2 Turn the curtain right side out and press, so that the curtain fabric turns to the back of the curtain for 2 cm (¾ in) down each side edge. Turn over the allowance at the top of the curtain (the same width as the heading tape you are using), mitring corners and trimming excess fabric. Turn under the end of the heading tape and position it across the top of the curtain so that all raw edges are covered. Topstitch in place. Double stitch over the ends of the drawstring tape to hold cords firmly.

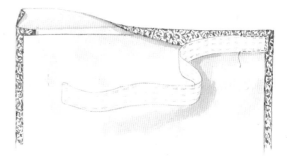

3 Pleat up the tape, insert hooks, and hang the curtains to check the length. Pin the hem in place after the fabric has dropped, and stitch by hand or machine.

For slotted tapes, pleated with hooks, calculate the fullness required according to the size of each pleat and the spacing between them. Make up the curtain in the same way.

To add a traditional trim down the leading edge of the curtain, topstitch or slipstitch bullion fringe to the finished curtain. For a frill, adjust the seam allowance down the side hem at the leading edge of the curtain and lining to 2 cm (¾ in). Make up a frill (page 201) and insert it between the fabric and lining.

For a bound edge, omit the seam allowance from the curtain down the leading edge. After joining the fabric to the lining down the outer edge, press. Tack the free side edge of the curtain to the lining. Bind the edges together with a wide strip of co-ordinating fabric.

All curtains hang better if you insert weights inside the hem.

MAKING TIE-BACKS

Tie-backs, to sweep curtains to the side of the window or to hold back bed drapes, may be made in a number of ways. Two of the most popular styles are shaped tie-backs with bound or piped edges, and straight, frilled tie-backs. For either type, hang the curtains and use a tape measure to judge the best proportions and position for the tie-backs. For shaped tie-backs, you will need a panel of the main fabric slightly larger all round than the finished tie-back, stiff buckram the same size as the finished tie-back, enough fabric to bind or pipe the edges, and lining fabric to back the tie-backs.

The frilled bands are made up from strips of fabric slightly longer and just over twice the width of the finished bands, interfacing to stiffen each band, and enough matching or contrasting fabric to make up a frill to the required depth.

SHAPED PIPED TIE-BACKS

Measure up and decide on a shape for the tie-back. Cut out a paper pattern and hold it in place to check the effect. For each tie-back, cut out fabric and lining 12 mm ($\frac{1}{2}$ in) larger all round than the pattern, a piece of interlining (if required) and a piece of buckram the same size as the pattern. You will also need sufficient piping (page 200) to fit around the seam line.

1 Lockstitch the interlining to the main fabric, leaving the seam allowance free. Lay the stiffening on the wrong side of the fabric, and stitch around the edge using herringbone stitch to hold the buckram in place. Position piping around the right side of the fabric and pin in place, then stitch on the seam line using a zipper foot. Press the raw edges of binding and fabric over the edge of the stiffening.

2 Turn under and press seam allowances all around the lining. Slipstitch the folded edge of the lining to the seam allowance of the piping. Sew a curtain ring to each end of the tie-back, close to the seam line or a centimetre ($\frac{1}{4}$ in) or so inside it. Hang the rings over a hook fitted to the side of the window. With larger, decorative knobs, you can use fabric loops to hold the tie-backs in place.

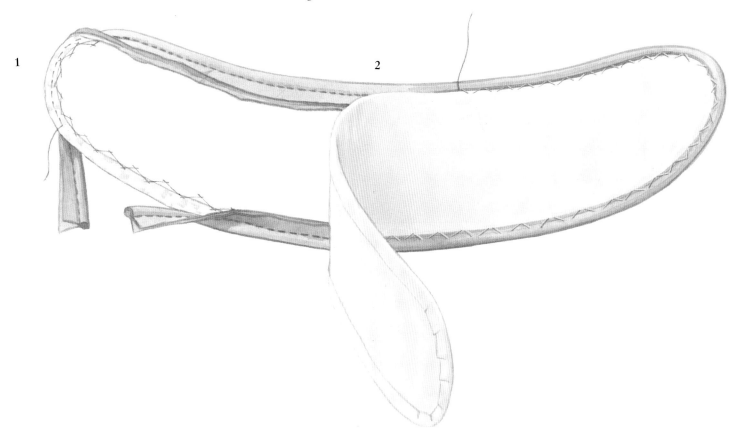

1

2

FRILLED TIE-BACKS

1 Cut a strip of fabric for the tie-back, twice the finished width, and allow 12 mm ($\frac{1}{2}$ in) turning all round. Make up a gathered frill to match the lower edge of the tie-back. Cut interfacing the same size as the finished tie-back.

Fold the strip for the band in half along its length and mark the fold line. Interface one half of the band, matching the top edge of interfacing to the fold line. Fit the gathered frill to the raw edge of the band, below the interfacing, and stitch in place, distributing fullness evenly.

2 Fold the band in half along the fold line, right sides together. Stitch at each end. Trim seam allowances, press and turn right side out, pushing out corners for a crisp finish. Turn under the seam allowance along the back of the band, and slipstitch to the frill.

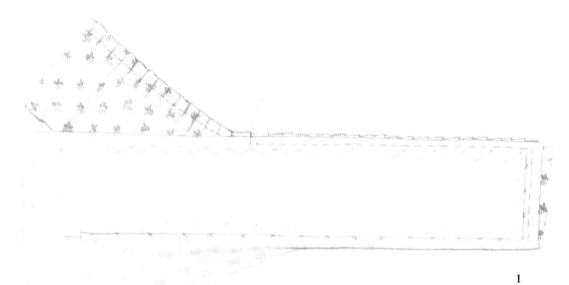

1

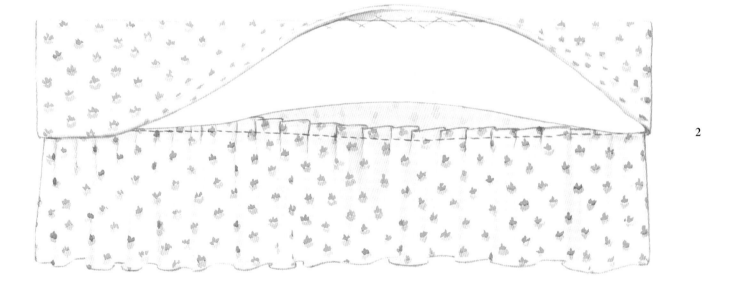

2

MAKING PELMETS (VALANCES)

Pelmets (valances) should be fitted to a shelf or box above the window. Once the shelf is up, you can plan the shape using a large sheet of paper to make a template. The pelmet (valance) must be deep enough to cover the curtain tracks and headings and should be up to one sixth of the depth of the window. To add fullness without cutting out light, gathered pelmets (valances) are often shaped to drape up to halfway down each side of the window.

For stiffened pelmets (valances), cut the main fabric 5 cm (2 in) larger all round than the template, and cut lining, interlining and stiff buckram the same size as the template.

For gathered pelmets (valances), calculate the finished (ungathered) width according to the type of heading tape used. As for curtains, use an exact number of widths of fabric to save wastage. Allow 10 cm (4 in) for the top turning and 5 cm (2 in) for the hem. Cut interlining to the finished size of the pelmet (valance) and a strip of interfacing for the heading the same size as the finished width if required. Cut the lining the same size as the main fabric, reducing the top turning and hem to 4 cm (1½ in). You will also need heading tape to gather the fabric.

Heavy bullion fringing can be added along the lower edge. For a bound edge, omit any seam allowance along the lower edge of the pelmet (valance) and lining. For a frill, allow a 15 mm (⅝ in) seam allowance along the lower edge of the fabric and the lining.

FITTING THE SHELF

1 Decide on the position for the shelf; you can either fit it close to the architrave around the window, or across the front of the opening of a recessed window, or make it wider and fit it well above the window to make the window look larger. Remember that the curtain itself will hang inside the box, so make sure there is room for the curtains to stack back on either side of the window where necessary.

Fit the shelf with angle irons, or screw it

directly to a wooden window surround if there is room. Use 12 mm (½ in) plywood or softwood, at least 10 cm (4 in) wide, and cut it the same width as the curtain track plus 5 cm (2 in) either end for clearance. For a box, screw 10 cm (4 in) square pieces of wood to each end of the shelf before fixing it in place.

2 Fit screw eyes around the outer edge of the lower side of a shelf so you can hang the pelmet (valance) from hooks, or stick the hooked side of Velcro (touch and close) fastening around the top of the shelf if you want to fit the pelmet (valance) that way.

MAKING A TEMPLATE

Use a large sheet of paper (lining paper or offcuts of wallpaper are suitable). Trim the paper to the length of the pelmet (valance) shelf and fold it in half down the centre. Sketch out a shape on the folded paper and cut it out through both layers.

Unfold the paper and tape it at the top of the window so you can check the effect. Make any necessary adjustments. This is now your pattern for cutting out the fabric.

If you are making a gathered pelmet (valance), you will have to 'spread' the shaping to allow for the fullness of the fabric. Take a second piece of paper to correspond with the finished size of the pelmet (valance) before it is gathered. Take a series of measurements, every 10 cm (4 in) or so, down the length of the first template, and transfer these measurements to the new template, spreading them apart according to the type of heading tape you are using: for example, a pinch-pleated heading takes twice the fullness of fabric, so allow for double the spacing between the measurements.

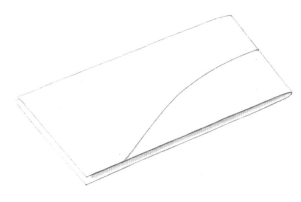

STIFFENED PELMET (VALANCE)

1 Lock the interlining to the main fabric. Position the stiffening on the interlining and herringbone stitch in place all round.

2 Fold the seam allowance of the main fabric over the stiffening, clipping and notching the seam allowance to reduce bulk and to help it to lie flat.

3 Turn under the seam allowance on the lining so that the panel is about 12 mm ($\frac{1}{2}$ in) smaller all round than the stiffened front panel. Slipstitch the folded hem of the lining to the seam allowance of the front panel all round.

Stitch a row of hooks to the inside of the pelmet (valance), or fit the looped half of the Velcro across the top, to fit it to the shelf. A straight pelmet (valance) can be attached to the shelf with 12 mm ($\frac{1}{2}$ in) tacks and the heads covered with braid or a strip of fabric to match or contrast, glued in place.

GATHERED PELMET (VALANCE)

Measure up and calculate fabric in the same way as for lined curtains, reducing the hem allowance to 5 cm (2 in) on the fabric and 4 cm ($1\frac{1}{2}$ in) on the lining. Bear in mind that you are making a single pelmet (valance), rather than a pair of curtains. For frilled pelmets (valances), allow 12 mm ($\frac{1}{2}$ in) seam allowance along the lower edge, and for a bound finish, omit the seam allowance.

1 Lock the interlining to the main fabric and stiffen the heading if required (page 196). Turn under the hem allowance on the lining and position the lining on the fabric. Stitch seams at each end. Turn right side out and press so that the main fabric forms even borders at each end of the pelmet (valance).

2 Turn the heading allowance to the wrong side across the top of the curtain. Turn under a seam allowance at each end of the heading tape, and position it across the top of the pelmet (valance). Stitch in place, double stitching across the ends.

3 Turn up the hem allowance across the lower edge of the pelmet (valance) and slipstitch in place over the lower edge of the lining. Draw up the heading tape and hang the pelmet (valance) with hooks and screw eyes.

For a fringed edge, topstitch bullion fringe along the lower edge.

For a frilled edge, after attaching heading tape, stitch the frill to the lower edge of the curtain, with right sides facing and raw edges matching, leaving seam allowances free. Press the frill away from the pelmet (valance), then slipstitch the folded lower edge of the lining to the wrong side of the frill to enclose all raw edges.

For a bound edge, make up the pelmet (valance) so that the lower edge of the lining, interlining and main fabric all match. Bind the edge, using bias-cut binding if the edge is curved.

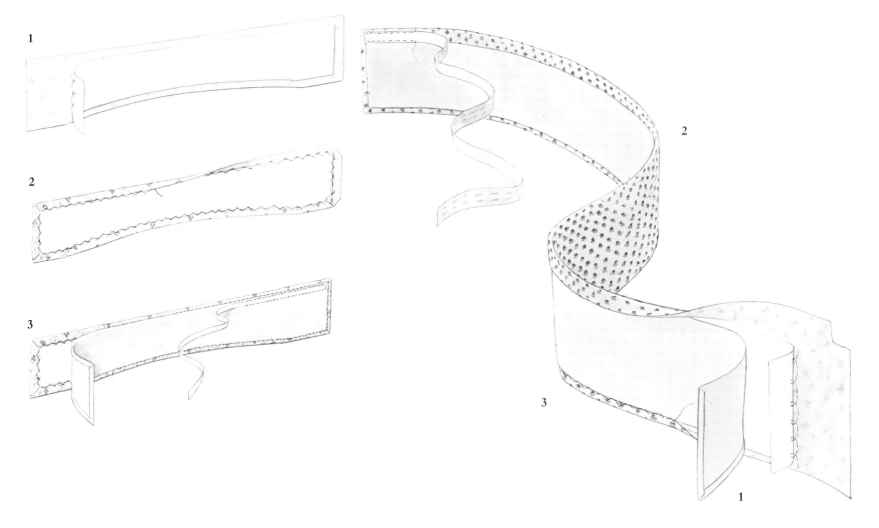

SOPHISTICATED *HEADINGS*

Traditionally, lavish draperies were only used in great houses. They signalled wealth and status for the owner; decoratively they gave presence and visual balance to the lofty height of the window frames. The proportions of a window dressing in relation to the size of a room are critical; dramatic drapes in the context of tall rooms and high windows will always look sumptuous, but in a small room with restrictions on scale, window schemes should be chosen with care. Keep to restrained, classical lines that will not be overwhelming.

Damasks and silks are ideal fabrics for a formal interior. Tall windows can take a commanding treatment such as swags and tails, or perhaps a festooned heading, full and rich with cascading tails laden with trimmings. A high profile window dressing like this should be used in a context where the colour scheme, furniture and accessories are equal to the opulence it provides. But swags and tails can be given a simpler look when the pleating on the swag is restrained rather than generous, the fabric has the cool perfection of heavyweight chintz, and the tails are pressed flat to reveal pleats and lining in geometric progression.

Opulent window treatments can be surprisingly simple to achieve but should be used boldly for a dramatic effect. Dress curtains can act as an ornate façade with inner draw curtains or blinds to provide privacy. Double curtains create a sophisticated effect in tones of the same colour or complementary patterns. Hang them together for the magnified effect of luxurious fabric or drape them asymmetrically with tie-backs. Curtains with a long drop can be caught twice as they fall. Or a single cord set high can reef up curtains in a manner reminiscent of eighteenth-century curtain designs. These schemes are ideal for semi-circular windows, or where curtains cannot be drawn.

Even the most spectacular designs are contrived from a standard repertoire of swags and tails, pelmets (valances) and draped headings. Once the

LEFT *A plain white curtain pole is employed in the Regency manner to display richly printed fabric draped to create the effect of swag and tails. White lace curtains make a telling contrast with the drape.*

BELOW *These windows are set comparatively low in the wall of this tall room. The heavy wool tassels pick out the strongest colour from the curtain stripes.*

ground rules have been mastered, most window dressings can be adapted to suit your own personal style. Swags, pelmets (valances) and lambrequins all have the panache to stand alone without curtains, and add a touch of theatre to a window in a hall or landing. A stylish heading can also set the mood of the room itself – a Gothic heading or a Neo-classical swag will establish a particular ambience.

Swags and tails lend authority to imposing windows. Although they have the appearance of a single fluid drape, the elements are cut separately and assembled at the window on a pelmet (valance) shelf. The swag can be cut on the bias, which gives it a naturally graceful swathe. The amount of fabric required varies enormously between a simple swag and one that hangs in deep voluptuous folds.

Companion to the swag are the tails that fall to each side of the window and sometimes at intermediate points when there is more than one swag. There is a wealth of tail designs from which to choose: spirals and flutes, asymmetrical tails that fold in from each side, or the more familiar form cut as a modified triangle and folded into a series of staggered pleats that reveal the lining, often in a contrast colour and pattern.

ABOVE *The considerable area of wall above this sash window gives scope for a draped heading that extends well beyond the window frame in an upswept swag. Tails overlay pleated curtains that tie back to flank the window seat. A plain white roller blind allows the careful lines of the curtain pleats to remain undisturbed.*

ABOVE *The molded plaster cornice around this bay has been employed as a decorative pelmet (valance) with swags and tails fixed behind it. Full length curtains hang between each window and end in a hemline cascade.*

RIGHT *The stunning rhetoric of double curtains takes full account of the shape and scale of these tall French windows which are flanked by lower windows on either side. The different heights are strongly maintained by the individual curtain poles from which hang outer curtains of dramatically sombre shot silk in laurel and brown.*

HAND SEWING CURTAINS

For pleated or draped curtains tailored precisely to your windows, with the pleats or drapes positioned to suit their size and shape, hand-made curtain headings are essential.

Particularly interesting effects can be achieved with vertically patterned fabric if you plan the size and spacing of pleats to match pattern repeats across the curtain. Triple pleats are appropriate when curtains are hung with rings from an exposed wooden or brass pole. By positioning a hook in the back of each pleat, the curtains hang so that the rings match the pleats.

Lining and interlining are essential; linings may be made from plain chintz, rather than standard lining fabrics, which will create a flash of colour where the tails hang in folds.

Extravagant, draped effects require careful sewing. The detailed measurements depend on the size of the window and the type of fabric you are using as well as the finished effect you aim to achieve. It may be necessary to experiment so that you can be sure the measurements you plan to use will suit the window and create the effect you want.

It is easier and more economical to make pairs of curtains from an exact number of widths of fabric. It also reduces the amount of sewing and pattern matching. Each curtain will require anything from $1\frac{1}{2}$ to 3 widths of fabric, unless the windows are unusually small or wide. Before you buy the fabric, do all your sums: you have to work out roughly how much fullness you need, decide on the number of widths of fabric, and then multiply that number by the total length required for each drop of fabric (including hem and turning allowances, and pattern matching). Then work out the precise spacing allowance (and the space between the end pleats and the edge of the curtain) before making up the curtain.

PLEATS BY HAND

Plan a suitable size and spacing of pleats and work out how much fullness this requires. For example, for triple pleats taking 25 cm (10 in) of fabric, spaced 15 cm (6 in) apart, the fullness is just under 3 times the width of the pleated curtain (because you need 40 cm/16 in to cover 15 cm/6 in of track).

To find out how many widths of fabric you will need for each curtain, multiply the distance the curtain is to cover by the fullness allowance, and divide by the width of fabric, rounding the figure up or down to the nearest half. Multiply by two (or the number of curtains) to give the total number of widths of fabric required.

Decide on the finished length of the curtains and add an allowance of 10 cm (4 in) at the top and at the hem and an allowance for pattern matching if necessary. Multiply the finished length by the total number of widths to give the amount of fabric.

Work out the total width of the made-up (unpleated) curtain by multiplying the number of widths required by the width of the fabric, subtracting 4 cm ($1\frac{1}{2}$ in) for turnings down each side edge of the curtain. To find the total number of pleats, take the finished (pleated) width of the curtain and subtract the space allowance at each side edge, say 5 cm (2 in). Then divide by the *planned* space between the pleats. Round up or down to the nearest whole number and add one. (Calculate

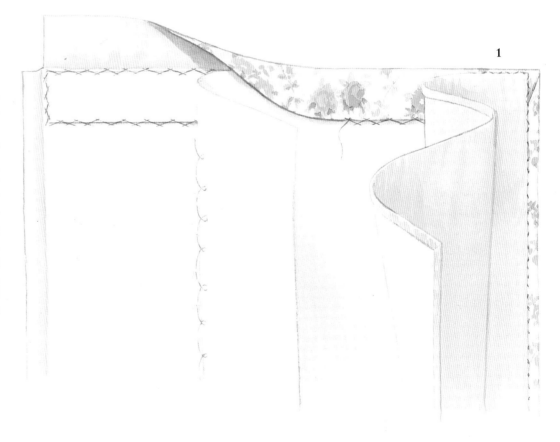

1

the adjusted distance between the pleats if you have rounded the figure.) Finally, check that the *planned* size of the pleats takes up all the fullness of the fabric. Make minor adjustments to the seam allowance and space at each side of the curtain to make measuring and marking up easier.

For lining, you will need enough fabric to make up a panel the width of the finished curtain, as calculated above. No extra side turning allowance is required. For the length, add 12 mm ($\frac{1}{2}$ in) top turning and 6 cm ($2\frac{1}{2}$ in) hem allowance. Interlining should be the same size as the finished curtain. Make up a curtain panel, matching pattern, and a lining panel, using flat seams and clipping into the selvedges. Make up interlining, using lapped seams (page 199). Cut a strip of interfacing (woven or iron-on) 10 cm (4 in) deep (or more, according to the depth of heading) to match the width of the finished curtain.

1 Mark the turning allowance at the top of the curtain. Apply interfacing across the top turning, aligning the top of the interfacing with the top foldline of the curtain. Position interlining on the wrong side of the fabric, leaving turning allowances all around. Lockstitch in place, then press the turnings at the top and sides of the curtain over the interlining and herringbone stitch in place.

Turn up and stitch a 4 cm ($\frac{1}{2}$ in) double hem across the lower edge of the lining. Turn under and press 2 cm ($\frac{3}{4}$ in) seams all round. Lockstitch lining to interlining, then slipstitch the folded edges of the lining to the folded edges of the curtain across the top and down the sides.

2 Turn up the hem of the curtain and slipstitch in place beneath lining.

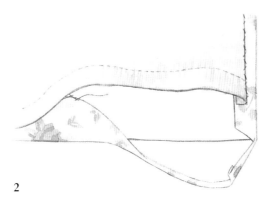

2

3 Use dressmaker's chalk to mark the pleat foldlines on the back of the ungathered curtain, according to the calculations.

4 Fold and stitch along the pleat lines in a straight line to 10 cm (4 in) depth, then

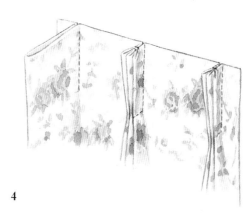

4

fold each pleat by hand. Stitch the base of the pleat by hand, and catch the inner folds together at the top. Insert spiked hooks into each pleat.

3

SWAGS & TAILS

Swags and tails are fixed to a shelf above the window. There are no text-book rules for proportions, but as with all window dressing, if you want plenty of light to come through the window, fit the shelf well above the window and extend it on either side. Normally, the first pleat of the tail should be at about the same level as the lowest point of the sweep of the swag.

When making your own swags and tails, it is worth using old sheets to make a mock-up or toile of the finished item. The upper edge should be about 50 cm (20 in) shorter than the shelf, and the lower edge about 20 cm (8 in) longer, according to the depth of the swag.

1 Decide on an appropriate depth for the toile, depending on the fullness required. Pin the toile across the top of the shelf to give the effect, pleating or gathering the ends. When you are happy with the arrangement, mark the fabric where it folds over the front edge.

2 Open out the toile and mark the seam line following the existing marks. Use this as a guide to cut out the fabric, allowing 4 cm (1½ in) turnings along the top and bottom edge, and 10 cm (4 in) for gathering and finishing down the angled side edges.

Make up the swag, lining and interlining if necessary, as for machine- or hand-made curtains, treating the upper and lower edges of the swag as the sides of the curtain. Gather or pleat the angled sides along the seam line and pin in place to check the drape. Topstitch, then trim the raw edges and finish by binding or zig-zag stitching.

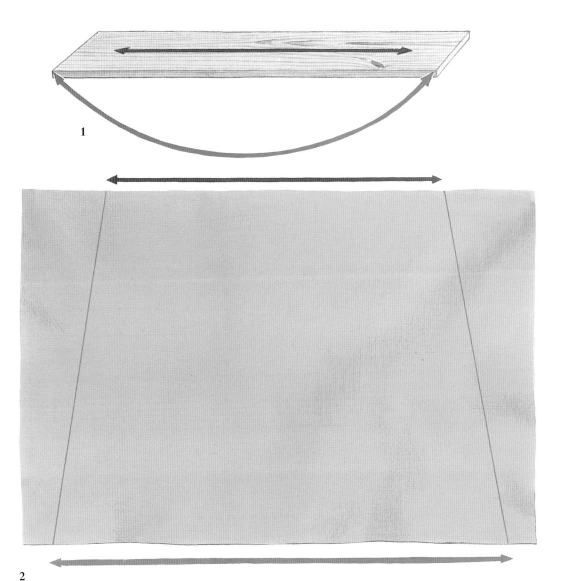

3 To make a toile for the tails, plan the width and spacing for the foldlines using a tape measure held along the top of the shelf. Decide on the inner and outer lengths of the tails and transfer all the measurements to the toile fabric. Cut out and check for fit.

4 Use the toile as a pattern piece, allowing 2 cm ($\frac{3}{4}$ in) turnings all around the sides and lower edge, and 10 cm (4 in) at the top edge. Cut lining to the same size as the main fabric.

Interline the main fabric panel, then position the lining on the tail, right sides facing, and stitch together all around the sides and lower edges. Trim seams, press and turn right side out. Press again, then mark and press the pleats into position. Check for fit, then topstitch pleats, trim raw edges and bind or zigzag stitch together.

5 Finally, fit the swags and tails in place, stapling them to the top of the shelf so that the tails overlap the ends of the swag.

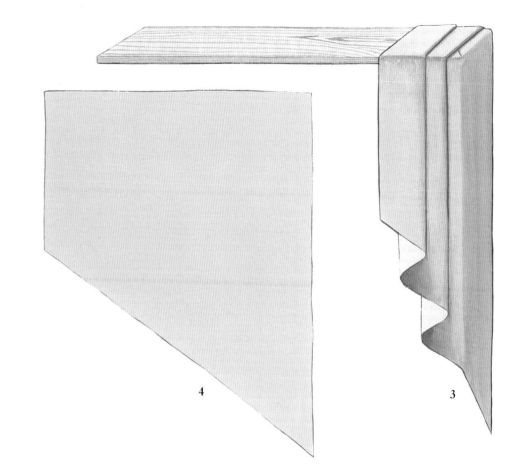

4

3

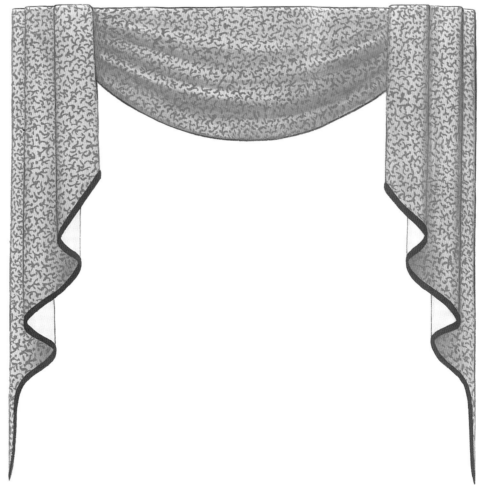

5

111

LACE & VOILE

The prettiest and most romantic of fabrics, lace gently filters light into a room whilst ensuring privacy. Usually light in colour, lace has distinctive qualities of texture and drape, spangling sunlight, creating shadows and fluttering in the breeze from an open window.

Muslin and voile, either plain or sprigged with flowers and garlands, can be turned into wispy swags or brief draperies to head a classic window, or they can be reefed up into festoons. But these fine fabrics drape gloriously when generous lengths are looped and swathed around curtain poles and allowed to descend in full-length cascades, or a full curtain can be knotted halfway-down to flare out again at the hemline. Sheer curtains can overlap across the full width of a window and then be tied back in graceful loops, one side set higher than the other and the overlapping edges accentuated with tassel trimming.

Figured lace should be used much more sparingly than muslin or voile. Lace curtains need very little fullness, in fact some panels look most effective when hung flat against the window using a cased heading or curtain rings and a slender pole. Lace panels with integral borders running round three sides sometimes have a lightweight drawstring tape across the top, stitched so that it doubles as a cased heading. Pelmet (valance) lace is also available and can add a further layer to a lace window treatment.

When voile or lace curtains are needed for privacy, sew cased headings and slot the fabric in unjoined widths (to avoid ugly seams) on to rods at both top and bottom, anchored within the window frame so that they hold the fabric lightly taut across the face of the glass. This method particularly suits French windows and glazed doors and is essential to hold fabric close to pivot and sloping windows.

RIGHT *Asymmetrically draped curtains provide screening by day and night. The heavy, off-white curtain is turned over the top of the muslin drape and stitched to form a casing, slotted onto a wooden pole across the top of the window. Tie-backs can be adjusted to control the amount of light filtering through.*

LEFT *Translucent cotton has been used for these simple cased curtains. The casings top and bottom are made with two lines of stitching, forming a 'stand' or heading. Simple ties draw the curtains in at the waist. A plain roller blind screens the top part of the window, and can be drawn down if necessary.*

RIGHT *A pair of lace panels has been fitted over a slim brass rod to hold these curtains close to the frame of these generous bedroom windows. The width of each curtain allows for gentle gathers but still shows off the pattern of the lace.*

MAKING LACE & VOILE CURTAINS

To show off intricate patterns on panels of lace, whether antique or contemporary, you need very little fullness. Use either a cased heading or clip-on rings to achieve this effect. Take particular care when measuring for lace panels: if they are hung by rings from a pole, measure from just beneath the pole; if they are hung from a plain track or rod, measure from the top of the fixture.

Headings for any type of sheer curtain fabric may be made in a number of ways, depending on the nature of the fabric and the effect you want. A cased heading, which enables you to slot the fabric onto a curtain rod or wire, is the simplest to make. For more formal gathers there are special lightweight curtain heading tapes.

Because of the transparent nature of the fabric, seams must be made as invisible as possible with borders arranged carefully around the edge of the curtains. Allow ample fullness with fine voiles and other fabrics – up to three times.

DOUBLE CASINGS

At French windows and glazed doors, it is advisable to fit rods or wires at both the top and bottom of the glazing so that you can anchor the lower edge of the curtain and prevent it getting caught in the door. This method is essential for pivot windows and sloping windows which follow the angle of the roof in a loft conversion, for example.

CASED HEADING

Measure the circumference of the rod or pole to be used to hang the curtain, and decide on a suitable depth for the casing, including an allowance for ease. Add a small allowance for a stand heading at the top of the curtain, and twice this amount for a top turning. The casing illustrated here is 2.5 cm (1 in) wide, with a stand of 12 mm ($\frac{1}{2}$ in). Allow 10 cm (4 in) for a 5 cm (2 in) double hem, and 2 cm ($\frac{3}{4}$ in) for a 1 cm ($\frac{3}{8}$ in) double side hem down each edge. Make up each curtain at least twice the width of the track it is to cover.

1 Join widths of fabric for each curtain, using narrow French seams (page 199). Turn under a 12 mm ($\frac{1}{2}$ in) wide double hem down each side edge and stitch in place by hand or machine.

2 Turn over and press a double 4 cm ($1\frac{1}{2}$ in) wide turning across the top of the curtain. Topstitch in place from the right side, stitching 12 mm ($\frac{1}{2}$ in) from the top fold of the curtain, and again close to the fold of the hem.

3 Turn up a 5 cm (2 in) double hem across the lower edge of the curtain and slipstitch in place.

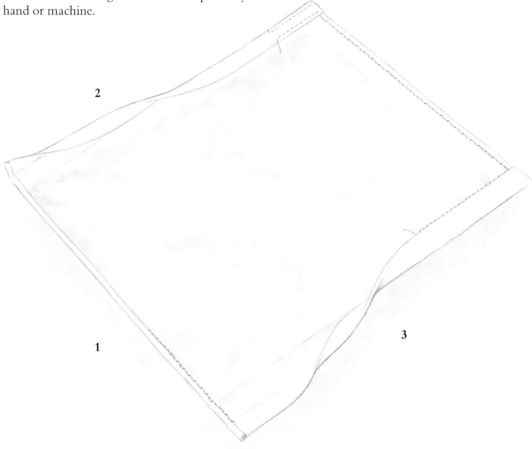

LACE PANELS WITH BORDERS

1 Where possible, use a single panel of lace for each curtain if there are borders down the side of the lace. When the border runs across the lower edge of the panel, make any adjustments to the length of the curtain at the heading to avoid having to turn up a hem. Trim the border if the side edges are to be joined. Make sure that the pattern will match across the widths at the seam line, and allow 2 cm ($\frac{3}{4}$ in) seam allowance. Join the widths with a French seam.

1

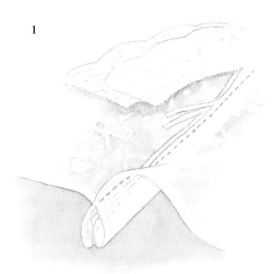

2 As an extra decorative device, you can use the border that has been trimmed to make a frill across the top edge of the curtain. Decide on the finished dimensions of the curtain, and cut out with the usual allowances, depending on whether you wish to make a gathered (taped) or a cased heading. When trimming the border from the side edge, include the same turning allowance as that required for your chosen heading. The total length of the strip for the trim must be the same as the total (joined) width of curtain fabric for each curtain. Position the border across the top of the panel of fabric for the curtain, and tack in place. If you are using a heading tape, turn over raw edges and cover with tape.

3 For a cased heading, make a double turning across both layers of fabric and stitch to form a casing.

2

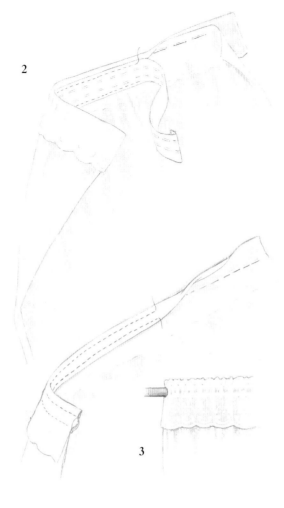

3

COTTAGE CURTAINS

Pretty, cottage-style windows cry out for a soft dressing. By using narrow strips of lace – pelmet (valance) lace – you can make curtains and frill all in one. For small windows, you will only need a single panel for each curtain. Decide on a finished measurement for the curtains and trim the top of the panels to size, allowing for turnings and stand heading. Cut

the lace to match the width of the pair of curtains, adding a total of 4 cm ($1\frac{1}{2}$ in) for side turnings. Decide on the finished depth of the pelmet (valance) and trim the strip of fabric, allowing 12 mm ($\frac{1}{2}$ in) for turning and an allowance for the stand.

Turn under 12 mm ($\frac{1}{2}$ in) double hems down the side edges of the pelmet (valance) and slipstitch in place. Lay out curtain panels, side by side, with the wrong side up. Position the pelmet (valance) across the top of the curtain, wrong side up with raw edges matching, and stitch. Press and turn the pelmet (valance) so the wrong side faces the right side of the curtain panel. Stitch a casing across the top of the curtain.

CURTAIN HEADING TAPE

To use curtain heading tape with lace and voile fabrics, the following allowances should be used for a pencil-pleated heading tape: fullness – up to three times; side hems – 4 cm ($1\frac{1}{2}$ in) per curtain; top turning – 8 cm (3 in); hem – 10 cm (4 in). Join any widths of fabric with French seams.

1 Turn under 12 mm ($\frac{1}{2}$ in) double hems down each side edge of the curtain and stitch in place.

2 Turn under 8 cm (3 in) across the top of the curtain and turn under 12 mm ($\frac{1}{2}$ in) at each end of the heading tape. Position the tape across the top of the curtain and stitch in place, double stitching over ends to hold cords securely.

3 Turn up a 5 cm (2 in) double hem across the lower edge of the curtain and stitch in place by hand or machine.

2

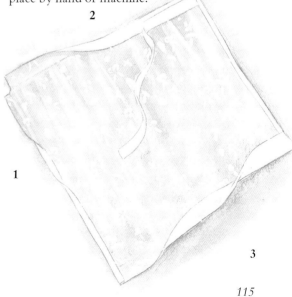

1

3

BLINDS

The clean classic lines of Roman and roller blinds are the ideal decorative accompaniment to the streamlined look of a contemporary room while the generous swathes of a festoon blind add softness without restricting natural light. Window blinds are usually functional as well as decorative, often engaged as working partners in combination window treatments. When dress curtains and drapes are only for show, the blind plays the active role.

Plain blinds

A roller blind pulls down to provide a flat screen to the window glass. Released, it disappears round its roller, so unless locked at an intermediate point down the window frame, its decorative presence is withdrawn during the day. Do not depend on it then for strong colour or pattern interest although in a child's room, for example, you could use a blind with a large motif. Roller blinds are simple and neat. They best suit rooms that share the same style, or windows that need one or other of their special functions. Blackout blinds are an asset to those who cannot sleep once dawn has broken; if you have sloping windows, roller blinds are one of the few systems that can be fitted successfully if they are secured at the bottom on a hook. At the grandly dressed window, a plain roller blind is the traditional innermost layer, drawn down to screen fine textiles and furniture from sunlight.

The Roman blind is simple too, and uses fabric with almost equal economy, but it has greater elegance and formality. These blinds are corded up the back and a wooden dowel, slotted into one or more horizontal channels, draws them up in pleats rather than soft scallops. They should be made in firmly woven cloth, preferably in plain colours or formal patterns such as stripes and plaids that enhance their character. It is important to the accuracy of the pleating that the grain of the cloth is true and, if it is a print, that the pattern is correctly aligned on the weave.

BELOW LEFT A carefully poised blend of set pieces – chaise longue, metal shelving, stylish objects – is put in the context of plain painted walls and boarded floor, indicative of the casual and the sparse. A Roman blind in a white dobby weave shares this elegance.

BELOW In a recessed window, the blind can be hung so that it fits against the glass; otherwise, it can be mounted on the frame or the wall immediately above. Yellow and white striped cotton has been used for these roller blinds which do not interfere with the window seats below.

Gathered blinds

An Austrian blind is also corded but looks like a curtain when it is let down. When the blind is drawn up it creates deep flounces across the head of the window. Austrian blinds were much used in the eighteenth century, either alone or behind ornate pelmets (valances). They need plenty of fullness, especially when the fabric is fine, or the scallops will look mean and undersized. For a more delicate effect, space the cording more widely or omit the cording altogether down each side so the blind looks like a swag with tails.

The impact of an Austrian blind is influenced by the fabric chosen for it. Natural calico or a fine plain linen adds a stylish simplicity to the natural exuberance of the flounces. In bold striped silk trimmed with bullion fringe, it will look dramatic and unassailably grand. In pastel-flowered chintz, bordered with lace or frill, the Austrian blind finds its most romantic expression.

Festoon blinds have twice the finished length gathered down the drop and little fullness across the width, creating a ruched effect rather than scallops when drawn up. When made up in a translucent fabric such as a light voile or fine sprigged cotton, festoon blinds can be left down permanently as a sheer screen.

LEFT The grand window in this converted bathroom is afforded privacy by a simple lace panel, flanked by further lace panels tied back with rope. The blind provides the pelmet (valance) and reduces the window height visually. Its tiny bobble edging echoes the shimmering transparency of the lace.

BELOW LEFT Bedhangings and window display make common cause in this opulent scheme in which festoon blinds are seen at their most exuberant. Frilled edges on both the curtains and the tie-backs match those on the blinds.

BELOW Roller or Roman blinds match the neatness of simple window shapes but when a softer effect is required, a single scoop Austrian blind is suitably charming.

Making Blinds

Roller blinds are the most economical and simple blinds to make, requiring a minimum of fabric and sewing. Choose a kit with the roller a size larger than the width of the window. Avoid making roller blinds that are wider than the fabric width you plan to use: the seams tend to make the fabric roll unevenly. You will need fabric stiffener to treat unstiffened material.

Roman blinds should be made from good-quality fabric: it must have an even weave and any printed pattern must be printed with the grain of the fabric. There are several methods for making Roman blinds: here we show a softly gathered one, with tapes running up the back of the blind, and a crisply pleated version, with dowels set into casings to keep the fabric and the pleated end straight.

To fit a Roman blind to the window, it should be attached to a wooden batten which can either be fixed directly to the window reveal or hung from angle irons fixed to either side of the window frame.

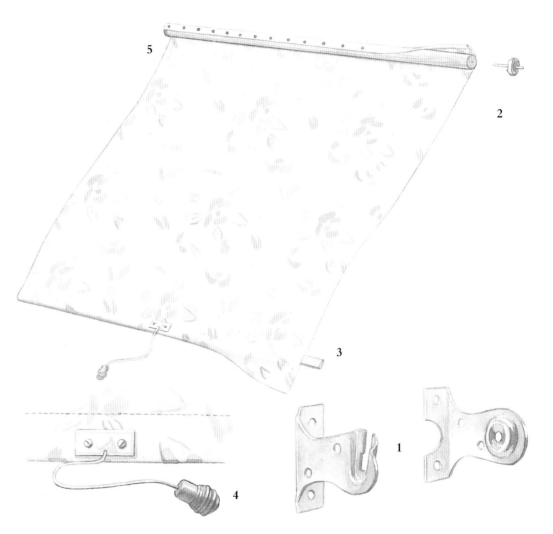

Roller Blinds

1 Fit the brackets on either side of the window. Check the instructions supplied: normally the slotted bracket goes on the left of the window and the round hole on the right.

2 Measure the distance between the brackets and cut the roller and bottom batten to size. Position the end plate over the cut end of the roller and tap in the pin.

3 Cut out the fabric so that it is 10 cm (4 in) wider and 20 cm (8 in) longer than the finished blind. Turn over and stitch a casing across the lower edge of the blind, deep enough to take the batten, plus an allowance for ease and shrinkage. Treat the fabric with stiffener, following the manufacturer's instructions.

4 When dry, trim the side edges of the blind to the exact finished width, following a thread of the fabric. Slip the batten into the casing and attach the string and acorn.

5 Turn over a narrow allowance across the top of the blind. With the fabric laid out right side up, and the roller across the blind with the round pin on the right-hand side, roll the top turning over the roller and tack in place. (Some kits have a strip of double-sided tape to hold the fabric.)

To tension the blind, roll up the fabric and hang the blind. Pull it down, then remove it from the brackets and roll it up half way. Hang the blind and pull it down again. Then test it: a second tug, and the blind should roll up to the top of the window. If it stops before it gets there, take it down and roll it up a little more.

If you want a decorated edge to the roller blind, the simplest method is to attach fringing along the bottom edge. Make the casing about 8 cm (3 in) from the edge, leaving enough depth to attach the decoration. Use double-sided tape to hold the fringe while you machine stitch in place.

For a shaped edge, make a paper pattern the width of the finished blind. Use tape to attach the pattern to the wrong side of the blind, draw around the shape with a light pencil or dressmaker's chalk and cut along the line. Finish with a zig-zag or satin stitch, binding or a fringe, or face with a piece of non-stiffened fabric, deep enough to be included in the casing.

UNLINED ROMAN BLINDS

Measure the window so you can calculate the amount of fabric you need (page 204). Take the finished width of the blind, and add a total of 6 cm (2½ in) for turnings. If you need to use more than one width of fabric, include an allowance for seams. Add 5 cm (2 in) for the heading and 11 cm (4½ in) for a hem.

To assemble the mechanism for drawing up the blind, you can buy a kit or use Roman blind tapes. Decide on a suitable spacing for the tapes – about 40 cm (15 in) apart, with the outer tapes 2.5 cm (1 in) from the edge of the blind. Multiply the number of tapes by the finished length of the blind. To calculate the amount of cord you need, add the finished length of the blind, half the width of the blind, and the distance down the side of the blind along which the cords should hang, and multiply by the number of cords. You will also need a curtain ring to fit to the bottom of each tape and a cleat attached to the window frame to hold the cords.

1 Turn under and press a 3 cm (1¼ in) turning down each side edge of the blind. Pin the tapes in place down the blind, evenly spaced, with the side tapes covering the raw edges of the turnings. Check that the loops on the tape are level across the blind with the first row of loops 22 cm (8½ in) up from the bottom.

2 Turn under 1 cm (½ in), then 10 cm (4 in) across the lower edge of the blind, enclosing the ends of the tapes. Machine stitch in place, then stitch tapes in place down each side, taking care not to catch the loops in the stitching. If necessary, you can fit a batten into the hem of the blind to stiffen it.

3 Cut the cord into suitable lengths for each tape. Fit a ring to each lower loop, then tie the end of the cord to it and thread up through every loop in the tape. Turn over 12 mm (½ in) at the top of the blind and fit the blind to a wooden batten, the same width as the finished blind.

4 Check the length of the blind, then fit the batten to the top of the window. Fit screw eyes into the lower edge of the batten and run cords through the eyelets.

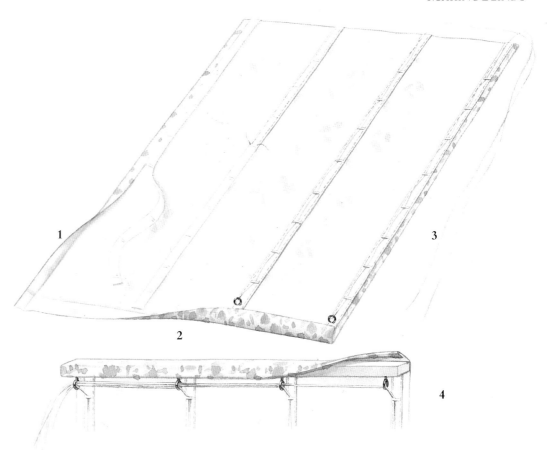

LINED ROMAN BLINDS

Cut the main fabric and lining to the size of the finished blind, plus 5 cm (2 in) heading allowance. If you want a decorative border, perhaps in a plain colour if the curtain fabric is patterned, make up a strip of straight- or bias-cut binding, long enough to bind the sides and lower edge of the blind. You will also need a length of fine wooden dowelling for each fold of the blind, the same width as the finished blind, and curtain rings and cords to draw the blind up. Space the cords up to 60 cm (24 in) apart, and buy enough curtain rings to hold each cord to each dowel casing.

Turn under and press a 1 cm (⅜ in) turning down each long edge of binding, and fold the binding in half. Position binding around the sides and lower edge of the main fabric with right sides together and the raw edge of the binding 4 cm (1½ in) from the edge of the fabric. Stitch in place, leaving an allowance for mitring at the corners. Press binding away from the blind.

Position the lining on the main fabric, wrong sides facing. Mark and stitch casings through both layers of fabric across the blind, spacing them evenly up the blind. The lowest casing should be the depth of the fold plus the border from the finished edge of the blind. Stitch from one folded edge of the binding to the other. Then slip the dowels into the casings and fold the binding over the edge of both layers of fabric. Slipstitch the free folded edge to the lining, enclosing the end of the dowel and forming neat mitres at the corners (page 200).

Stitch rings to the back of each casing, at the point where the cords cross them, and fit the blind as before.

MAKING GATHERED BLINDS

Austrian blinds borrow many of their construction details from curtains. Special tracks are available, together with tapes and cords in kit form. The blind is drawn up in the same way as a Roman blind. Since the heading is gathered, the width measurement of the fabric is not critical, but allow plenty of fullness for an extravagant effect. Lining adds luxury, and a piped frill gives a delicate finish.

Festoon blinds are usually unlined and may be made with similar kits, but the blind shown here is a variation on a more traditional method. Ribbon or decorative cord is threaded through casings in the blind to gather it up, with the usual cords held by rings at the back of the blind.

LINED AUSTRIAN BLINDS

For a lined Austrian blind, allow at least 1½ times fullness for both fabric and lining. Cut the main fabric so that it is at least 4 cm (½ in) wider than the lining. If you have to join two widths of fabric, cut one width in half lengthways and join the selvedges to the main panel of fabric to avoid positioning a seam down the centre of the blind. The length of fabric for the blind should be the length of the finished blind plus 12 mm (½ in) seam allowance at the lower edge and 2 cm (¾ in) at the top edge. Cut the lining fabric 2 cm (¾ in) shorter than the main fabric. Make up a length of piping (page 200) the width of the finished (ungathered) blind, and cut enough fabric to make a frill at least 1½ times that measurement.

1 With right sides of fabric and lining together, and the top of the lining 2 cm (¾ in) lower than the top of the fabric, stitch down the side edges. Press seam allowances towards the lining. Stitch the piping to the lower edge of blind, leaving turning free.

2 Make up and gather a frill (page 201) to fit the lower edge of the blind, distributing fullness evenly. Pin the frill in place over the piping, then pin the lining over the frill and stitch through all layers of fabric. Turn blind right side out. Press.

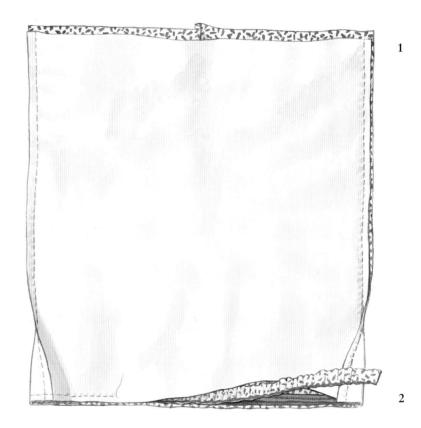

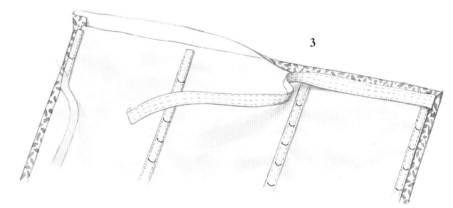

3 Position the tapes down the back of the blind, spacing them about 60 cm (24 in) apart. Turn over 2 cm (¾ in) at the top of the blind, trimming excess fabric from corners and mitring them (page 200). Position heading tape (page 100), covering the top of the vertical tapes. Stitch all tapes in place. Run cords through the loops in the tape as for Roman blinds (page 119). You may want to hang the blind first (according to the type of track used) so that you estimate correctly the amount of cord needed for each length. The cord running through the row of loops furthest from the cleat which will hold the cords will need to be longer than the cord nearest the cleat, for example. The cords are all pulled together and tied to the cleat to hold the curtain part way up so that it hangs in swags.

FESTOON BLINDS

1 Cut out the fabric for the blind, joining widths if necessary, to make a panel allowing at least 1½ times fullness both across the blind and down its length.

Turn under and press 2 cm (¾ in) double hems around the sides and lower edge of the blind and make up and attach a topstitched frill (page 201) for all three sides. Make a cased heading at the top of the blind to fit a pole placed across the window (page 114).

2 Decide on a suitable spacing for the channels and make a row of buttonholes in the blind, just below the cased heading, one for each channel. Cut strips of fabric for the casings 4 cm (1½ in) wide, and turn under and press 6 mm (¼ in) down each side edge and across the ends. Pin and tack the casings to the back of the blind and topstitch in place.

3 Estimate and cut the lengths of the cord or ribbons and thread them through the channels, bringing each one out through the buttonhole at the top. Stitch across the lower edge of the casing to hold the cords firmly in place. Draw up the blind to the required length. Stitch a short length of matching cord or ribbon to the front of the blind, just below the buttonhole, and tie the ends together to form a decorative bow.

4 Stitch rings to the back of each channel, every 20 cm (8 in) or so, down the length of the blind. Tie the ends of the cords to the lowest rings and thread up the blind in the usual way. Slot the heading onto a rod or pole and fit screw eyes to a batten behind the rod or pole to carry the cords across the top of the window.

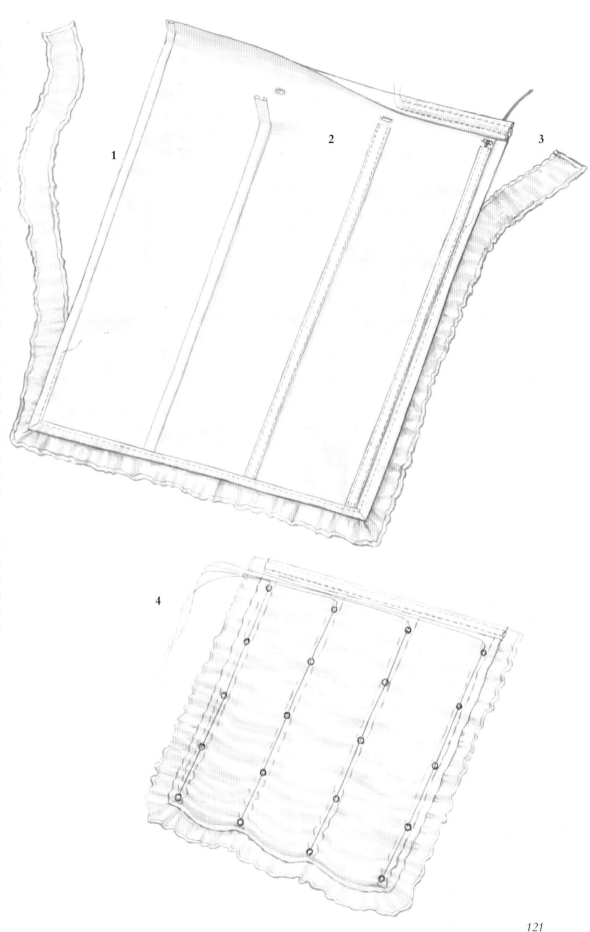

INDIVIDUAL TREATMENTS

Special situations call for a particular kind of window dressing. Where an unattractive view needs to be screened or privacy is required, café curtains reminiscent of French brasseries come into their own – a decorative alternative to muslin and voile. Made in the same way as standard curtains, and hung from metal or wooden poles or rods placed halfway up the window frame, they can have a variety of decorative headings.

Arched windows are a beautiful architectural feature and care should be taken to show them off. Cased headings can be used in such situations: curtain fabric is threaded on to wire which is then fixed into place, accentuating the shape.

Locations other than windows can benefit from a curtain treatment. A full-length curtain hung from a decorative pole above a doorway will provide an extra element of warmth in the Victorian tradition; or do away with internal doors altogether and use curtains reefed up to one side instead. Cupboard doors can be given an elegant finish by infilling the glazed area with fabric gathered onto curtain wires.

Shower curtains need special treatments too: they can be hung from ceiling-mounted curtain track, or fixed by hooks and rings from a pole or rod. Use shower curtains or light cotton lined with waterproof fabric.

ABOVE *The convention of door curtains began in medieval times to exclude draughts; a concern enthusiastically taken up by the Victorians. Gliding on wooden rings from a dark stained pole that matches the door itself, this curtain uses a Victorian design, repeated on the wallpaper and floor tiles.*

LEFT *This tiny bathroom window can be given a voluptuous window treatment because of its wide sill. The small frilled curtains fit the space perfectly without interfering with the inevitable bathroom accessories.*

RIGHT *The cupboard doors have been cleverly utilized in this dressing room by lining the once glazed panes with fine fabric gathered at the top and bottom onto curtain wires and hung inside the frames. The folds of the fabric offer a textural dimension while hiding the clothes and accessories from view.*

LEFT *A bedroom well lit by wide windows has inner curtains in white voile to filter the sunlight. The main curtains are gathered along a white pole and draped back as a symmetrical duo, covering a good deal of the window but not enough to cast the room into shade. The charming floral print is given a mark of formality with the cord and tassel tie-backs.*

RIGHT *An arched window must be dressed to mirror its shape. This means either fixing a curving track or handpleating the heading to follow the line of the arch. Curtains that curve can never be drawn; they must be either tied or draped back. By looping back these curtains to show a contrast lining and edging, a rival symmetry is offered within the frame of the arch.*

MAKING SPECIAL HEADINGS

Café curtains may be made in the same way as curtains, with a cased, slotted or hand-made heading. A scalloped heading, with or without pleats between the scallops, is another popular finish. These curtains are usually hung from rods fitted across the window. There are many styles to choose from: a simple, scalloped heading can be used to form a flat curtain looped over a pole. Pinch pleats between the scallops, hooked to rings on the pole, give a more formal effect.

Ready-made shower curtains are normally made in a plastic fabric. Shower curtaining is available by the metre for making up curtains yourself. You can create a soft effect by using cotton for the outer layer of the fabric and a plain white or coloured plastic or plasticized fabric on the inside.

SCALLOPED & FACED HEADINGS

Decide on a suitable fullness – one and a half times the window width is usually sufficient. Allow 4 cm (1½ in) for side hems, a total of 35 cm (14 in) for loops and facing and 10 cm (4 in) for hems.

1 Turn under 2 cm (¾ in) double hems down each outer edge and turn under and press a narrow turning across the top edge. Stitch in place.

2 Turn over 25 cm (10 in) to the right side of the curtain across the top edge to form the loops and facing. Decide on a suitable depth for the scallops and length for the loops, say a total of 20 cm (8 in) – and a suitable width for the loops, say 5 cm (2 in), spaced 10 cm (4 in) apart. Make up a paper template and mark the scallop seam line along the top of the curtain. Stitch along the marked seam line, then cut away the fabric from the scallops, layering seam allowances.

3 Turn the facing right side out and stitch the ends of the loops to the curtain. Hang the curtain and check for length, then turn up the hem by hand.

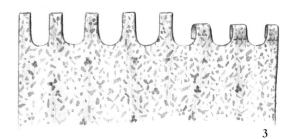

3

PLEATED HEADINGS

Allow extra fullness for this style, to suit the size and spacing of the pleats. A suitable allowance is 25 cm (10 in) for pleats and 10 cm (4 in) for the scallops. Allow 12 mm (½ in) seam allowance across the top of the curtain. Include the same side turning and hem allowance. For the lining, allow the same fullness and top turning, but omit the side turning allowance and reduce the hem allowance to 6 cm (2½ in). Join widths of fabric if necessary.

1 Turn up and stitch a 4 cm (1½ in) double hem across the lower edge of the lining. Position the lining on the fabric, right sides facing, with the top of the lining matching the top of the curtain. Join side edges. Press seams towards the centre of the curtain.

2 With the lining centred on the curtain, use a template to mark the seam line across the top of the curtain and stitch the scallops in place, stitching across the top of the curtain 12 mm (½ in) from the raw edges between the scallops. Trim excess fabric from the scallops and layer the seam allowance.

3 Turn the curtain right side out and press. Mark a stitching line and form pleats (page 109). Insert hooks, hang curtains and check the length. Turn under 2 cm (¾ in) and then 8 cm (3 in) and stitch the hem, mitring corners (page 200).

1

2

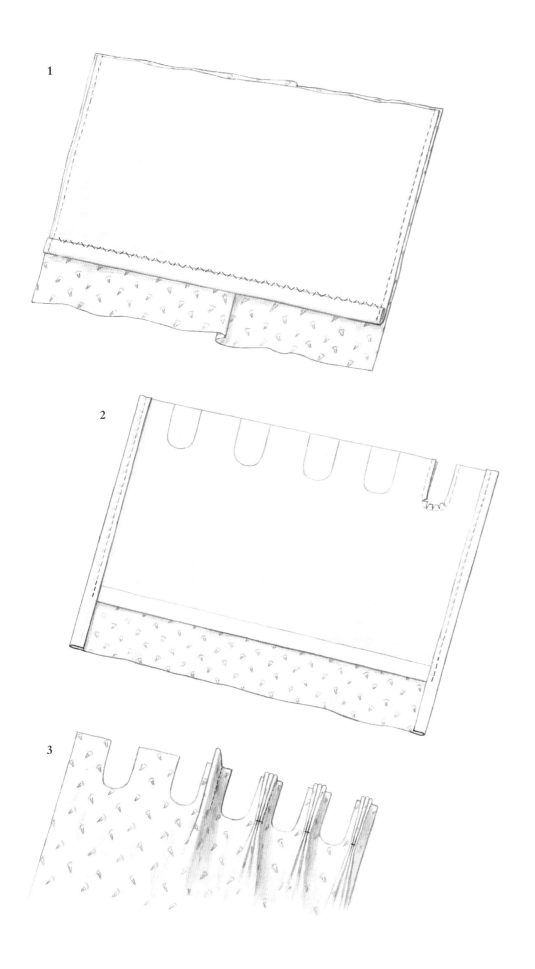

SHOWER CURTAINS

Decide on a suitable fullness for the curtain – say $1\frac{1}{2}$ times. Allow 8 cm (3 in) for 4 cm ($1\frac{1}{2}$ in) double hems down each side edge and the same for a 4 cm ($\frac{1}{2}$ in) double hem across the lower edge. Include a 12 mm ($\frac{1}{2}$ in) seam allowance across the top edge. Cut waterproof fabric to the same dimensions. When stitching plastic, a layer of tissue paper on top of the fabric helps prevent the needle sticking.

1 Turn under 2 cm ($\frac{3}{4}$ in) double hems down the sides and a 4 cm ($1\frac{1}{2}$ in) double hem across lower edges and stitch, mitring corners. Position lining on the fabric, wrong sides together, and stitch, positioning the seam 12 mm ($\frac{1}{2}$ in) from the top raw edge. Turn the curtain right side out and finger press the seam.

2 Stitch a casing the diameter of the shower rod, positioning the first row of stitching 12 mm ($\frac{1}{2}$ in) from the top edge.

Another simple method is to sew rings to the top of the hemmed shower curtain. Place rings about every 10 cm (4 in) and sew firmly. The rings then slide on to the shower rod.

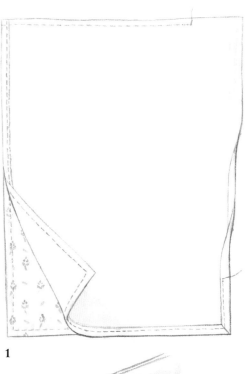

1

2

SOFT FURNISHINGS

CUSHIONS

Cushions, though small, have the potential to pull a scheme together with accents of pattern or colour. The easy charm of printed linen or chintz covers responds to the zest of complementary pattern on cushions – perhaps a stripe or diamond motif. Plain chintz or satin weave cushions can be used to pick out and heighten secondary colours in a room, or they can provide a striking contrast.

Decorative techniques

Cushion covers can be decorative in their own right, displaying creative techniques such as patchwork, appliqué and outline quilting, stencilling or fabric painting. Trimmings give a cushion cover a professional finish: piping in matching or contrasting fabric outlines the shape; flat borders and gathered or pleated frills act as frames; tasselled fringes or heavy silk cording are suitably lavish for velvets, tapestries and brocades.

Themes from the past

A profusion of cushions, piled upon a sofa or window seat, conveys a sense of comfort, even though furniture is now so thoroughly upholstered that cushions are primarily used as accessories. It was not always so. Until the sixteenth century seating had no upholstery and most chairs no back to lean on either. It was the cushion that provided a softer seat; they were the precursors of the flat squab cushion we still tie to kitchen or dining chairs.

Embroidering covers for cushions was one of the accepted occupations for women in noble households, and cushions remain objects for colourful decoration. One of the most popular embroidery effects was crewelwork. Cushions were also covered in velvet or silk damask or in the carpet-like Turkeywork. History repeats itself and the pendulum of style has swung back, renewing interest in decorative effects of the past – the embroidered and kelim-covered cushions we see on many sofas today take their brief from earlier fashions.

LEFT *Cushions provide a vivid tableau set against the polished oak of a wooden settle. The simple, square shapes have been given a variety of decorative treatments: neatly striped cushions have been piped in matching sapphire blue, others display the use of an inner border in a co-ordinating pattern, while a striped twining leaf print, piped in contrasting crimson, pulls all the colours together.*

BELOW *Conservatories share the outdoor colours of blue sky and green landscape, a colour theme taken up here by flowers and foliage on the curtains. A woven willow sofa with snugly fitting piped seat cushion has the additional comfort of chintz covered scatter cushions lodged against either arm – their colour a mirror to the sky on bright summer days.*

RIGHT *Draped wool throws and a variety of cushions evoke comfort and style in this boldly schemed sitting room. Print cushions reflect the pattern and colour in the other furnishings. Prominent accents are the warm texture of needlepoint and the animal magic of white heraldic lions on a crimson cushion.*

Designing your own cushions

Cushions can be made from scratch, which gives complete freedom of choice in the matter of shape and filling. This will be necessary when cushions are to fit a window seat or follow the shape of a chair seat, but for scatter cushions you can choose from a wide range of ready-made shapes and sizes. Sometimes scatter cushions do need to be custom-made to match the size of a fragment of antique textile, or when making cushions with a theme – children love cat or flower-shaped cushions.

The inner covers of cushions are made of calico, sateen or down-proof cambric, according to the filling that is to go inside. Feathers have always been the élite filling for cushions and their supreme softness and natural resilience is unchallenged, but feathers can work their way out through some weaves. Fibrous kapok can become lumpy and foam chip fillings are unavoidably so. Lightweight polyester cushion pads have the advantage of being washable, but they do not possess the supple quality of feathers. For thin squab cushions and deeper box or welted ones, choose a foam filling but check that it matches flammability safeguards.

Most furnishing fabrics and even some dress fabrics are suitable for covering scatter cushions, but for chairs or window seats use firm woven cottons or linens, or even fabrics of upholstery weight if they are not too thick. For sheer extravagance, delicate lace or hand-painted cushions are the ultimate accessory.

ABOVE *The appliqué and antique linen cushions are just for show in this nursery. Shaped cushions, like the pair of ducks, can be made in practical fabrics with washable stuffing and double as soft toys.*

BELOW *The two frills of different widths on this round cushion co-ordinate with the soft floral print of the cushion panels. The topstitched frill, which forms a skirt to the softly padded window seat, is trimmed with a rouleau strip over the line of gathering stitches.*

RIGHT & BELOW *Elegant treatments for the end of a sofa or chaise longue include firm support in the form of a bolster cushion. The scatter cushions take on a softer look with deep frills around the square cushions and plain piped edges.*

BELOW RIGHT *Squab cushions are made with ties stitched into the seam at the back corners to hold the cushions in place. The ties match the contrast binding around the deep frill.*

MAKING CUSHIONS

Any cushion starts with a cushion pad. To calculate the amount of fabric and work out the pattern for a cushion, measure the pad and plan the main panels of fabric allowing 12 mm ($\frac{1}{2}$ in) seams all round. For shaped cushions, either welted or plain, cut a paper template to fit the area exactly. If the cushion is an unusual shape – for a chair seat or a heart shape, for example – fold the paper in half before cutting it out to ensure it is symmetrical.

COVERING A BLOCK OF FOAM

Using calico, cut a top panel and base panel to fit the foam block, allowing 12 mm ($\frac{1}{2}$ in) all round for seams. Cut a strip of fabric for the welt on the straight grain, to fit all around the foam (see below). Join the ends to form a circle and fit it tightly around the foam. Clip into the seam allowances at corners and position the top and base panels in place. Tack together at the seams, leaving an opening in one edge. Remove the pad, stitch seams and press, then turn right side out. Insert the foam pad and slipstitch the opening by hand.

ENVELOPE METHOD

This is a quick method suitable for calico covers or simple fabric covers with no piping.

Start by measuring around the block of foam, to give the total amount of fabric required to wrap around the block. Add 3 cm ($1\frac{1}{4}$ in) seam allowance. Measure the length of the foam block and half-way down the welt at each end. Add 3 cm ($1\frac{1}{4}$ in) to give the total width of fabric required. Cut out a single piece of fabric to this measurement.

1 Join the top and bottom edge with a flat seam, leaving a 30 cm opening in the centre, or setting a zip into the seam if required. This forms a tube.

2 Slip the tube over the foam pad, wrong side out, and pin a seam at each end. The seam line should be positioned in the centre of each end panel, and be slightly shorter than the panel, allowing half the depth of the end panel at each end to make a neat mitre. Remove the cover from the foam, tack and stitch the seam, then make short diagonal seams to form a neatly mitred end. Trim away the excess fabric from the seams, turn right side out and press. Replace the foam pad in the cover and stitch up the opening, or close with the zip.

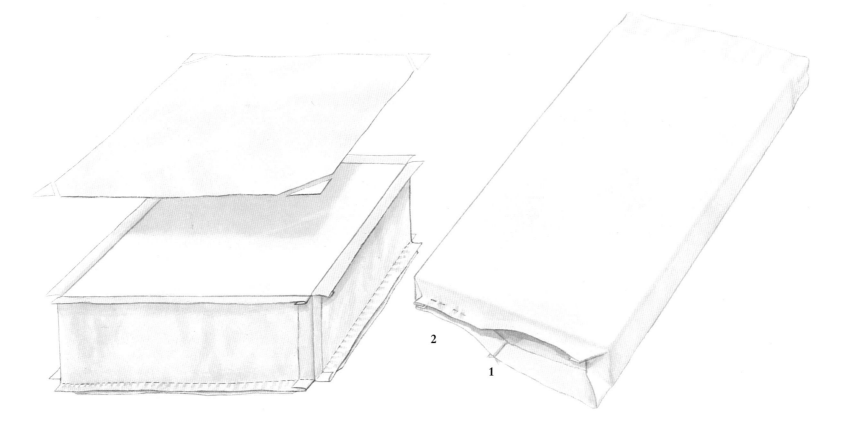

SCATTER CUSHION

1 Cut out the top cushion piece from fabric, allowing 12 mm (½ in) seam allowance all round, and make a paper template from it. Cut the paper across where the zip is to be inserted (about a third of the way down), and spread the pieces 2.5 cm (1 in) apart to allow for the zip. Make a template of this shape and use it to cut the fabric piece for the back. Insert the zip (page 201).

2 Apply any decorative trims to the front panel of the cushion. Position piping or a frill around one cushion piece if required, raw edges together, the piping or frill facing the centre of the cushion piece. Tack and stitch in place.

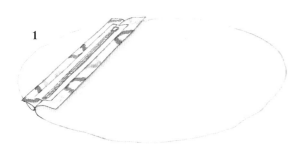

With the zip open, right sides facing and raw edges matching, sew around the cushion. Turn right side out. Press before inserting the cushion pad.

BOX CUSHION

1 Cut out a fabric panel for the top of the cushion, making a template if necessary. Include a 12 mm (½ in) seam allowance. For the back, cut two panels of fabric to fit the cushion allowing 2.5 cm (1 in) extra for the zip to be inserted across the panel (page 201).

2 Make up a welt to fit tightly around the cushion pad. Clip into the seam allowances at the corners. If the cushion is round or awkwardly shaped, cut the welt on the bias to make it easier to fit.

3 Fit piping all around the upper and lower panels if required. With right sides facing inwards, fit the top and base panel to the welt and pin. If the cushion is to be tied in place, make up fabric ties and pin them into the seams at the back corners. Remove the pinned cover by opening the zip and machine stitch the seams. Clip seam allowance across the corners and notch curved seams as necessary (page 198).

The zip can be inserted into the welt in which case measure up for two lengths of fabric to make up the welt, one that extends around adjoining corners by 5 cm (2 in) both ways. This piece needs to be 2.5 cm (1 in) wider than the other welt piece so that it can be split down its length to insert the zip.

BOLSTER CUSHION

Before cutting the fabric, decide whether any pattern should run along or around the cushion. Cut a rectangle of fabric long enough to wrap around the bolster pad, with 12 mm (½ in) seam allowance down all sides. Make the rectangle into a tube to fit around the pad, setting a zip into the seam. Fit on to the pad wrong side out, and clip into the seam allowance.

Cut a circle of fabric for each end of the cushion, including the same seam allowance. Apply piping or frills around the edge if required. Fit the circles on to either end of the tube, wrong side out, and tack along the seam line. Remove the cover from the pad and machine stitch seams. Layer and notch seam allowances and press towards the circles. Press, then turn right side out and press again before inserting the cushion pad.

You can decorate the end of bolsters with tassels, rosettes, covered buttons etc.

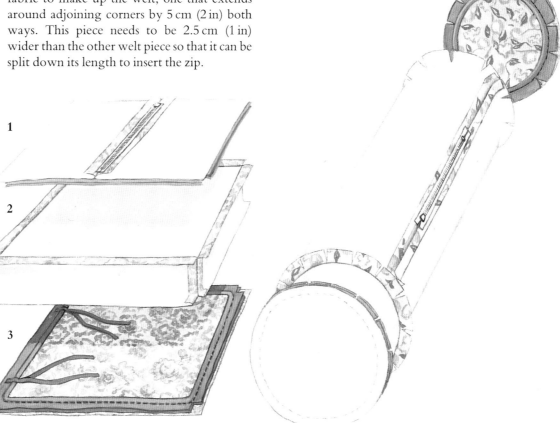

LOOSE COVERS (SLIPCOVERS)

Whether you want to change a colour scheme or revitalize a favourite chair, loose covers (slipcovers) are the ideal furnishing solution. Their practicality also endears them to areas of heavy use, such as family rooms, where covers that are removable and can be washed or dry-cleaned come into their own.

Loose covers (slipcovers) were first made in the eighteenth century as a form of protective covering for fine silk and velvet upholstery. They were frequently made in dimity, a gingham-like cloth, and many paintings of interiors show that their fit was far from tailored. This informal, unfitted style is echoed by the throwover, used for both chairs and sofas – a skilfully draped length of cloth, sometimes an old embroidered or linen tablecloth or antique bedspread, well tucked in down the sides and around cushions, but neither cut nor sewn. A few darts can be added for shape and to keep it in place, but when piled high with cushions, a throwover suggests casual informality.

A tailored loose cover (slipcover), with matching or contrasting piping to outline the shape of the chair or sofa and a straight valance with inverted pleats at the corners, will lend a neat, formal look that is almost indistinguishable from an upholstered piece. But the loose cover (slipcover) is most often associated with a more mellow formality, with chintz and linen covers in classic floral patterns that age gracefully. Gathered valances and plump cushions add to the sense of ease and comfort.

Choosing fabric

The right quality fabric will help to achieve a good-looking finish. It must be strong, but also light enough to take decorative piping and a well-pressed seam line, so avoid materials such as velvet, tapestry or tweed because of their bulk. Woven and printed cotton and glazed chintz are ideal for light occasional use but try a more durable fabric such as a heavy cotton weave or linen union for hard wear. If your chosen fabric is not shrink resistant, and covers are to be washed rather than dry-cleaned, pre-wash all materials, including piping, before making up.

Start with a plain fabric or a print with a small all-over pattern, which is easier to match or position than fabrics with large designs and bold motifs. These should be centred on covers.

RIGHT *The zest of wide stripes gives presence to a sofa partnered by curtains and cushions which use the same stripe to underlay a flower print. It is imperative when working with any striped fabric to make sure that the pattern matches across the seams.*

BELOW *Chintz covers look more tailored and important when given a box-pleated skirt and piping set into the seam lines. The advantage of being able to remove the covers for laundering or dry-cleaning is especially significant when the fabric is a light, plain colour.*

Right *Even though they make a point of hiding the legs, there is nothing remotely Victorian in the inspiration behind these floor-length slipover covers for dining chairs. The chairs may be basic, but the covers provide tailored camouflage with all seams piped and a contrast lining within the inverted corner pleats.*

Below *A gathered skirt on a chair cover diffuses formality. The advantage of using a plain fabric such as this coral cotton is in the substantial block of solid colour it contributes, and it obviates the need for pattern matching. A lightweight cloth, so long as it is firmly woven, allows for well defined seams and neat, slim lines of piping.*

MAKING LOOSE COVERS (SLIPCOVERS)

Tailored or casually fitted covers are a practical and traditional finish for upholstered furniture. You can add a range of different trims to set the style of the cover, picking up themes used elsewhere in the room. The simplest finish is a drawstring casing around the lower edge of the chair, with a tape threaded through it to draw the edge of the cover under the chair. Skirts and fringed trims can be added according to the effect you want.

Piping emphasizes the structure of a piece of furniture and adds formality. It can be combined with a skirt with inverted pleats at the corners to give a tailored finish. Deep bullion fringing can also be stitched around the lower edge of the cover to hide unsightly legs.

Loose covers (slipcovers) are not difficult to make but they are bulky and awkward to handle. Tackle simple shapes first – an armless chair is a suitable project for a beginner. The basic method involves cutting rectangles of fabric to cover the chair or sofa, and then constructing the cover on the chair with the fabric inside out. By fitting the panels inside out, it is easy to mark and tack seam lines. Fit and stitch the various sections of the cover in turn, following the sequence described here.

AN ARMLESS CHAIR COVER

Draw a scale plan and work out a cutting layout for the panels of fabric, checking that the grain runs up and down the chair, and from front to back across the seat. Then calculate how much fabric you will need from the scale plan (page 207). Cut out rectangular panels for the back, outer back and seat of the chair to the appropriate measurements. Mark the centre of the back panel, seat panel and chair with lines of pins.

1 Pin the back panel on the chair, wrong side out, matching the pinned lines.

1

2 Fit it around the top of the chair with stitched darts or tucks if necessary.

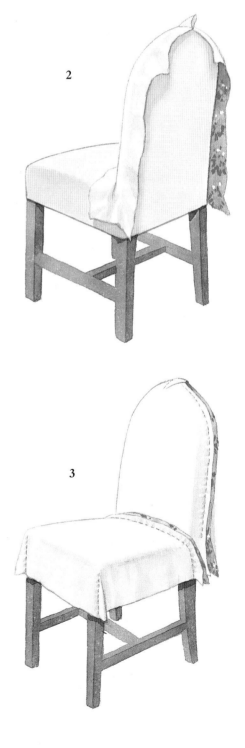

2

3

3 Fit the outer back panel to the back of the chair in the same way, and pin and mark the seam line around the top and sides of the back of the chair. Remove the cover and pins and apply piping to the seam line around the back of the chair. Tack the seam, then stitch, leaving an opening down one side edge if necessary to fit the cover.

Pin and fit the seat panel in the same way. Stitch the seams, inserting piping (page 200) if required. Fit the back of the cover and the seat on the chair again and tack the seam between the two. Stitch the tacked seams. If there is a crack between the upholstered back and the seat of the chair, shape the seam line so you can tuck in the flap.

4 For a gathered skirt, cut the fabric to twice the length of the edge the skirt is to be joined to and join the fabric to make a long strip, allowing 10 cm (4 in) for the hem, a 12 mm ($\frac{1}{2}$ in) seam allowance along the top edge, and a 2.5 cm (1 in) allowance at the ends of the strip for finishing. Press under the turning allowance at the ends; press under a 2.5 cm (1 in) turning along the lower edge, then turn up and stitch an 8 cm (3 in) hem along the lower edge. Gather the raw edge and fit the skirt around the edge of the seat and stitch in place, neatening seam allowances together. Set a zip into the opening at the back corner.

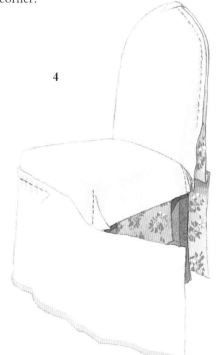

4

A Skirt with Inverted Pleats

This method of measuring and folding pleats in a skirt gives a crisp finish. It can be used on a simple armless chair, with pleats falling from each corner of the seat to the floor, or on a skirt around the lower edge of an easy chair or sofa. There is no need to hem the bottom as the fabric is doubled.

1 Cut a strip of fabric for each side of the skirt, adding 11 cm ($4\frac{1}{2}$ in) at each end for the pleat and seam allowances. The fabric should be twice the depth of the finished skirt, plus a 2.5 cm (1 in) seam allowance. For three of the corners, cut an underlay of fabric 22 cm (9 in) wide, and the same depth as the main part of the skirt. For the corner where the opening is to be, make the underlay from two separate panels, allowing an extra seam allowance where the fastening is to be attached.

Fold the side panels in half along the line of the hem, wrong sides together, and press. Repeat for the underlays.

2 Turn under and press the 11 cm ($4\frac{1}{2}$ in) turnings at each end of the side strips. Butt the folded edges of the side panels together, and position the turnings over the underlays, so that raw edges match. Pin and stitch the raw edges together, taking 12 mm ($\frac{1}{2}$ in) seams, and trim seam allowances. Neaten raw edges together. Leave one seam unstitched at the corner where the opening is positioned. Tack across the top of the pleats.

Fit the skirt around the lower edge of the seat panel or cover, and stitch in place. Layer the seam allowances and press them upwards. Fit the zip or hook-and-eye tape down the opening. On a simple armless chair, continue the fastening down the opening in the skirt. On an easy chair or sofa with an applied, short skirt, fit the fastening to the main part of the chair, and turn under and neaten the allowances down the centre of the corner pleat.

2

1

ARMCHAIRS & SOFAS

There are so many different styles and finishes for covered furniture that it would be impossible to explain all the steps in making every type of cover, but there are some general principles that you can adapt to suit the particular shape you are covering.

1 If you are using a fabric with a bold pattern, position a motif in the centre of each of the main panels of the chair or sofa, on the back or back seat cushion(s), on the centre of the seat, the front seat panel and over the top of each arm. It will be easier to do this if you find and mark the centre of the chair to start with, and align each motif as you work.

Join the sections of each part of the chair as you fit them, then join them all together when you have trimmed and finished the seams. The usual order is to start with the inner and outer back sections, shaping darts at the corners or taking tucks to ease fullness on a rounded shape. Then fit the arms, the inner panel to the outer panel first, then the front panel. Next fit the seat and front panel together at the front of the seat, then fit the sides of the seat to the lower edge of the inner arms, and the ends of the front panel to the front arm panels.

Finally, join the arm and seat sections to the back, first along the back of the seat, then over the arms and finally down the outer corners. If it is a wing chair, make up the wing sections first, then fit them to the inner back panel.

Always follow the rules for trimming and clipping into seam allowances (page 198), and press and finish each seam as you stitch it. It may be difficult to finish the seams once further sections have been joined.

2 Where seams cross, taper any piping into the seam allowance, trimming the cord from the piping to reduce bulk so that you can stitch seams across each other.

3 On most styles of sofa, you will have to join widths of fabric to make up the full width of the back, seat and front panels of the cover. Use a full width of fabric down the centre of the panel, with narrow strips joined selvedge to selvedge down each side. Slip-tack the seams to ensure any pattern matches.

Allow panels around the sides of the seat and down each back corner to tuck into the cracks between the upholstered sections of the chair or sofa to hold the cover in place. Do not trim

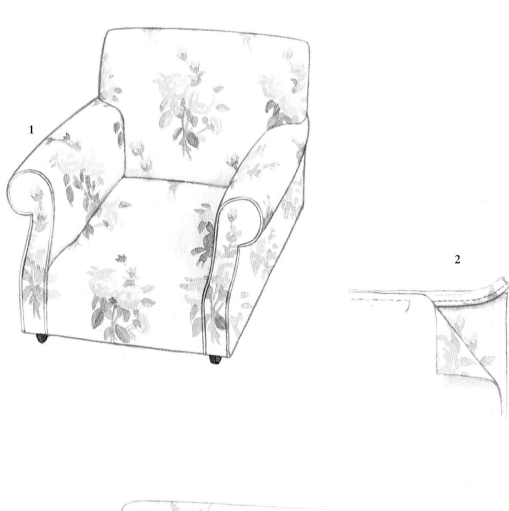

the seam allowance from these tuck-ins until you have tacked the cover and are happy with the fit.

4 There are many different shapes for the arms of chairs. For simple, rectangular shapes, there is often a gusset over the top and front of the arm. If you have to join strips to make up the gusset, position the seam at the front angle of the arm. For heavily stuffed, curved shapes, gather the fabric over the head of the arm and fit it to a front panel shaped to match the outline of the arm.

5 Around the lower edge of the cover, allow a 20 cm (8 in) turning under the chair. Clip away the fabric to fit around the legs or castors of the chair leaving a 6 mm ($\frac{1}{4}$ in) seam allowance. Then neaten the edge with a strip of fabric cut on the bias. Make a casing all around the lower edge and thread a tape through it to draw the cover tightly under the chair or sofa.

6 Down the opening edge at the back corner(s), allow a wider seam allowance and press the turnings towards the back of the chair. Fit hook-and-eye fastenings or a zip by the overlapped method (page 201).

7 Before fitting a valance, mark the level of the valance on the outside of the cover with chalk or pins, checking it is the same height from the floor all round.

For a gathered valance, make up a strip of fabric allowing at least $1\frac{1}{2}$ times the measurement around the chair. Neaten the sides and lower edge with a 12 mm ($\frac{1}{2}$ in) wide double hem. Gather the long raw edge. Position the valance on the cover, with right sides facing and the valance lying upwards, so that the seam lines match. Stitch in place, then press the valance downwards.

8 For a crisp finish on a tailored valance, cut the lower part of the cover off just below the marked height of the valance. Make up the valance and re-join the strip you cut off to the seam joining the valance and cover, sandwiching the top raw edge of the valance between the cover and the lower strip with the casing. Stitch together, then layer the seam allowances and press them upwards.

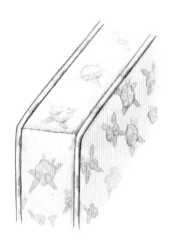

4

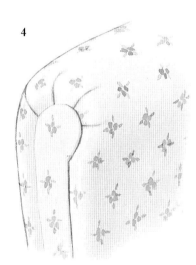

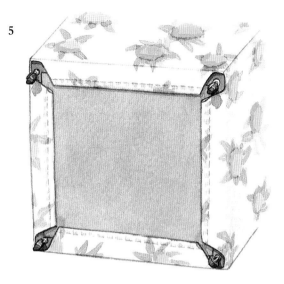

5

6

7

8

UPHOLSTERY

The elegant curves of a Regency chaise longue or the strong outline of a high-backed dining chair demand tight covering to emphasize their shape, or to take in techniques such as deep buttoning. The whole spectrum of fabric types can be used for upholstery from the heaviest velvets and tweeds and the intermediate weight linens and cottons to moiré and satin.

As fitted upholstery is less easy to clean than removable covers (slipcovers), pastel weaves and prints on a light background will benefit from a stain-resistant finish and fitted armcaps will protect fabric from heavy wear. Thick, patterned tapestry in rich colours is a practical and decorative alternative.

Basic principles
In its most basic form, upholstery is a panel of fabric fitted over any tight, calico-covered, padded surface. More advanced upholstery skills take in the fitting and shaping of the padding as well as the application of the top cover. Various combinations of stuffing and padding are used. The most basic is the padded seat in which a thick layer of foam is cut to fit a seat panel and then held in place and slightly shaped by a tight calico cover, tacked under the edge of the seat panel.

Formal chair seats are constructed on a base of webbing stretched across the frame of the seat and covered with a layer of coarse canvas to support traditional padding, usually horsehair and cotton wadding, or modern foam and polyester substitutes. Upholstery may also contain springs in the seats and arms of chairs and sofas and occasionally in the seats of traditional upright dining or occasional chairs.

A drop-in dining chair seat is a good initiation into the skills of upholstery because the work is limited to a small surface. Dining or occasional chairs with fully upholstered backs are a more advanced task. A tight calico cover is seamed or cut and shaped to fit around the back, allowing ease at the seat, before it is tacked in place.

Decorative trimmings
Covering fabrics are nailed to the framework of upholstered furniture leaving at least the lower edge visible. Brass-headed furniture tacks can be used as a decorative disguise, following early traditions where nails were used in a variety of complex patterns. Braid or gimp can also be stapled or glued over tack heads, or adopt the more flamboyant historic practice of using fringing around chair edges or footstools and tassels on arm ends and bolsters.

BELOW *Damask has a long pedigree as an upholstery cloth. Originally woven in silk or wool, it is now often printed in cotton. The elegance of the figured weave and the deep bullion fringe on this sofa is in keeping with the traditional status of both furniture and setting.*

LEFT *The chaise longue is a showpiece for which tight covering is required to give clarity to its elegant shape. Although velvet is the most traditional covering, printed cotton makes a refreshing change. A footstool is upholstered in a related print.*

BELOW *An upholstered sofa reveals every stitching line and every section of fabric as being closely tailored to the shape of the piece. The tailored look is softened here by fullness at the corners where the straight skirt is gathered into gentle flares.*

ABOVE *Antique tapestry on a period chair can be re-created with modern interpretations of traditional fabrics.*

ABOVE *Deep buttoning is one of the options that tight upholstery offers. A sharply pleated skirt provides a notional valance.*

ABOVE *On this dining chair, the padded seat is finished with a simple gimp trimming, appropriate with the striped cotton.*

Upholstering a Seat

Upholstery Tools

You will need some special tools if you plan to tackle the construction, as well as the finish, of upholstery. Webbing can be stretched more efficiently if you use a webbing stretcher which grips the webbing so you can pull it taut over the frame (or improvise with a block of wood). Use upholstery tacks and a fine hammer to fix the webbing, canvas and calico in place. The horsehair is held in place with large, loose stitches (bridle ties); you will need a heavy, straight or curved upholstery needle to do this. A finer curved needle is useful for slipstitching fabric in place – both the calico cover and the top cover of the chair.

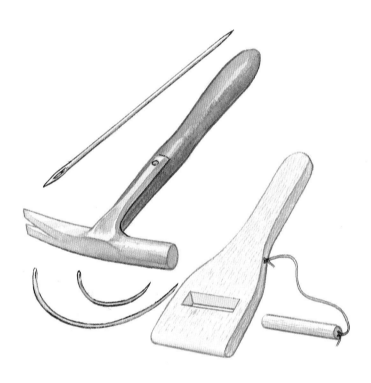

Covering Fabrics

It is essential to use firmly woven fabrics for upholstery; it must hold its shape when stretched and not allow tack heads to slip through the weave. Velvet and heavy tapestry fabric, brocade and silk, dobby weave and linen, and plain or woven patterned cottons can all be used for upholstery. The amount of use the upholstery has to undergo and the decorative scheme of the room are other important considerations in choosing a fabric.

The two dining chair seats discussed here illustrate some of the principles of simple upholstery. The method for covering a drop-in seat shows how calico and cover are attached, and can be adapted if the upholstery is fixed directly to the frame of the chair.

The overstuffed chair seat takes the technique a step further, showing how to replace the webbing and re-fit the padding, as well as finishing the cover. The methods apply to drop-in seats, and upholstery fitted to panels on the back or the arms of a chair. The style of the chair dictates where the fabric should be fixed: it may be fitted in a recess on the frame of the chair, with a carved or shaped wooden trim; or it may wrap around the seat of the chair, so that trimming is decorative rather than acting as a mask for tack heads.

Always cut the panels of fabric so that the crosswise grain runs parallel to the front and back rails, with the lengthwise grain running down the centre of the chair. Temporary tacking is a professional technique used in upholstery which involves holding the fabric taut with a few strategically spaced tacks while you fit the permanent tacks.

RE-COVERING A DROP-IN SEAT

1 Cut a panel of calico, allowing at least 20 cm (8 in) all round to wrap around the sides and under the seat.

Lay out the fabric, wrong side up, and centre the chair seat on the panel. Wrap the fabric around the drop-in seat, tightening it over the front and back rails first. Knock in temporary tacks at the centre front and back, then wrap the fabric tightly around the sides and use tacks at the centre of each side.

2 Nail the fabric down each side of the underside of the seat, spacing the tacks about 5 cm (2 in) apart, to within 5–10 cm (2–4 in) of each corner. Wrap the corner of the panel of fabric over the frame and tack in place, close to the corner of the seat.

3 Make an inverted pleat around the corner so that you can wrap the side turnings together to form a neat mitre. Tack in place. Repeat to fit the fabric outer cover, positioning motifs centrally if the fabric has a bold pattern.

4 Trim away excess fabric. Cut a piece of canvas or black linen upholstery fabric to the size of the underside of the seat, adding 12 mm ($\frac{1}{2}$ in) all round. Turn under and press 4 cm ($1\frac{1}{2}$ in) turnings all around the canvas and tack them in place underneath the seat to cover the raw edge of the seat fabric.

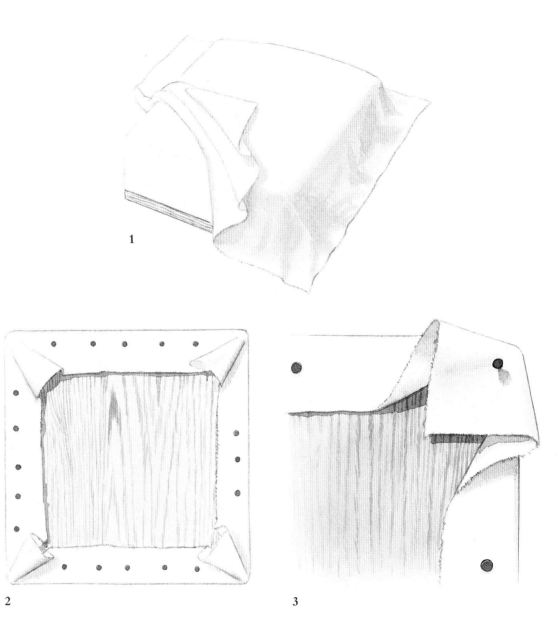

1

2

3

4

REPAIRING AN OVER-STUFFED SEAT

Strip off the old covering and webbing, noting how it was constructed and reserving stuffing and padding for re-use if possible. Use a tack lifter to lever out tacks.

1 Traditional seats have a basketwork of webbing across the base of the seat. Do not cut webbing to length: position the end of the first strip to be fixed with the raw edge level with the inside of the frame of the chair and fix in place with three tacks, close to the outer edge of the rail.

Fold the webbing back over the end, and fix with two more tacks inside the first three. Use a webbing stretcher or wooden block to stretch the webbing across the seat, and hold in place with three tacks, close to the outer edge of the fixing rail.

Trim the webbing 4 cm (1½ in) from the tacks and fold over and fix the end with two more tacks inside the previous three. Repeat for all the strips of webbing. The gap between the webbing strips should be less than the width of the webbing. Work from front to back across the chair, then weave the crosswise webbing over and under the first strips as you work.

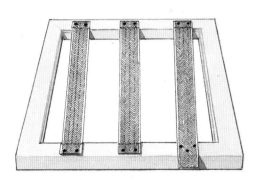

2 Cut a piece of canvas for the lining, allowing a 2.5 cm (1 in) turning all around. Stretch the canvas across the frame, with the grain running parallel to the front and back rails. Hold in place with temporary tacks at the sides and corners and when you are happy with the fit, knock in the tacks. Turn in the allowance and tack in place every 5 cm (2 in) or so all around the chair.

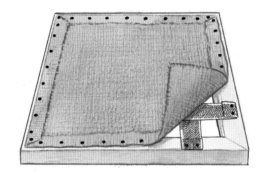

3 Make a series of large backstitches (known as bridle ties) around the edge of the canvas. Tease out horsehair and arrange it on the seat, tucking it under the loops around the edge. Build up the centre of the seat and ensure that the frame is well padded.

4 Fit calico over the seat, fixing it firmly along the straight back edge of the seat first, then stretching it to the front and then the sides of the chair. Hold it taut with temporary tacks as you work. Around the legs, cut into the fabric at the corners, and wrap it firmly around the seat, without straining it at the corners. Tuck in the fullness at the front corners and turn under the fabric in line with the top of the leg before tacking in place. Trim away fabric close to the tacks.

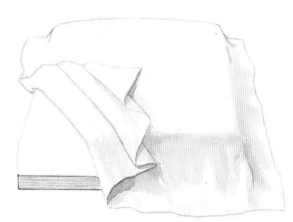

5 Lay a padding of cotton wadding or wool interlining over the calico so that it wraps over the edge of the frame. Trim excess fabric at corners. Fit the cover in the same way as the calico: the top cover may be held in place with brass upholstery tacks, closely spaced, or with ordinary tacks. Some styles have to be fixed along the outer edge of the side and front rails; others can be fixed under the frame of the seat.

6 Glue a plain woven or decorative braid trim to the edge of the upholstery to hide any tacks that show and make a neat join between the frame of the chair and the fabric. Fit a base of canvas or calico for a neat finish.

UPHOLSTERY TECHNIQUES

The details of stitching and fitting covers depend on the style of the chair or the shape you are covering, but there are some general principles which apply to any shape. The most important rule is to make a careful note of how the original cover was fitted, including the positioning of webbing and springs, so that you can reassemble the chair in the same way. Keep the original fabric covering for use as a pattern when you come to cut the new fabric. Always include a generous turning allowance so that you have plenty of fabric to grip as you stretch it in place. It can always be trimmed if necessary. If you plan to tackle more involved upholstery techniques, you may find it easier to use a staple gun to fit the fabric to the frame.

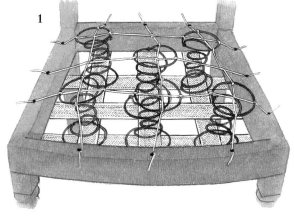

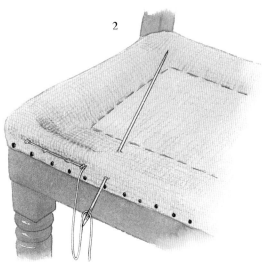

GENERAL HINTS

1 To attach springs, first fit a basketwork of webbing to the underside of the chair frame (rather than the top, as described for dining chairs). Position the springs on the webbing, centring them at the points where the strips of webbing cross. Stitch the springs to the webbing intersections. The springs are then lashed in place with twine. Drive tacks half way into the frame at the end of each row of springs. Tie the twine to the tacks and thread the twine across the top of each spring to the other side of the frame. Hammer the nails in to hold the twine firmly. The springs should be slightly compressed. Cover with a layer of hessian, tacking it to the top of the rails and stitching it to the springs again with twine. Continue as for an un-sprung seat.

2 To make a rolled edge, an extra layer of fabric is included in the stuffing. The horsehair is held in place with a layer of scrim (hessian type fabric), which is fitted to the lower edge of the rails. Around the edge of the seat, stitch the scrim to enclose a roll of stuffing. Topstitch the roll in place, enclosing stuffing in the roll made by the stitches. Fasten the thread at one corner of the chair with a couple of backstitches and then grip a roll of stuffing through the scrim at the outer edge of

the seat. Stitch it in place with a row of topstitching, angling the needle as you stitch so that the lines of stitching are almost continuous on both sides of the roll. The stitches should hold the roll firmly in place over the edge of the frame.

The next step is to use more stuffing to pad the centre of the chair inside the roll, holding it to the scrim with bridle ties. Then cover with calico, wadding and the top cover as before.

When covering a chair with an upholstered back and/or arms, always start with the seat section of the upholstery, stretching the webbing to hold padding or springs. Normally, the back (and arm) sections have a hessian backing only: no webbing is needed to hold the stuffing in place.

Leave the hessian backing untacked across the lower back edge when you fit it. This enables you to fit the seat covering to the back of the back rail. Fit webbing and springing to the seat, then fit hessian over the springs. Fit the stuffing and form a rolled edge on the seat of the chair, then finish the calico cover,

wadding and main cover on the seat, nailing them firmly to the outside of the back rail.

Fit stuffing to the back of the chair, using extra bridle ties, and finish with calico over the front. To neaten the back of the chair, you will need a panel of fabric shaped to fit, with a 2.5 cm (1 in) turning all round. Press under the turning and slipstitch the panel in place around the sides and top of the chair. Fit the cover to the back of the chair as for the calico cover.

To anchor the stuffing to the frame, knock tacks halfway into the frame, and then tie loops of twine between the nails. Knock the nails in to hold the twine and tease the horsehair under the loops in the same way as described for bridle ties. The stuffing is held in place with scrim tacked to the frame.

You will have to make pleats around the top of a shaped arm or back. The roll of the arm or back is stitched in place as for the seat, and more horsehair laid over the depressions before the calico cover is fitted. The front arm gusset has to be slipstitched in place in the same way as for the back of the chair.

TABLE LINEN

Pure linen will always have its place at a formal dinner table as a partner to porcelain, silver and sparkling cut crystal. Napkins should be made in fabric with some absorbency. Again, linen is the ideal choice. As napkins are reversible, the fabric needs to be plain or a woven design such as a gingham or stripe. Hems should be neatly unobtrusive unless they are contrast bound, scalloped or trimmed with lace or crochet.

The cut of the cloth
Match table linen to curtains and they will draw that colour or pattern into the room scheme, or if cushions provide pattern contrast in a sitting room, cloths for side tables could be matched to them in a strong supporting role. Tables, sideboards and even mantelpieces were once draped with cloths, often in thick fabrics and heavily fringed or overlaid with layers of linen and lace. Even in our much simpler interiors, the full-length cloth over a side table can add style to a room. Though the table beneath may be of humble chipboard, when draped with an antique kelim or a paisley print in rich colours, and used as a base for a collection of objects, it becomes highly decorative.

A full-length circular cloth can be cut over long so that it swings out at the hem. A knee- or floor-length edge can be bound, frilled, padded or fringed. Cloths can be used in tandem: a small circle or square can be laid as contrast over the main cloth; Madras muslin can be draped or knotted over a creamy cotton or dark contrasting base cloth, and lace can be swagged over gathered voile for a romantic bedroom.

Side tables with sweeping overcloths have a place in the sitting room as an alternative to conventional wooden occasional tables to hold lamps, books and objects. In the bedroom they can take on the role of bedside or dressing table, perhaps hiding a portable television beneath the skirt. Such an elegant table provides a useful surface in the hallway by a front door.

ABOVE *An airy, uncluttered room has the table set almost in the manner of an altar in front of a high window screened by voile. Rectangular tables are the least easy to cover successfully with a long cloth. Here the dramatic intention is well served by a hand-embroidered table cloth.*

RIGHT *Pink chintz cloth, chosen for an occasional table in a drawing room, is cut slightly long to give more emphasis to the flare. The hemline is defined by a tasselled fringe set just up from the floor.*

LEFT *Still-life on a table top has its arrangement underlined and subtly exploited by a paisley decorated shawl slung across the table which partly conceals and partly reveals the shape and style of the piece of furniture. The objects present an artful symmetry, even when the drape of the cloth apparently quarrels with gravity.*

LEFT *When a full-length cloth is made for a large circular table, the fabric must be heavy to hold its shape; light fabrics tend to drift. A quilted coverlet can translate successfully from the bedroom to make an attractive overcloth of weight and substance.*

RIGHT *A celebration calls for a table setting to match. The fitted top cloth is held in place with a scalloped border.*

MAKING TABLE LINEN

Simple linen or cotton tablecloths can be made up with any number of different finishes: bold, bound edges; fine, hand-rolled hems; a simple, topstitched double hem. Trim them with appliqué ribbons or lace, cording, drawn thread work or embroidery. Napkins should have a simple finish that will withstand repeated laundering. Cotton blended with polyester makes a good easy-care cloth.

Fabrics that are woven with no distortion of the lengthwise and crosswise grain (so they run at right angles to each other) are easier to cut out and to handle. Follow a thread when cutting out and marking hem lines.

For a richly padded, floor-length circular cloth, careful measurement (page 207) and cutting is essential. The cloth may be lined and interlined, with a thickly padded or faced hem.

TABLECLOTH & NAPKINS

Decide on the finished size for the tablecloth and add a suitable allowance for the seam. For a bound hem, no allowance is needed; for a rolled hem, 6 mm ($\frac{1}{4}$ in); for a double hem, anything from 2 cm ($\frac{3}{4}$ in) to 20 cm (8 in). Cut out a panel of fabric for the cloth, ensuring the corners are exact right angles. (Use the side and end of a table as a guide when cutting out.) Flat fell seams are used to join any widths of fabric.

1 For a bound edge, cut bias strips of fabric twice the depth of the finished binding with 6 mm ($\frac{1}{4}$ in) turnings down each long edge. Press under the turnings and fold the binding in half, right side out. Attach the binding by hand or machine, easing around corners.

2 For a rolled hem, make a line of machine stitching 6 mm ($\frac{1}{4}$ in) from the raw edge of the fabric. Roll the edge of the fabric between the thumb and forefinger of one hand as you stitch the hem with your other hand.

3 For a double hem, turn under the depth of the hem, trimming away fabric at the corners for a smooth finish. (The corners may be mitred, or finished with overlapping hems.) Stitch the hem by machine, close to the folded inner edge of the hem. You can also use a zig-zag stitch over the folded inner edge of the hem, or stitch from the right side with a zig-zag stitch, applying cording along the line of stitching.

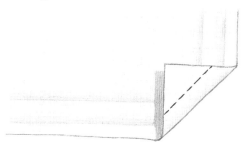

4 Decide on suitable dimensions for the napkins. For maximum use of fabric, cut an exact number of napkins (say three or four) across the width of the fabric. Use one of the methods described for finishing table cloths to neaten the edges of the napkins.

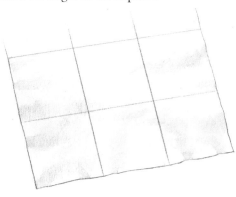

A CIRCULAR CLOTH

1 Decide on a finished diameter for the cloth: for a full draped effect, make the cloth slightly longer than twice the height plus the diameter of the table. Decide on a suitable finish and include a hem allowance. For a lined cloth, include a 5 cm (2 in) turning all around the outer edge. To interline the cloth, the best method is to cut a separate circle of interlining to fit the table and place under the cloth. This saves cleaning problems.

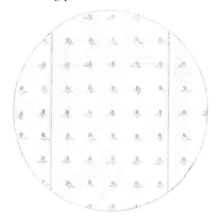

Cut enough widths of fabric to make a square with each side the same measurement as the diameter of the fabric required for the cloth. In most cases you will have to join widths of fabric. Position a full width of fabric down the centre of the cloth and join strips to each selvedge to make up the width, matching the pattern carefully by slip-tacking (page 196) if necessary.

2 Fold the fabric into quarters, wrong side out, and lay it on a carpeted floor. To make a paper pattern, take a square of paper the size of the folded fabric. Use a drawing pin (thumb tack) to hold a string at the centre of the paper in the corner of the fold, and tie a pencil to the other end of the string so that you can mark the radius of the paper pattern (including seam allowance). Pin the pattern to the layers of fabric, draw a pencil line along the curve and tack just inside the line. Cut out through all layers at once. With thick pile or slippery fabrics, cut through only two layers at a time.

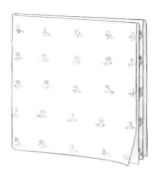

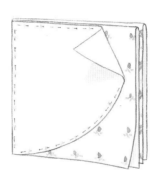

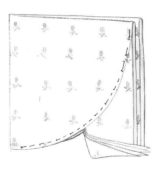

3 For a lined cloth, cut a circle of lining the same size as the main fabric. On both circles of fabric cut notches all around the edge at regular intervals (2.5 cm/1 in) to allow the hem to lie flat. Turn under 2.5 cm (1 in) all around the lining and the main cloth. Lock-stitch the lining to the cloth if it is large. Position the lining on the cloth wrong sides together and slipstitch the folded hems together. Press, without making a crease in the hem of the cloth.

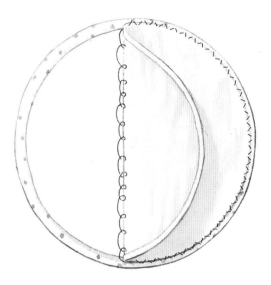

A faced hem gives a crisp finish to a circular cloth. Cut the fabric into a circle as before, allowing a 1 cm ($\frac{3}{8}$ in) turning. Cut a 2.5 cm (1 in) wide strip of fabric on the bias to match the circumference of the finished cloth. Press under 6 mm ($\frac{1}{4}$ in) down each long edge and join the ends (page 200), or you can purchase binding. Position the binding around the hem of the cloth, right sides facing, and stitch so that the fold of the binding is 1 cm ($\frac{3}{8}$ in) inside the raw edge of the fabric. Press, then turn the hem allowance and binding to the inside and press again. Slipstitch the free folded edge of the binding to the main part of the cloth, easing in the fullness as you work.

The cloth may also be finished with a simple topstitched hem, and trimmed with braid or bullion cord at floor level.

BEDS & BEDLINEN

Bedspreads

For centuries, sumptuous bedspreads, coverlets and quilts have been important elements of bedroom furnishing. Crimson silk worked with gold thread was the stuff of royal fourteenth-century quilts; Henry VIII's bed also boasted splendid covers quilted in gold and silver; humbler Tudor households made do with embroidered linen and serviceable woollen blankets. Washable, brightly printed Indian chintz bedspreads, known as palampores, were first seen on European beds over 300 years ago and were imported from Madras by the East India Company; contemporary regal four posters, however, favoured more elaborate bedspreads of damask and velvet. Marriage quilts were something special – Victorian girls would spend years stitching their own – and in colonial America, betrothed girls would be expected to stitch at least twelve everyday quilts as well as a marriage quilt for a trousseau.

Styles, colours and fabrics

Bedspread fashions may come and go but for cottage and attic bedrooms a traditional patchwork quilt teamed with a simple iron, pine, or painted bedstead is a recipe for success. Grand, more formal beds can take a dressed-up patchwork quilt. A frilled or pleated valance showing below gives a variety of different effects. The fabric could echo or contrast with colours in the quilt, bedhead, window dressing or upholstery fabrics.

Quilts and bedspreads in children's rooms in pastel-coloured fine cotton prints with broiderie anglaise edgings look enchanting appliquéd with alphabet or animal motifs. For more unusual appliqué inspiration, say, in an Edwardian-style child's bedroom, Kate Greenaway's characters would also look appropriate worked in typically muted grey-greens, blues, cream and terracotta.

Lace and crochet bedspreads always look feminine and pretty, providing a soft, glamorous contrast to sturdy brass and iron bedsteads.

RIGHT *A chunky hand-crocheted bedspread, fine bedlinen, simple net curtains and a smoothly painted metal bedstead provide the ingredients of a fresh, understated bedroom.*

LEFT *A throwover can enhance or disguise the bed and the bedding – it is the perfect means of bringing the bed into a room scheme. This linen and lace throwover evokes romance and elegance; linen lasts forever if well looked after.*

BELOW *Cot quilts of finest cotton lawn in pastel colours make a fairytale coverlet for a baby. Matching cot bumpers add a practical note by providing a necessary barrier to the cot frame.*

Fortunately, it is not hard to find new versions of authentic nineteenth-century lace designs as these are still being made. A fine white or cream voile or lace 'overspread' with a gathered skirt can cover an existing chintz quilt for an exciting new look and give added protection at the same time. Throwover bedspreads consisting of a simple hemmed sheet are useful in informal bedroom schemes and are quick and easy to make. For grander beds needing a more luxurious, finished look throwovers can be quilted and lined with a complementary co-ordinating fabric in a tiny geometric print. Alternate bedcovers according to the season with a heavy quilt for winter warmth and a light cotton cover for the summer.

A tailored bedspread with a panelled or pleated skirt lends dressed-up dignity to a four poster. In one-room apartments and spare bedrooms the bed needs to blend in unobtrusively as part of a seating arrangement. Suitable fabrics here could be a plain linen union or cotton repp; tartan or paisley prints in sophisticated burgundy, navy, charcoal and bottle green will also work well. To add interesting detail, pick out the piping and pleats in a fabric to match the curtains and upholstery.

LEFT *Nothing evokes a country bedroom atmosphere more than a simple chequerboard patchwork quilt worked in brilliant colours. Early American, Shaker and Amish patchwork quilts were made from fine cotton or woollen fabric recycled from old clothes and blankets. Quilts were family heirlooms handed down to each generation and were a unique record of a family's history.*

LEFT *An alternative to duvets and bedspreads is to have plain top blankets and bedlinen in a matching colour. Deep, frilly, floral-printed valance skirts give these beds a celebratory 'dressed up' air. Neatly folded eiderdowns at the foot of each bed lie ready to be pulled up when chilly winter nights draw in.*

RIGHT *Patchwork quilts are extremely versatile – the perfect answer for those wanting to cover a grand four poster bed without making it appear too formal. The colours of the American quilt here are cleverly echoed in the pretty frilled canopy valance and patchwork cushion.*

MAKING BEDSPREADS

By making your own bedspreads, you can ensure a good fit and perfect match to other furnishings in the room. You can devise your own finishing touches and embellishments – quilting in patterns outlining the print of the fabric, or adding an unusual trim, piping or binding, for example. When measuring up for a bedspread (page 206), note whether the pillows and bedding should be in place.

When cutting out fabric for a double bedspread, it is important to position the seams down either side of the top of the bedspread, close to the sides of the bed: this avoids having an unsightly central seam and gives a more professional finish to the cover.

Fitted covers lie more smoothly on the bed if the top panel is lined and interlined; the sides need not be lined, although this gives a smart finish to tailored covers.

A THROWOVER

This simple, floor-length throwover cover has rounded corners at the foot of the bed, and is lined and interlined. Decide on the overall finished dimensions of the bedspread: it can just touch, or trail on to the floor.

1 Cut out the fabric to make up the main panel, allowing 5 cm (2 in) turning all around the sides and lower edge, and 2.5 cm (1 in) across the top. Cut the interlining with a 2.5 cm (1 in) turning around the sides and lower edge, but no turning allowance across the top. The lining should be 5 cm (2 in) smaller than the main fabric around the sides and lower edge, with the same turning across the top.

If you need to make seams in the layers of fabric, position a full width of fabric down the centre of the bedspread with narrower widths joined selvedge to selvedge down each side edge. Use flat seams for the main fabric and lining, and abutted seams (page 199) for the interlining. Round off the lower corners of the panels, using a large plate or paper template, and check that the corners match.

Position the interlining on the wrong side of the main fabric and lockstitch in place (page

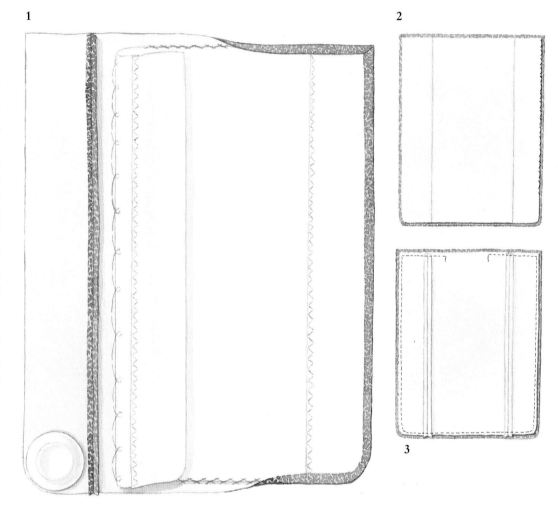

196), leaving the appropriate turning allowance all around. Herringbone stitch the interlining to the main fabric around the outer edge. Turn under and press the seam allowance across the top edge of the main fabric, over the interlining.

2 For a hand-finished cover, turn up the 5 cm (2 in) hem allowance on the main fabric, rolling the interlining up without pressing a crease. Press under a 2.5 cm (1 in) turning all around the lining. The lining may be fitted by hand, or stitched by machine.

Position the lining on the wrong side of the fabric and lock to the interlining. Slipstitch the lining to the main fabric all around the sides

and edge of the cover, close to the edge of the interlining.

3 For a machine-stitched lining, position the lining on the interlined fabric, right sides together. Open out the turnings in both layers of fabric and pin and tack together, taking 2.5 cm (1 in) seams.

Ease the fullness of the main fabric into the seam around the curved corners. Stitch together, leaving a 50 cm (18 in) opening in the top edge. Turn the cover right side out and press, without pressing a crease into the hem of the interlined fabric. Slipstitch seam allowances together along the opening to give a professional finish.

FITTED COVER WITH INVERTED PLEATS

This cover has a top panel with piped edges, and a straight skirt with inverted pleats at the corners of the foot of the bed. Calculate the finished measurements for the bedspread – the overall length and width of the top panel and the depth of the skirt.

1 Cut a rectangle of fabric for the top panel, allowing a 12 mm ($\frac{1}{2}$ in) seam allowance all round. Cut a piece of lining fabric the same size. Cut and join the sections for the skirt, adding 40 cm (16 in) for pleats at each corner. Allow a 12 mm ($\frac{1}{2}$ in) seam allowance along the top edge and 5 cm (2 in) for double hems all around the sides and lower edges. Make up sufficient piping to fit all around the sides and lower edge of the top panel (page 200).

Join fabric to make up a top panel if necessary. Round off the corners at the foot of the bed for a less severe shape. Position piping all around the sides and lower edge of the top panel and tack and stitch in place using the zipper foot, taking a 12 mm ($\frac{1}{2}$ in) seam allowance. Clip into seam allowances as necessary to fit the piping around the corners.

If the corners are rounded, lay the cover on the bed and mark the position of the pleats at the corners of the top panel with pins.

2 Turn under 2.5 cm (1 in) double hems down the sides and along the lower edge of the skirt, mitring the corners. Measure and pin pleats to fit at the corners of the bedspread, then stitch across the top of the pleats, just inside the seam line. Position the skirt around the sides and lower edge of the bedspread, with right sides facing and raw edges matching. Clip into the seam allowance of the skirt at the corners if necessary to help the fabric lie flat. Pin and tack in place, following the line of stitching which is holding the piping in place. Layer the seam allowance.

Position the lining over the top panel, right sides facing and raw edges matching, stitch across the top edge, and turn the lining to the wrong side. Turn under 12 mm ($\frac{1}{2}$ in) all around the lining and slipstitch in place, enclosing the raw edges of the top panel, the skirt and the piping.

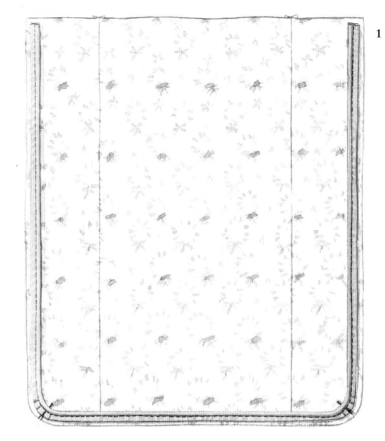

MAKING QUILTS

A simple throwover bedspread in quilted fabric gives a smart finish and provides an extra layer of warmth over blankets or a duvet. In warmer weather, the quilt and a flat top sheet alone provide ample bed covering.

Although ready-quilted fabric and ready-made quilts are available, by quilting your own fabric, you can alter the spacing, direction or even the shape of the quilting to suit the fabric. A straight striped fabric, for example, is particularly effective quilted with parallel lines of stitching, following the stripes of the fabric. For more elaborate detail, shape the quilting to outline bold motifs in a pattern.

QUILTED THROWOVER

Cut a panel of main fabric, the size of the finished bedspread plus 10 cm (4 in) all around. Cut wadding and lining fabric (preferably in a contrast fabric, as the throwover is reversible) to the same size.

1 Join widths of fabric with a flat seam, and butt widths of wadding together, joining them with zig-zag stitch or by hand with herringbone stitch. Sandwich the three layers together, with the wadding in the middle and the main fabric and lining right side out. Tack together all around the outer edge. Make lines of tacking stitches diagonally or in parallel lines across the panel, about 10 cm (4 in) apart.

2 Quilt up and down the panel by machine. Trim the quilted panel to the finished measurements of the bedspread and round off the corners if required (page 157). If the bedspread has to fit over the frame of a bed, cut out the corners so that you can arrange the overhang neatly around the bedposts at the foot of the bed. Cut lengths of binding on the bias, making one strip long enough to fit all around the outer edge of the quilt and one to fit across the top. Join lengths as necessary. The binding should be about 8 cm (3 in) wide. Turn under and press 2 cm ($\frac{3}{4}$ in) down each long edge, and fold in half and press. Position binding around the outer edge of the quilt and stitch in place by hand or machine.

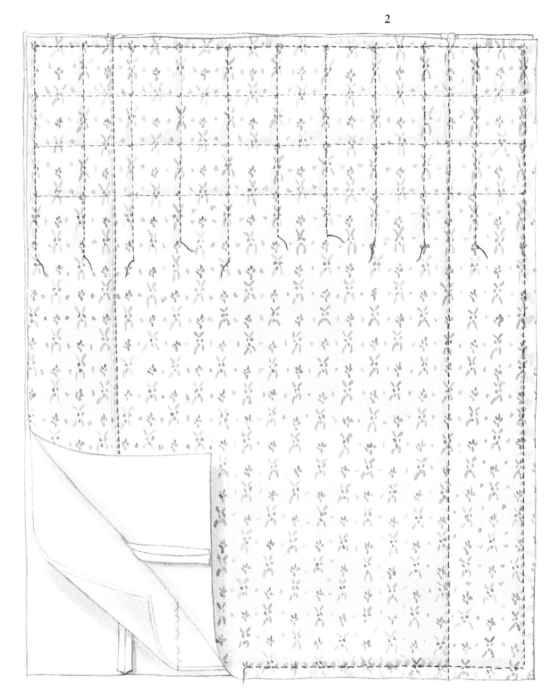

2

1

For variations of pattern, plan the arrangement of squares on graph paper before you start, using crayons or coloured pens to organize the colour sequences. You can increase the number of fabrics you use so that the whole is graded in tone from the centre outwards.

Choose three or four co-ordinating fabrics and cut them first into strips, 12 cm (4¾ in) wide, and then into squares of the same measurement. Press under 1 cm (⅜ in) wide turnings all around each square.

Take the first two squares, in two different fabrics, and join with a flat seam. Join further squares to the opposite free edges, keeping the different patterns in the same order. Join enough squares to make a strip the length of the finished quilt.

Make up further strips until you have enough to fit the width of the quilt. Plan the strips so that each one starts with a different fabric in the sequence. Press all seams open and clip across corners of seam allowance.

Join the strips in the same way as the squares, being careful to take precise 1 cm (⅜ in) seam allowances. Check the arrangement of the strips before stitching so that they form diagonal bands of pattern. Press the seams open.

Make up the quilt with a plain backing panel and a piece of wadding the same size as the patchwork panel, and bind the edge.

When joining triangles to form a square, match the raw edges carefully or the resulting seam will be incorrectly aligned.

3 If the quilt is to fit over a brass or wooden bedframe, cut out the corners of the quilted fabric to accommodate the bed posts before applying the binding.

PATCHWORK COVERLET

Patchwork was originally developed as a method of re-cycling fabrics, but has developed into an art form.

This basic machine method based on simple shapes like the square and triangle is a time-saving way to re-create the effect. Quilting can be done after all the patches are sewn together.

Cut out all the shapes with the same seam allowance so that they match up at the seam lines when the units, or blocks, of smaller patchworks are sewn together into the final throwover. The instructions here are for the simplest throwover made from squares that are all the same size (or you can assemble triangles to the same size as the squares).

BEDLINEN

Wealthy medieval households spun and wove their own bedlinen which was stored in huge oak linen presses smelling sweetly of woodruff and lavender. Bedlinen was considered so precious it was included in wedding dowries and wills; rich travellers took their sheets and pillows with them when they went to stay with friends. And while embroidered silk 'oversheets' adorned royal beds, practical linen sheets went underneath.

Satin sheets were reputed to have made a brief appearance in Tudor times in Britain through the auspices of Anne Boleyn who brought them back from France. However, cotton sheets were not introduced until the end of the eighteenth century and remained white throughout the nineteenth century, although the edges were often elaborately embroidered and trimmed with lace and ribbons. It was not until the 1960s that deep-dyed colours and sumptuous floral printed cotton bedlinen first appeared; duvets from Germany and Scandinavia were also introduced and revolutionized styles in modern bedlinen.

Styles and fabrics

Bedlinen should be seen as part of the whole bedroom scheme. Colours, styles and patterns in duvets and pillowcases should either match, complement or contrast with other bedroom furnishings such as the curtains, blinds or a bedspread. It also helps to think of successful combinations: pure, crisp white cotton sheets with delicate lace, scalloped or picot edges always look marvellous against rich mahogany or walnut bedheads and Empire-style beds. Flower-sprigged cotton duvets and valance frills are pretty and practical on a divan in a young girl's room or a spare bedroom. Sheets and pillowcases patterned with bold cabbage roses can complement a white lace and crochet bedspread or perhaps co-ordinate with a smaller geometric trellis, a striped bedspread and matching curtains or an Austrian blind. Sofabeds in a living room, study or one-room apartment could have a set of bedlinen that complements the upholstery: midnight-blue sheets and pillowcases with a light quilt in a bold paisley pattern could either match or co-ordinate with the sofa covers.

By making your own bedlinen, you can add special decorative touches, making it truly individual – details such as tucking and cording in a contrasting colour for pillowcase and sheet borders. Borders of co-ordinating fabrics or plain fabrics in a contrasting colour also look attractive. A time-honoured favourite is to have plain sheets and pillowcases discreetly monogrammed in satin stitch with your initials. A few embroidered flowers, leaves or bows do wonders for a plain white pillowcase corner.

BELOW *A simple, tie-on padded headboard in a plain fabric lends a clean, uncluttered line to this bedhead and sets off the quilted throwover and striped gathered valance to perfection. A loose-covered bedhead is also practical as it can be taken off for cleaning. Having pillowcases in a colour or pattern that matches the headboard fabric gives a 'finished' look.*

RIGHT *Duvets are the perfect bedcover for beds with head- and footboards that can be awkward to make. Cover styles can be purely functional or sumptuous, designed to be permanently on show. A cotton cover is eternally fresh and summery and particularly flattering seen against the polished wood bedstead.*

BELOW *Besides adding a pretty, feminine touch, gathered valances also provide flattering camouflage for unsightly bases, bedlegs and underneath storage. The cotton and lace valance softens this metal bed frame. Valances in fabrics that match or co-ordinate with the rest of the bedlinen always look smart – alternatively, choose a valance in a colour that echoes other colours in a room.*

BELOW *A fitted, tailored valance with bound detailing offsets this bedlinen, with its exuberant pastel print, to perfection. The frilled pillowcases give just the right amount of light relief – a frilled valance as well would have been too fussy.*

MAKING BEDLINEN

When making your own bedlinen, where possible apply any decorative touches before finishing the seams. Decoration is best limited to borders and edgings (it is uncomfortable to sleep on when used elsewhere). Use full width fabric for the reverse of the duvet and bottom sheet to avoid uncomfortable seams.

Cording and pin tucks are described here – other finishes are described elsewhere: appliqué page 203), frills and piping (page 201).

Sheets and duvet covers should be made up in sheeting width fabric – normally 228 cm (90 in) wide. If you want to use a print which is not available in sheeting width, just use it for the parts of the bedlinen that will show – the borders all around the pillowcase or along the top edge of the duvet, for example.

Choose washable fabrics. Linen is luxurious, but demands time and effort to keep it at its best; cotton or a cotton/polyester mix are more practical alternatives. Where possible, use enclosed seams to prevent fraying during laundering.

CORDING

Use fine cotton cord, in white or a colour to match or contrast with the fabric. Thread the machine with an appropriate colour: if you use contrast cording, use a contrast colour in the needle; the bobbin thread can be matched to the fabric so that the stitching is less obvious on the underside. Set the sewing machine to a medium length and width zig-zag stitch and fit the cording foot on the machine. (This has a hole to guide the cording thread under the needle.)

Mark the position of the cording with chalk or a line of tacking threads on the right side of the fabric. Thread the end of the cord into the foot and position the edge of the work under the foot of the machine. Stitch along the marked line, feeding the cord under the foot, so that the zig-zag stitch holds the cord in place. Two parallel lines of cording, 6 mm ($\frac{1}{4}$ in) apart, are a simple, effective touch.

TUCKING

Decide on a suitable width and spacing for the tucks: they may be stitched close to the folded edge of the fabric for a very narrow tuck (pin tucks), or up to about 15 mm ($\frac{5}{8}$ in) from the fold for a wider tuck. Calculate the total number of tucks and allow twice the width of each tuck when working out how much fabric you will need. Add an extra allowance so that you can trim the panel accurately when making up the item.

Mark out the tucks across the top and lower edge of the area to be stitched. With large areas, such as a duvet cover, mark across the centre of the fabric as well. For pin tucks, mark the centre of each pleat. For wider tucks, mark the stitching lines of each tuck. Press the pleats into the fabric, following the marks. With wide pleats, fold the fabric so that the marked stitching lines come together.

Stitch each tuck in turn, using the presser foot of the machine or the throat plate markings as a guide when positioning the stitching. There is no need to finish the ends of the threads as they will be enclosed in seams or hems. Trim the fabric to the required size, ensuring the tucks are positioned centrally.

A DUVET COVER

1 Measure the duvet to be covered and cut out two panels of fabric, allowing 5 cm (2 in) for seams and ease all round. Decorate the top panel of fabric before trimming to size. If you have to join widths of a patterned fabric for the top panel, position a full width down the centre of the cover and strips of equal size down either side. Join widths with a flat fell seam, slip-tacking first if there is a difficult pattern match.

Join the two panels of fabric using a French seam. Across the lower edge of the cover, end the seams 20 cm (8 in) in from each corner to make an opening for inserting the duvet. Press the folds of the seam allowance across the opening to provide the hem.

2 Turn the cover inside out again. Across the opening, position the popper tape (or whatever fastening you wish to use to contain the duvet – Velcro strips, press studs, buttons etc) and cover or hem the raw edges. Ensure that the opposite halves of the opening match and secure the fastening in place. Turn right side out and press.

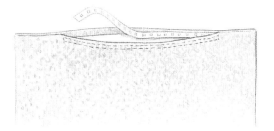

A PLAIN PILLOWCASE

1 Cut out a strip of fabric, twice the length of the pillow plus a total of 30 cm (12 in) for turnings and tuck in. Allow 2 cm ($\frac{3}{4}$ in) seam allowance down each long edge. At the tuck-in end, turn under and press 15 mm ($\frac{1}{2}$ in) and then 10 cm (4 in) to make a broad border. Stitch in place and add cording or any other trim if required. At the tuck-in end, turn under and press a 15 mm ($\frac{1}{2}$ in) double hem

PILLOWCASE WITH BORDER

For a crisp, flat edging to a pillowcase, the front should be cut from one panel of fabric and the back cut from two panels, one to cover the main part of the pillow and the other to form a tuck-in.

1 Cut out the front panel, allowing 6 cm ($2\frac{1}{2}$ in) – or whatever width you want – all around for the border and seam allowance. Cut out the main back panel, omitting the border allowance down one short edge. Cut the tuck-in panel the same width as the main panel and 23 cm ($9\frac{1}{2}$ in) deep.

Turn under a 2 cm ($\frac{3}{4}$ in) double hem down the short edge of the main back panel and on the smaller back panel. If you want a more traditional fastening, make buttonholes along the hemmed edge of the main back panel. Position the main panel over the tuck-in, with the wrong side of the main panel facing the right side of the back panel so that they make up a panel the same size as the front panel of fabric. Tack together within the seam allowance where the panels overlap.

Position the back on the front, right sides facing, and pin together all around the outer edge. Stitch, taking a 1 cm ($\frac{1}{2}$ in) seam allowance.

and stitch in place by machine. Turn under and press a 15 cm (6 in) wide tuck-in.

2 Fold the fabric in half so that the finished edge of the border matches the fold of the tuck-in, wrong sides together. Pin and stitch down each long edge, taking a 1 cm ($\frac{3}{8}$ in) seam. Trim seams, press and turn inside out. Complete the French seam, taking the same seam allowance as before. Turn right side out and press.

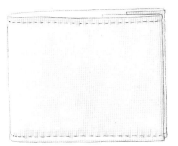

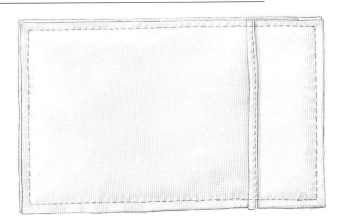

2 Turn right side out and press. Topstitch all around the pillowcase, positioning the stitching 5 cm (2 in) inside the previous seam line to make a flat border. Add cording or trimming along the seam line if required, and sew on buttons or other fastening.

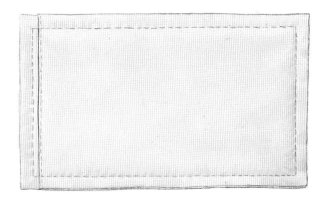

HEADBOARDS & VALANCES

A SLIP-ON HEADBOARD COVER

Simple headboards are normally made from wooden panels, with slotted struts to attach to the base of the bed. Simple, slip-on covers are easy to make and can be removed for washing when necessary. If you want to cover a plain wooden board, use quilted fabric to give a soft, comfortable finish. If the headboard is already padded, you can use plain chintz.

Measure the headboard and decide on suitable finished dimensions for the cover. If the headboard is an elaborate shape, cut a template to make cutting out easier. Cut out front and back panels – allow 12 mm ($\frac{1}{2}$ in) for seams, and up to 2.5 cm (1 in) for ease around the top and side edges, particularly when working with quilted fabric. Allow 2.5 cm (1 in) along the lower edge. If the existing headboard is more than 5 cm (2 in) thick, cut a gusset to fit all around the sides and top edge, allowing 12 mm ($\frac{1}{2}$ in) for seams and 2.5 cm (1 in) at each end. Cut piping (page 200) to fit the seams around the sides and top edges, and binding to fit across both lower edges and across the gusset if there is one. Cut four ties, 5 cm (2 in) wide and 15 cm (6 in) long.

1 Fit piping around the sides and top of the front panel, clipping into the binding to fit it around corners if necessary. Fit piping around the back panel as well if there is a gusset.

2 Join front and back panels, right sides facing and raw edges matching, sandwiching piping in between. If there is a gusset, fit the front and back panels to each long edge. Turn right side out and press.

3 To make up ties, fold and press under 12 mm ($\frac{1}{2}$ in) down each long edge, fold in half and press, then stitch down the centre of each strip.

4 Bind the lower edge of the cover, catching ties into the stitching about a third of the way along each long edge.

ADDING A RUCHED TRIM

Tightly fitted covers for padded headboards can be decorated in a number of ways: the instructions here are for a 15 cm (6 in) wide ruched border, made from a strip of gathered fabric, topstitched around the outer edge of the cover and edged with piping.

Cut out front and back panels for the headboard, including piping, binding, ties and gusset if required. For the ruching, cut three strips, 18 cm (7 in) wide, one for each side and one for the top, allowing at least one and a half times the length for fullness. You will also need extra piping to fit around the inner edge of the ruched strip.

1 Gather each long edge of the strips for the ruching and join the ends with one short side section at each end of the top section. Mitre the corners. Mark a chalk line, 16 cm ($6\frac{1}{2}$ in) inside the raw edge of the front cover panel. Position the piping around the marked line and tack in place. Tack the inner edge of the ruched strip in place, taking a 12 mm ($\frac{1}{2}$ in) seam allowance, with right side of ruching facing piping and right side of cover, and the outer edge of the strip towards the centre of the cover. Stitch in place.

2 Trim and layer seam allowances, and press ruching so that the free raw edge matches the raw edge of the cover. Position piping around the outer edge and tack in place. Pin and tack the back of the cover in place over the piping and finish as for a slip-on cover.

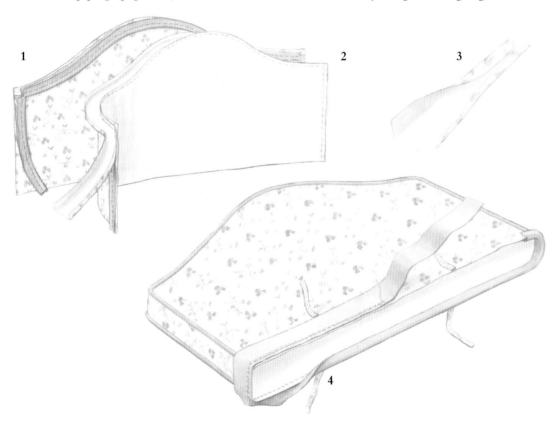

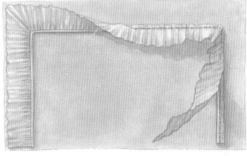

A FRILLED VALANCE

Valances give a tidy, co-ordinated finish to beds, covering the base and hiding unsightly legs. They can be made in a number of ways – with a frill or inverted pleats at the corner, for example. Valances with inverted pleats can be made in the same way as fitted bedspreads (page 157). If you use a lining fabric to cover the top of the mattress, cut a border of the main fabric about 15 cm (6 in) wide all round so the lining fabric won't be seen.

Measure the bed without the mattress in place: the valance fits over the base of the bed, beneath the mattress (page 206).

Cut a centre panel to fit the top of the bed, allowing a 12 mm ($\frac{1}{2}$ in) seam allowance around the sides and across the lower edge, and a 10 cm (4 in) turning and flap allowance across the top of the panel. Join widths of fabric together if necessary.

1 For the skirt, cut strips to fit around the sides and across the lower edge, allowing at least one and a half times fullness. Allow a 12 mm ($\frac{1}{2}$ in) seam allowance along the top edge, and 5 cm (2 in) for 2.5 cm (1 in) double hems along the lower edge. Join strips if necessary. Cut separate strips if the valance has to fit around a frame. Neaten the ends of the skirt, turning under a 12 mm ($\frac{1}{2}$ in) double hem at each end. Turn under a 2.5 cm (1 in) double hem along the lower edge.

2 Mark the centre of each skirt section with a pin at the top edge. Run lines of gathering stitches through the top of the skirt. Turn under 6 mm ($\frac{1}{4}$ in) double hems along the top 10 cm (4 in) of each side of the main panel. Clip into the seam allowance and stitch in place. Turn under a 2.5 cm (1 in) double hem across the top of the panel.

3 Mark the centre of each side and the centre of the lower edge of the top panel with pins. Position gathered skirt section(s) around the side of the top panel, aligning pins. Tack and stitch in place. Neaten raw edges together and press towards the skirt.

4 Some beds are made with wooden frames, such as four posters or beds with wooden headboards and footboards. In this case, make up separate skirt sections for the sides and foot of the bed so that you can fit the valance around the legs at the foot of the bed.

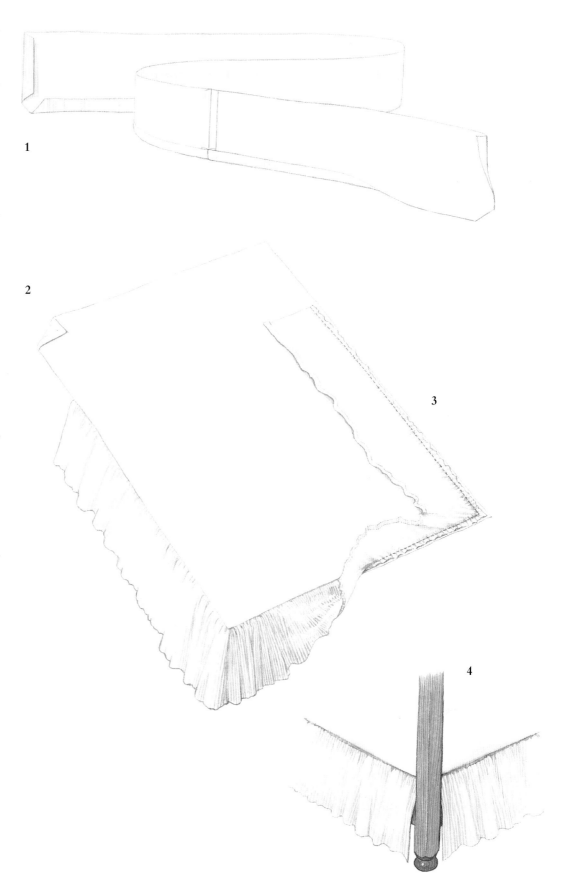

1

2

3

4

Bed Drapes

Medieval and Tudor four poster beds took bedroom insulation seriously; detachable bed hangings and curtains were mostly of wool and hung on iron or horn rings. Later crewelwork bed curtains became fashionable; the handsome examples by Abigail Pett, depicting mythical beasts, formalized fruit and flowers, can still be seen in the Victoria and Albert Museum, London. The first imported Indian cotton chintzes were immediately popular as bed drapes although the wealthy still preferred silk damask and brocade. Styles were elaborate with heavy gold fringes, tassels and tie-backs.

The Regency and Empire periods favoured reclining daybeds with simpler fixed 'dress' drapes rather than curtains that closed. These 'dress' drapes of light voile, spotted muslin and silk were often swept over a single knob or fitted to a corona and they can easily be re-created today.

Victorians returned to brass four posters with heavy velvet curtains but around the 1860s decided that it was unhealthy to have curtains enclosing the whole bed. As a result, half-testers consisting of two upright poles and fixed 'dress' drapes became popular.

The Arts and Crafts movement headed by William Morris saw a revival in heavy carved four posters but cotton and linen bed drapes were light and frivolous by comparison. Morris would sometimes combine as many as four specially co-ordinated fabrics for the pelmet (valance), curtain, curtain borders and tie-backs.

By the twentieth century smaller, scaled-down four posters were the hallmark of the country-style bedroom. Chintz drapes with deep pelmets (valances), frills and scalloped edges were the order of the day. A great variety of tie-back styles including bows were also much in evidence.

LEFT *Tropical mosquito nets are the inspiration for these bed drapes, which are looped over the bed frame and fastened with Velcro to keep the folds in place. This idea works best with modern four poster beds and needs light, see-through fabrics such as muslin, voile, lace and fine silk.*

ABOVE LEFT *A luxurious tented canopy can be achieved relatively quickly and easily with a decorator's staple gun. Pick fine fabrics that can be easily pleated. Tacks can be covered over with rosettes, braid and ribbon. These lined drapes have been hitched up to resemble leg-of-mutton sleeves.*

ABOVE *Converting a simple timber bed frame to a four poster is a relatively simple carpentry job. Clever fabric wrapping and the use of decorative braids, ribbons and artificial flowers can conceal rudimentary deal posts and give a four poster a festive air.*

LEFT *A deep frilled and bound pelmet (valance) with a curtain at the bed head is all that is needed to 'dress up' this four poster. The pretty painted posts here have been left exposed.*

Drapes for today

In most rooms bed hangings that match or co-ordinate with the window curtains create a harmonious effect. If your window curtains use several fabrics and are very elaborate, you can simplify the whole effect and alter the balance of pattern by reversing the fabric order: the plainer lining fabric of the window curtains can be used for the main part of the bed drapes. The window curtain fabric can then be used for small, co-ordinating touches such as binding, frills or tie-backs on the bed hangings.

If your decorative scheme follows a particular period or imitates the style of a certain country, choose an appropriate finish for the drapes. For example, you can imitate draped, swagged eighteenth-century styles with a pole extending out from a wall above the bed, a long panel of fabric can then be draped over and clipped either side of the bed; this style looks especially good with an Empire-style single bed. For a canopy reminiscent of the tropics, drape fine muslin or voile from a large hook fixed above the bed: a hoop can then be added to stretch the fabric away from the centre of the bed. For American country drapes, choose simple prints to make full gathered curtains and tie these to the bed frame with ribbon or fabric ties.

RIGHT *Closely co-ordinating fabrics for upholstery, cushions, blinds, bed drapes and linen create a restful scheme in this bedroom. The floral prints are counter-balanced by simple treatments – Roman blinds, bordered pillows and ungathered curtains with fabric ties to fit them to the simple four poster bed. Notice how the lining of the four curtains has a white background and is also used for the top pillow and sheet.*

ABOVE *A neo-classical style is conjured up with an elaborately veneered bed and furniture, a simple colour scheme and soft drapes. Four panels of lace have been gathered up so that the cords in the heading tape can be tied to a hook fitted to the ceiling. A cone of fabric fits over the top. The window dressing continues the lace theme.*

RIGHT *Bed drapes gathered into a corona lend a grand, Empire-style air to a bedroom. Smaller bedrooms with low ceilings, however, may find that this attractive, semi-circular corona takes up less space than circular ceiling-fixed versions. The drapes here would also look good in a creamy spotted muslin or a lace with matching cream bedlinen.*

Fitting Bed Drapes

There are many ways to drape a bed but even before you decide on the style, you need to plan how to fix the drapes. If you have a four poster bed, you can choose either dress drapes which hang down each post, drapes which close like curtains to enclose the bed, a pelmet (valance) which goes around three sides at the top of the posts, or a canopy; or you can combine all three. If the canopy has a long frill, this replaces the separate pelmet (valance). If your bed has no posts, you can hang poles from the ceiling joists or hang a curtain track directly on to the ceiling and use this to surround the bed with fabric.

Draping a Four Poster

Even if you aren't planning to draw the curtains around the four poster, it is a good idea to fit the drapes and pelmet (valance) to curtain wire for easy removal for cleaning. If the bed isn't valuable, you can fit screw eyes directly into the wooden bars and the drapes can be hung from these using curtain heading tape and hooks, or curtain wire.

1 Decide where to hang the drapes and fit curtain wires (on screw eyes): fit one for the back curtain across the inside of the bar at the head of the bed, and short lengths for the side curtains extending up to 50 cm (20 in) from the head and the base of the bed and across the foot on the underside of the frame. For full curtains, fit lengths along each side of the bed, and across the foot, along the underside of each bar.

2 Make the drapes as for lined curtains (page 101), using one width of fabric – you won't need much fullness (unless you plan to draw the drapes). The lining and the main fabric should be the same width so that the drapes look as good from the inside as the outside. If you decide to put frills down both sides, think of the drape as a huge pillowcase with frills down two sides.

Use fabric rather than a purpose-made lining for both the outside and the inside of the curtains, either matching or contrasting. Fin-

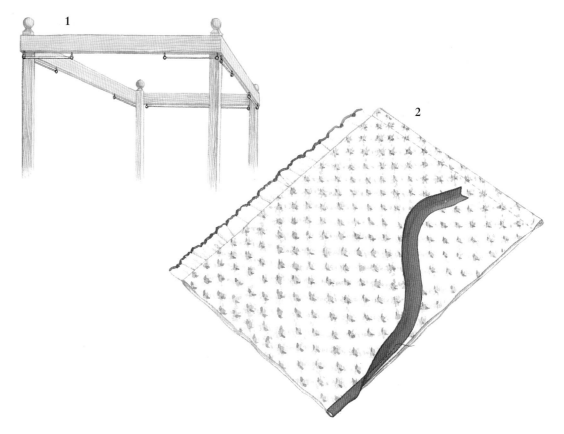

ish the side edge with a frill or binding and stitch a casing across the top of the curtain to slot on to the curtain wire (page 114). Or tack and sew curtain heading tape along the inside top edge of the drape, draw up the tapes and attach curtain hooks which hook on to curtain rings or screw eyes fixed to the frame. Hang all the curtains by whichever method you have chosen and turn up the hems, stitching by hand for a neat finish.

Making a Pelmet (Valance)

Measure the total length for the pelmet (valance) down the sides and across the foot of the bed. Decide on a suitable finished depth – say 30 cm (12 in). Allow at least one and a half times the total length for fullness, adding a 12 mm ($\frac{1}{2}$ in) seam allowance along the top edge. Cut out the pelmet (valance) in both the main fabric and the chosen lining. Lay the lining strip on top of the outer strip, right sides facing, and stitch a seam at each end. Insert a

frill, or turn right sides out and finish the lower edge by binding the raw edges together.

A simple method of fixing a pelmet (valance) is to make it as for a window pelmet (valance) – see page 104 – using curtain tape with hooks to attach it to the bed frame. You can make up three separate curtains – two for the sides and one for the foot of the bed.

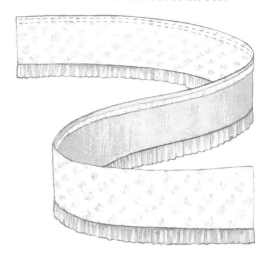

Making a Canopy

A canopy with a frill is made in much the same way as a valance that sits on the mattress (page 165) except that it is hung across the four poster. Choose two layers of a fabric such as voile, or similar light-diffusing fabric, for the canopy, with 12 mm (½ in) seam allowance all round. No frill is needed across the head of the bed.

Measure up and make three pelmets (valances) as before, but omit the casing allowance and gather the unfinished edge of each pelmet (valance). Fit them around one panel of the canopy with the right side of the valance facing the right side of the canopy. Distribute the fullness evenly, increasing fullness slightly at the corners. Tack in place.

Lay the second panel of canopy fabric on top of the frilled panel and stitch together all around the edges. Continue the stitching around the top of the canopy, leaving a 50 cm (20 in) opening at the centre of the head of the bed. Trim seam allowances and turn right side out, then press. Topstitch through the voile and seam allowances, continuing topstitching across the opening at the top.

If the four poster frame has finials at the top of the uprights, cut a hole in each corner of the voile canopy large enough to fit over the finials and neaten the edges by hand or with binding or piping.

Empire-style Canopy

These are draped over a pole which is hung from the ceiling at a right angle to the head of the bed.

1 Measure the distance from the floor on one side of the bed over the pole to the floor on the opposite side of the bed. Add a total of 30 cm (12 in) for ease and hem allowance. Cut two lengths of fabric, one top fabric and one lining, and position them on top of each other, wrong sides together. Tack them together down each long edge.

2 Mark the centre of the panel at the position where the pole is, and stitch a casing through both layers of fabric. Bind the long raw edges together on either side of the opening. Add extra binding along each edge of the opening.

3 Fit the drape on to the pole and mark the hemline. Turn in the hem allowance at the ends of the panel and slipstitch together by hand.

Make tie-backs (page 102) to hold the canopy back against the wall on either side of the head of the bed.

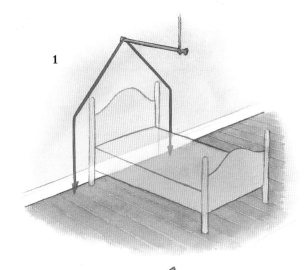

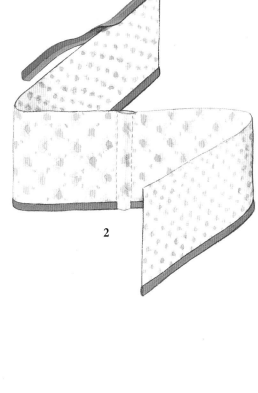

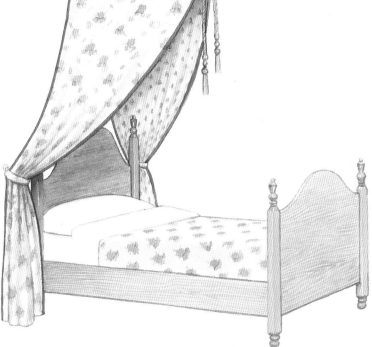

NURSERY BEDDING & ACCESSORIES

In a nursery, some accessories, though functional, can be decorative too and as they are on a small scale, you can try out techniques such as appliqué or patchwork (page 203) for the first time.

Padded bumpers around the head of a cot keep out draughts and prevent babies from knocking their heads on the bars. A fabric storage pocket can hang from the end of the cot or changing table and hold all the paraphernalia for nappy changing.

Nurseries should be fresh and clean, so choose fabrics carefully, making sure they are washable.

QUILTED & FRILLED MOSES BASKET

1 Cut a paper template to fit the base of the basket, and another to fit the sides, making darts or tucks where necessary.

Cut two base panels in fabric, allowing 12 mm ($\frac{1}{2}$ in) seams all round. Cut a piece of wadding the same size as the template. Sandwich the layers together and tack around the edges and across the centre. Quilt by machine (page 202), working around or across the panel. The rows of stitching need not be closely spaced.

2 Using the template as a pattern, make up side panels twice in fabric with a 12 mm ($\frac{1}{2}$ in) seam allowance along the lower edge and 20 cm (8 in) top turning. Make up the same shape in wadding, with no seam allowance. Fit the wadding between the fabric side panels and tack along upper and lower edges. Quilt the sides of the lining: this is particularly effective if you make vertical rows of stitching, spaced 5–10 cm (2–4 in) apart, using a narrow zig-zag stitch. Make a line of stitching around the top of the side panels, level with the top of the wadding.

Press under a 12 mm ($\frac{1}{2}$ in) turning around both layers of fabric. Stitch together close to the edge, then again 2 cm ($\frac{3}{4}$ in) from the first line of stitching to make a casing. Add a topstitched frill beside the casing.

3 Fit the base to the side panels. Insert elastic into the casing to hold the lining in place.

If the basket has handles, mark and cut a slot in both layers of fabric for the handles to slip through. Make two diagonal snips at each end of the slash, and press under a narrow turning all around the opening, or bind with a bias strip of contrasting fabric (page 200). Slipstitch folded edges together.

A FITTED COT SHEET

Not all cots are standard sizes, so you may find it helpful to make your own fitted sheets for the nursery. If you use stretch towelling, you can be sure of a tight fit.

1 Measure up the cot mattress (page 206). Cut out a single panel of stretch towelling, allowing the depth of the mattress all around, plus an extra 15 cm (6 in) to wrap under the mattress and for turning. With the right side of the fabric facing the mattress, pin the seam lines at each corner. Tack the seams, then remove the cover from the mattress and stitch the seams. Trim the fabric from the seam allowance and neaten the raw edges together.

2 Turn under a 12 mm ($\frac{1}{2}$ in) double hem along all the raw edges. Stitch the turnings in place, beginning and ending stitching 8 cm (3 in) from each corner seam. To make elasticated corners, take four pieces of 6 mm ($\frac{1}{4}$ in) wide elastic, each 10 cm (4 in) long. Pin the elastic over the turnings at each corner of the sheet, and stitch in place with a zig-zag stitch, stretching the elastic as you stitch.

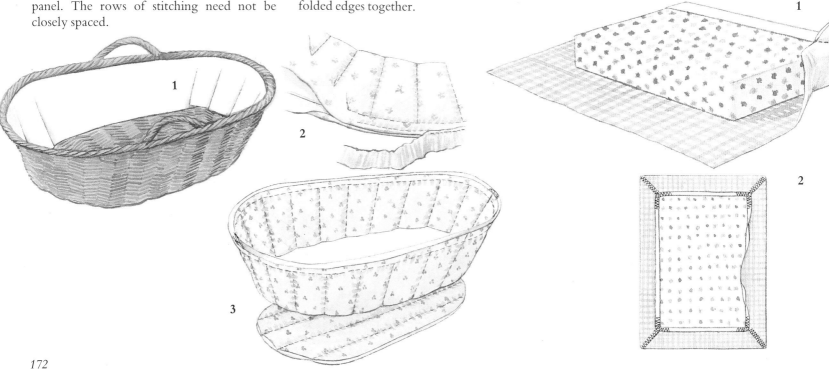

A COT BUMPER

Use washable fabrics and quilt the bumpers with heavyweight polyester wadding. The instructions here are for a bound edge – but bumpers can equally well be finished with a frilled or piped edge.

Measure across the inside of the top and half way down the sides of the cot. Decide where the ties should be positioned – the top edge of the bumper should be tied to corner posts and to bars half way down the side of the cot. If the cot has a solid headboard, make long ties which can fasten around the back of the headboard.

Cut main panels of fabric and a layer of wadding to the finished measurements. Join widths of fabric with flat seams and the wadding with a lapped seam if necessary. Cut a 15 cm (6 in) wide strip to bind the edges of the bumper; these strips need not be cut on the bias since they do not have to be eased around curves. Cut four ties, 20 cm (8 in) long and the 5 cm (2 in) wide.

1 Sandwich the wadding between the two panels of fabric, right sides outwards; pin, then tack together all around the edges. Tack at intervals to hold the layers in place while you stitch the quilting – tack along the length of the bumper for vertical stitching, or up and down for horizontal quilting (page 202).

2 Turn under 2.5 cm (1 in) down each long edge of the binding. Position on the inner side of the quilted panel, with the raw edge of the binding 2.5 cm (1 in) from the edge of the panel, right sides together. Stitch along the fold line, making tucks to turn the corners. Turn the binding over to the outside of the quilted panel and slipstitch in place by hand or machine just inside the previous line of stitching.

3 Make up ties by turning in 12 mm ($\frac{1}{2}$ in) down each long edge and then folding in half. Press and stitch, turning in the ends. Stitch the centre of each tie to the appropriate point on the outside of the binding by hand. Do not make the ties too long; if they were to come untied, they could become entwined around a baby's neck.

POCKET STORAGE

A simple fabric pocket storage system, hung on the back of the door or at the foot of the cot, can be used to store baby-changing equipment or small items of clothing.

Decide on a suitable overall size for the storage system: about 60 cm (24 in) wide by 100 cm (40 in) deep is suitable for most needs. Plan the size and number of pockets: the instructions here are for three rows of pockets across the width of the panel, 30 cm (12 in)

deep. Use a single thickness of chintz, or a double thickness of lighter fabric. Cut a panel of fabric for the back panel the size of the finished overall piece. Cut three strips for pockets making the length of each strip the same as the width of the panel, and adding 2.5 cm (1 in) across the top for a double hem, and 12 mm ($\frac{1}{2}$ in) turning across the bottom. Cut sufficient binding or bias cut fabric to bind the outer edge of the back panel, and make two loops from fabric or binding to hang the storage pockets from the corner posts of the cot or from two hooks on the back of the door.

Turn under a double 12 mm ($\frac{1}{2}$ in) hem across the top of each pocket strip and stitch. Turn under and press a 12 mm ($\frac{1}{2}$ in) seam allowance across the lower edge. Position the three strips across the front of the back panel, spacing them evenly apart. Tack in place down the sides and across the lower edge. Topstitch in place. Mark the width of each pocket across the strips, and tack down the marked lines. Topstitch in place, reinforcing the end of the stitching at the top of each pocket by sewing a few stitches in reverse.

Position binding around the outer edge of the front panel, making a pleat at each corner to form a neat mitre. Position the ends of the strip for the corner loops between the binding and fabric at each top corner. Stitch in place, enclosing the sides of the pockets and stitching across the end of the loops. Turn binding over to the back of the panel and stitch the folded edge in place by hand or machine.

For deeper pockets, allow an extra 2.5 cm (1 in) for each pocket along the length of the strip. Turn and stitch the top hem and press the seam allowance under along the lower edge. Before stitching the strip in position, mark the stitching lines for each pocket and make a 6 mm ($\frac{1}{4}$ in) deep tuck on either side of each line. Make similar tucks 2 cm ($\frac{3}{4}$ in) from each end of the pocket strip.

Tack the tucks in place. Position the strips across the back panel and stitch in place as before, so that the ends of the tucks are held in by the base stitching. Remove tacking and bind the edge (page 200).

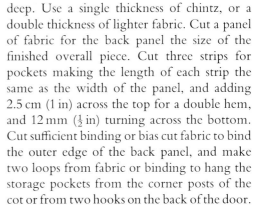

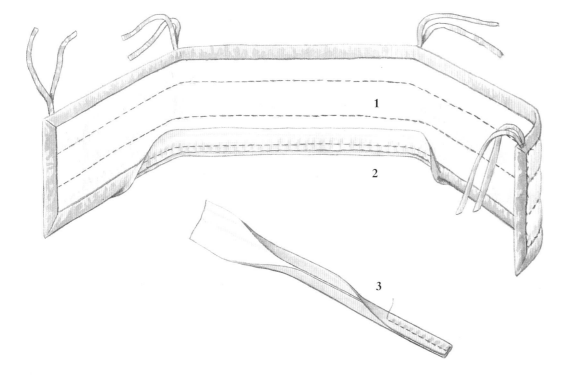

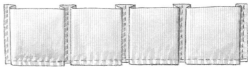

Accessories

CO-ORDINATION & GROUPING

One of the easiest ways to give cohesion to a group of accessories and ornaments is to pick a theme. It may be a colour, a subject, or a similar shape, although the things you collect need not necessarily be in the same style or period. Start with a core of items with some connection and keep your choice flexible. A thoughtful, eclectic mixture can reflect truly individual taste; in a collection of jugs, for instance, a few genuine, antique examples will blend in beautifully with new, reproduction jugs of any period.

Colour grouping

Grouping ornaments and accessories by their colour is a powerful way to highlight a colour scheme. You could choose cushions, lampshades and picture frames in antique, muted soft colours that pick up one of the tones in a rug, carpet or wallpaper. Select your colours carefully: coral ceramic vases and lampbases contrast well in a smoke-blue living room scheme. In a predominately apricot bedroom, accents of soft aquamarine could be introduced – in delicately embroidered cushions and decorative glass.

Collecting ornaments in the same colours, such as blue and white jars, bowls and plates, and displaying them against a matching backdrop brings a welcome freshness. Conversely, a collection of brilliant saffron yellow plates on a dresser can make a predominately cool blue and white kitchen scheme feel sunny and Mediterranean. Large blue and white ginger jars were a favourite early-Georgian accessory offering a welcome focal point and light relief to many heavily carved mantelpieces. A pair, or group, of blue and white ginger jars can still do the same for traditional mantelpieces, or use them to bring a classical touch to a modern setting.

Covering old blanket chests and screens, small card and wooden boxes and metal wastepaper bins in fabrics that either co-ordinate or blend in with the rest of the furnishings helps to link some of the more disparate elements.

Extra touches

Collections and accessories can be witty and tongue-in-cheek. An assortment of necklaces can enhance the necks of plain glass and pottery vases. A *trompe l'oeil* painted cat on a fire screen with a collection of needlepoint cat cushions makes an amusing point. If you haven't much wallspace on which to hang all your objects, consider displaying them on a freestanding fabric-covered screen – the panels are perfect for pinning up collections of old Valentine cards and dolls' hats. Antique toy and games collections can be carefully displayed in special perspex cases to great effect. Medals, coins, stamps, old pieces of lace and fans can be framed in deep box frames.

BELOW *Bring the garden into your home with clever plant arrangements to give the feeling of a conservatory. Instead of pictures, a group of florist's plaited wreaths and garlands emphasize the green feeling and create a focal point.*

LEFT *Being bold and making a strong visual statement works. Massing this collection of Chinese ginger jars on a sideboard creates a much more dramatic effect than placing them singly about the room.*

BELOW LEFT *A group of idiosyncratic objects create a dramatic still life, brought together with a flourish by the curves of a marble mantelpiece.*

BELOW *Dressing-table accessories that are in constant use need to be carefully ordered to achieve maximum effect. Here, a terracotta bust makes an amusing, impromptu hatstand and the jaunty Staffordshire figure offsets the symmetrical dried flower arrangements.*

ABOVE *Stage manage your collection and think in blocks of colour. Any object for displaying should make a strong visual statement. Here, white flower arrangements link a row of* cool pastel ceramics. The painting above contains similar honey tones to the wooden building blocks and painted wooden cow. Texture and shape also play their part.

ABOVE *Circular tables covered with a floor-length cloth offer endless display opportunities. For extra protection and added sparkle the top can be covered with a piece of plate glass cut to size.*

LEFT *A leafy orchid and a trio of botanical prints placed on this bedside table create an interesting 'background screen' of colour and pattern, giving cohesion and definition to a collection of objets trouvées.*

ABOVE & RIGHT *Open shelves are a perfect framework for displaying a collection. Decoy ducks are at home alongside ethnic carvings and pictures; stone carvings depicting classical motifs and geological specimens are cleverly divided and set off by neat white blocks of arranged books and catalogues.*

LEFT *The height of this dried flower arrangement creates a dramatic foil for a pair of china Staffordshire dogs which add a touch of whimsy to this collection. Family pictures are more at home on a table top than hanging on a wall.*

ABOVE *These flowers pay tribute to the colours in the curtain fabric and make a simple table-top arrangement spring to life. A generous bowl of fragrant pot-pourri is an essential ingredient of country-house style.*

THROUGHOUT THE *HOME*

Collections of items built around a relevant personal theme can add great style to every room in a house. Globetrotters are particularly lucky with *objets trouvées*: plates and glasses in different styles from different countries make spectacular shelf displays. Cushions and wallhangings in ethnic fabrics can highlight a room scheme and bring back memories. Old leather luggage sporting original labels makes a wonderful display in a redundant fireplace.

Some rooms such as the bathroom suggest obvious accessory themes: a nautical air with groups of polished pebbles, tropical sea shells, dried urchins and starfish arranged on a large dish and teamed with sailing prints and pictures. A glass jar filled with seashell guest soaps is another marine touch.

In a bedroom with flowery fabrics or wallpaper, follow the floral idea through with generous arrangements of fresh, dried or silk flowers, baskets and bowls of pot pourri and heaps of cushions embroidered with flowers.

In living rooms create an eastern flavour with tabletop collections of jewel-coloured Indian papier mâché boxes and intricately carved ivory and jade oriental perfume bottles for light relief. A group of palms in ceramic Chinese cachepots also emphasizes the eastern feeling.

In a dining room or large family kitchen, fruit or vegetables may hold the key – a table centrepiece of ceramic fruit in a ceramic bowl, cabbage plates on the walls and reproductions of old Dutch paintings burgeoning with glossy apples and half peeled lemons. Kitchens also lend themselves to 'theme' displays of antique cookware: old copper pans and jelly moulds can blend in quite happily with new stainless steel pans. Or hang up your own kitchen utensils as a *batterie de cuisine* together with bunches of fragrant herbs.

RIGHT *Oil paintings do not necessarily have to be seen in stately drawing rooms and art galleries. They can look just as good in less formal settings. This country kitchen with its pleasant blend of old and new furnishings provides the perfect homely ambience for an eighteenth-century family portrait.*

LEFT *A traditional blanket box, padded and upholstered in a pretty fabric and sited at the foot of the bed, offers practical storage for extra bed linen and towels as well as comfortable bedroom seating.*

RIGHT *Toy chests, like this one upholstered in a pretty fabric, are perfect storage containers for dolls and teddy bears.*

Studies, libraries and hobby rooms are perfect places for displaying framed photographs, botanical prints and cartoons. Display the paraphernalia that goes, say, with being a musician: old music hall scores and battered brasss percussion instruments can take pride of place; metronomes have unusual shapes, often made in fine woods, and they can provide a strikingly unusual display.

Hallways are particularly good places to display a 'theme' collection. A set of old school boaters hung on a wall together with school photographs and other educational memorabilia can reflect your family's past.

Accessorizing children's rooms calls for wit and originality. A beautiful toy – a wooden rocking horse, for example – is a delightful focal point and could spark off the inspiration for the rest of the décor: rocking horse motifs could be appliquéd on to cushions and echoed in a frieze. Similarly, a beautiful doll's house with some embroidered sampler cushions and a framed sampler picture is a pretty theme for a young girl's bedroom.

Accessories in bedrooms can be functional too. Blanket boxes, linen chests or presses and baskets provide storage and look pretty.

LEFT *The colours in the wallpaper have been picked out in a picture frame and mount to great effect and provide a handsome backdrop for dressing-table accessories and objets trouvées of wood and tortoiseshell.*

RIGHT *Plain white painted shelves provide a disciplined grid for displaying all kinds of collections. In the dining room, ordinary everyday cookware with its classic, clean lines is left out on show.*

LEFT *Classical shapes in a monochrome scheme of pristine white, matt black and chrome are appropriate in a modern streamlined bathroom.*

ABOVE *Fabric screens provide wonderful decorative camouflage and usefully divide one area and activity from another. This screen is made up of fabric gathered on to poles at the top and bottom of the panels.*

BELOW *Large fabric-covered blanket boxes and chests can lead a useful double life by providing extra living-room seating as well as storage for books, magazines, hobbies and games.*

RIGHT *In this Edwardian-style bathroom the accessories have been carefully matched to the period. The light fittings, towel rail and mirror surround are matched by an unusual antique fabric-covered screen which discreetly separates the bidet and w.c. from the washing areas.*

LEFT *Mixing informal and formal objects creates a pleasing decorative style. Blue and white china and a wicker log basket blend happily with a walnut Queen Anne-style side table and antique silver.*

Boxes & Screens

Old cigar or crystallized fruit boxes – even strong card boxes – can be softly padded and covered with fabric. Line them with felt or wallpaper, and use them on dressing tables or desks. Hat boxes provide decorative storage containers; blanket boxes, decorated with a paint finish or padded and covered with fabric, perhaps with a buttoned top, can co-ordinate with other furnishings and add to the storage capacity, provide extra seating or a resting place for a tray.

Screens are decorative, movable objects that can delineate areas in a large multi-purpose room, or simply provide an elegant accessory. If you do not have a frame, you can make a simple one from three rectangular frames of softwood, covered with panels of hardboard, and hinged together so they can be folded into a concertina.

Covering a Box

1 Cut a piece of wadding to fit the top of the box. Stick it in place with fabric glue at each corner. Measure the top of the box and to each dimension add twice the depth of the sides of the lid, plus a total of 2.5 cm (1 in) for turning. Cut a piece of fabric to these measurements.

Position the lid upside down centrally on the wrong side of the fabric. Mark the position of the box. Mark a point measuring 6 mm ($\frac{1}{4}$ in) diagonally outwards from each corner. Cut out a square of fabric at each corner, following the position of the marked point. Snip to the corner of the lid. Press under the narrow turning. Position the lid on the fabric again and turn up the sides. Glue in place, then turn the sides to the inside of the box and glue.

2 Cut a piece of felt or wallpaper to the internal dimensions of the lid plus the depth of the sides all round. Mark the internal dimensions on the wrong side of the fabric or paper. Cut a square out of each corner, in line with the marked lines. Fit the lining into the lid and glue in place. Repeat this method to cover the base of the box, omitting the wadding.

If the lid fits too snugly to turn the edge of the fabric over the inside of the box, trim it to fit neatly around the outside and finish by covering the raw edge with ribbon or braid, glued in place.

If you are working on a hinged, flat-topped box, remove the hinges and cover each part of the box separately. Attach a piece of the ribbon or a fabric loop to the front of the lid to make a handle to open the box.

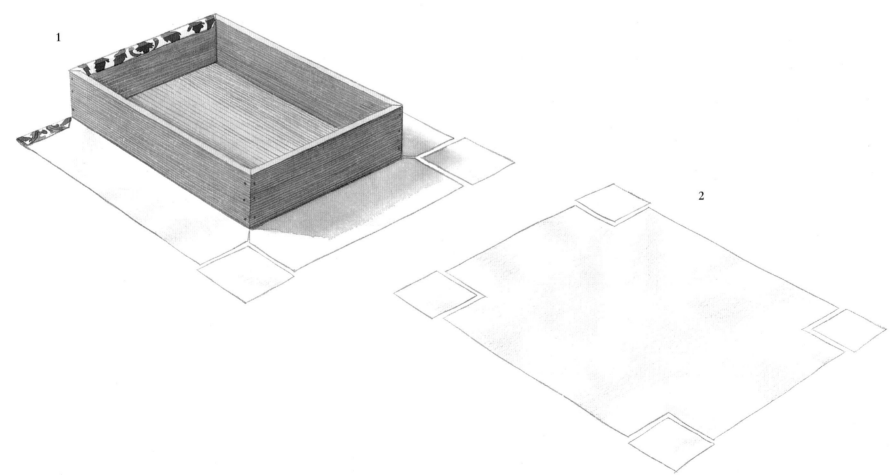

COVERING A SCREEN

Take the hinges off the screen and cover each panel separately. Measure each frame of the screen. If it has a shaped top, cut a paper template.

To save sewing a cover, cut each fabric panel slightly larger than the frame and wrap each panel over the edge, stapling in place. Cover the raw edges and staples with decorative braid, held with decorative brass upholstery tacks, small-headed tacks or glue.

1 To sew a screen cover, with a gusset, measure the depth of the screen and make up a strip of fabric to fit all around the sides and top of the frame, allowing 12 mm ($\frac{1}{2}$ in) along the sides, and 5 cm (2 in) at each end.

Cut a panel of fabric for each side of the frame, allowing 12 mm ($\frac{1}{2}$ in) turnings all round and 5 cm (2 in) along the lower edge. Pin the gusset fabric in place up the sides and across the top of the fabric panels. Tack in place. Clip into the seam allowance at the corners, then stitch the gusset. Press the seam allowances towards the gusset. Then turn right side out.

2 Slip the cover over the frame of the screen and wrap the ends of the gusset inwards. The cover should be stretched tightly over the screen; check for any puckering. Turn under a narrow turning along the lower edge, wrap it over the other raw edge and hold in place with tacks or staples. Repeat for the remaining panels. Replace the hinges.

1

2

LAMPSHADES

Many modern lampfittings look good in traditional settings: ceramic or wooden candlestick bases with card or fabric shades are readily available in an increasing range of colours and styles. Pick a lampshade and base that suit the style and scale of the room: ceramic lamp bases in traditional ginger jar shapes now come in a huge range of richly coloured glazes to blend or match almost any paint colour and fabric. Team bases like these with plain cream or white fabric, or card coolie shades for country house and traditional town house living rooms; pleated fine cottons and silk drum shades also look elegant here. Smaller versions of coolie or drum shades in cottagey flower prints teamed with simple wooden or round ceramic bases lend a cosy touch to informal sitting rooms and bedrooms. Shiny black coolie card shades teamed with clean cylindrical or spherical bases in matching black, cream or terracotta look good in modern living rooms; Chinese pierced ceramic bases with special

silk shades complement eastern-looking room schemes perfectly.

Paper shades

Pleated paper shades are easy to make and, depending on the paper, look right in almost any scheme. Plain white or coloured card, marbled papers, scraps of wallpaper and decorative wrapping papers backed on to white card can be threaded through with fine cord or narrow ribbon to great effect. Other card lampshades you can make yourself are simple drum or coolie shapes taped over a wire frame.

A pretty nineteenth-century idea due for a revival is to cut out a simple floral motif in white paper to make a small shade for a wall fitting or bedside lamp. A hand-painted or stencilled border pattern, inspired perhaps by a motif from a furnishing fabric or wallpaper in the room and applied to the edge of a ready-made plain coolie shade adds a personal touch.

BELOW LEFT *Plain card shades in 'coolie' styles are readily available in a huge number of colours and sizes and blend in happily with most décors. A small hand-stencilled pattern on the edges can give them an individual look.*

BELOW *Candlestick-style bases vary enormously from turned wood and delicately sponged columns to brilliant rose embellished lacquerwork. Here, carved wooden barley twist stems show off cream pleated shades to perfection and add a hint of frivolity to dark, richly coloured schemes.*

Something old, something new

It is also worth hunting around junkshops for
small marbled, opaque and painted glass
lampshades which look wonderfully atmospheric
in small bedrooms. Reproduction glass
lampshades and bases are also a good investment –
rustic candleholders, Victorian and Art Nouveau
oil lamps with glass shades wired for electricity
and grand gilt Corinthian column lampbases with
patterned glass and paper drum shades. Painted
metal and card lampshades in dark green, claret
red and black look good on traditionally styled
wall light and chandelier fittings; these are
eminently suitable for modern studies, libraries
and dining rooms that are styled with a touch of
tradition.

LEFT *Pleated paper shades
blend happily with
traditional and modern
decorative schemes. This
lampshade shape also suits
a variety of different bases,
from the tall ceramic ginger
jar base shown here to
squat spherical and tall
candlestick styles.*

ABOVE *The pleated and
bound fabric shade is a
traditional look for
bedrooms and living rooms.
Fine chiffon, silk or cotton
in plain white, cream or
pastel colours are the
fabrics that work best with
this style.*

RIGHT *Wall-fixed lamp
brackets such as these can
take a number of different
shade styles but small card
or metal coolie shades give
fittings a modern look that
is still in keeping with
more traditionally styled
dining rooms, studies and
hallway schemes.*

Making Lampshades

These styles are for simple frames: you can buy them ready to cover, or strip the covers off old shades that are the right shape but the wrong colour for the base and the room scheme. For the techniques shown here, you will need conical or coolie shapes, with a suitable fitting to hold the shade on the lamp. If you are buying a frame, it is a good idea to choose plastic-coated wire, which will not rust.

A Pleated Paper Lampshade

A simple shade should be made from stiff card. You can buy plain colours from art shops, but if you want to use a pattern (wrapping paper or wallpaper, for example) to blend with other furnishings, use lightweight white card and paste the patterned paper to it.

1 Measure the circumference of the lower ring and multiply by 1½–2, depending on the fullness required. Measure a vertical strut, and add 2.5 cm (1 in) for a slight overhang at the top and bottom of the shade. Cut a piece of stiffened patterned paper to these dimensions.

2 Decide on a suitable size for the pleats: 12 mm (½ in) will suit most frames, but you may want to make the pleats smaller for very small shades. Mark the pleat fold lines vertically down the card lightly in pencil, working across the width of the panel. Use the back of the blade of a pair of scissors to score the card: score every other fold line on the right side of the shade, then turn over and score the alternate lines on the back of the card.

Fold the card concertina-wise, following the scored lines: this is easier if you use a metal rule as a guide, folding the card crisply over the ruler.

3 Trim the end folds (or waste) so that you can lap one end neatly over the other, and glue in place.

4 Use a fine punch to make holes in the pleats, 12 mm (½ in) from the upper edge of the card, centring the holes between the fold lines. Thread cord or ribbon through the holes. Fit the shade over the frame and draw up the cord. Tie the ends in a decorative bow, or fasten ends together inconspicuously inside the shade.

5 To hold the shade to the frame, use a strong thread to stitch over the cord and the frame between each pleat. You can finish the lower edge in the same way for a firmly fitted shade.

Binding the Frame

By binding the frame with tape, a fabric cover can be stitched to the lampshade frame. Use a narrow, firmly woven tape in unbleached cotton. If you follow the order shown, you will only have to secure one end of the tape with stitching.

When the whole frame is bound, tuck one end of the tape under the last loop, turn under and stitch it in place to give a firm finish.

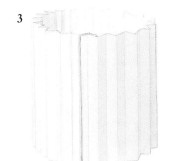

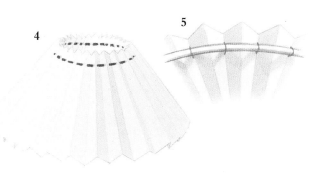

STIFFENED FABRIC SHADE

For a crisp effect, stiffen the fabric with heavy iron-on woven interfacing (buckram). Binding in a contrasting colour gives a neat finish.

1 Use the frame to draw a paper pattern for the shade; mark a straight line the same length as a strut and position the strut along it. Then roll the frame over the paper, marking the position of each ring as you go with a series of dots. Join the dots to make smooth curves. Allow a 2 mm ($\frac{1}{2}$ in) overlap at the end.

Cut the pattern out and check that it fits before cutting out the shade in two pieces, allowing a single overlap on each piece.

Cut iron-on interfacing to the size of the paper pattern and the fabric with a 6 mm ($\frac{1}{4}$ in) turning all round. Cut bias strips 2 cm ($\frac{3}{4}$ in) wide, plus 6 mm ($\frac{1}{4}$ in) turning down each edge, and long enough to go around each ring plus a turning at each end. Press turnings under.

2 Fuse the fabric to the interfacing, leaving the turnings free. Position the binding around the top and bottom of the panel so that the raw edge of the binding is 12 mm ($\frac{1}{2}$ in) from the edge of the panel and stitch in place on the fold line of the binding.

Wrap the turning of fabric over the stiffening and fit the shade over the frame. Glue the overlap in place. Slipstitch the fold of the fabric to the bound frame all around.

3 Fold under the opposite edge of the binding and turn under the ends so that they meet neatly. Wrap the binding over the frame and slipstitch or glue in place.

A PLEATED FABRIC SHADE

Measure the circumference of the bottom ring on the shade and multiply by $1\frac{1}{2}$ to give a slight fullness. Measure the height of the frame along one of the struts. Cut a rectangle of fabric to these measurements, adding 2 cm ($\frac{3}{4}$ in) turnings all around. Cut strips of binding fabric as for the stiffened shade.

1 Join the ends of the fabric with a 2 cm ($\frac{3}{4}$ in) seam; trim and neaten the seam allowances and press open. Working from the wrong side of the fabric, make a line of gathering stitches all around the top and lower edge of the fabric, picking up only a couple of threads of fabric and spacing the stitches

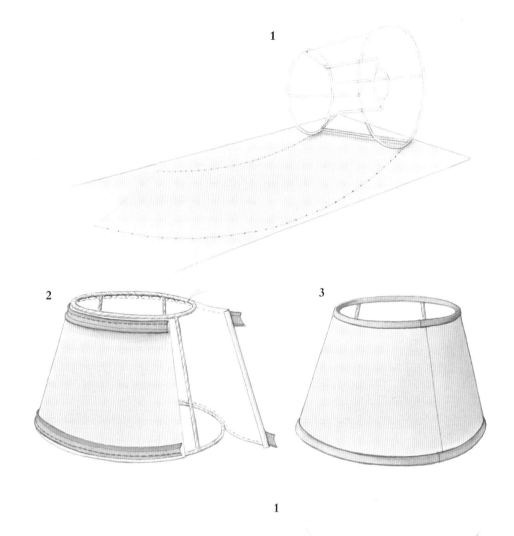

evenly – about 2 cm ($\frac{3}{4}$ in) apart. The exact spacing depends on the weight of the fabric and the amount of fullness that has to be taken in around the top ring. Divide the fabric into four equal sections and mark these points at the top and bottom.

2 Slip the fabric over the frame, and hold in place with clothes pegs positioned so they are equally spaced around the frame. Draw up the gathering threads so that the fabric fits around the frame and neatly arrange the pleats that form, pressing them all in the same direction with your fingers. Pin the pleats to the taped frame, then oversew the shade in place all around the top and bottom rings.

Trim away the fabric close to the stitching, then stitch the binding over the rings and stitch in place by hand or glue over the rings.

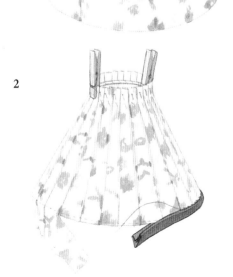

PICTURES & WALL HANGINGS

Owning a modest number of pictures, prints and photographs brings a personal art gallery within your reach. Achieving a professional look is often a question of careful hanging, grouping and proportion. As with everything else, there are fashions in picture hanging. Traditional picture rails can be used to provide a more formal interior scheme. Camouflage picture cords with lengths of wide satin, moiré or velvet ribbon or strips of glazed chintz. Large picture hooks can be hidden with generous opera bows or rosettes.

Grouping

Frames in the same colours and finishes give uniformity to a collection of differently-shaped pictures. Framing disparate subjects with the same colour mounts also gives unity to a collection.

Another attractive way to group pictures is to revive the eighteenth-century practice of dividing a wall into picture panels using simple wood beading or wallpaper borders to 'frame' your pictures. A classical wallpaper border such as egg and dart molding on pale grey or yellow painted walls could be a perfect foil for a set of engravings with birds' eye maple frames. Similarly, a chinoiserie fretwork wallpaper border on red painted walls could enhance a set of Chinese paintings with black lacquer frames. Narrow wood beading picked out in a colour or perhaps a stencilled acanthus motif could also make effective wall panels.

Placing all the pictures and objects you intend to hang up on the floor is an easy way to plan the grouping. Move your groups of pictures around until you are satisfied and then stand away from them. You can also plan groups of pictures and objects successfully by sketching the shapes out carefully first on a piece of squared paper. When hanging pictures over a piece of furniture such as a sofa, bedhead, chest of drawers or a fireplace you will also need to consider how much space to leave above and below, both for practicality and visual effect.

LEFT *Hanging a set of pictures in this rectangular format requires care and accuracy: the sofa width governs the length of the picture base line.*

BELOW *The combination of fine brass chains and a slim pole looks elegant and is a traditional way of hanging pictures. An inexpensive version would be to have a thin brass pole or a painted or stained wooden dowel rod.*

RIGHT *These charming, nostalgic twenties' prints in their oval frames repeat similar shapes in the Art Nouveau settle beneath. Hanging and centring this pair of pictures vertically forms a more satisfying composition than if the pictures had been placed side by side.*

BELOW *A classic eighteenth-century idea was to use silk bows and rosettes to disguise picture cords and hooks on picture rails. It was also a way of making a particular object the focal point of an elaborate display. The colours in the fabric bow are matched to those of the border pattern above.*

BELOW *A gallery of black and white prints pasted on to the wall is unified with* trompe l'oeil *black and white frames and a bold printed swag which gives a central focal point to the whole arrangement. Instead of lining the prints up horizontally, they are centred in vertical rows.*

FRAMING PICTURES

Professionals cut window mounts from thick art board, specially designed for the purpose. The white board has a coloured facing, and should be cut with an angled mount cutter, making neatly mitred (bevelled) corners. This is a very difficult task, requiring specialist tools, so you may prefer to cut a mount from thinner card, coloured all the way through, which is easier to handle.

Choose colours to tone with, or set off the subject. White or vellum is a safe choice, but creams and greys of all shades, as well as soft pastels, can be effective. Always consider the colour of the paint or wallpaper which forms the backdrop, as well as the colours of any other mounts in the room.

Ready-made frames are available, mainly in simpler styles – clip frames, simple wooden frames, aluminium kits. Look out for interesting second-hand frames. Check the back of the frame before buying if you intend to renovate it. The backing should be held in by small 'sprig' tacks and the joint sealed with gummed paper. If you can see how the picture is fixed in, you can judge how easy it will be to replace.

CUTTING MOUNTS

First decide on the proportions of the mount: if you are fitting the picture into an existing frame, the old mount can be used as a guide. Cut the mounting card to fit the frame exactly. To help plan the position and size of the opening, cut a paper template to represent the area of the picture you want to frame. Position it centrally on the mounting card. If the proportions of the picture and frame are such that you cannot arrange the 'window' with an even border all around, make the border wider along the lower edge of the picture. The border at the top should normally be the same width as the side borders.

Mark the position of the window very lightly in pencil on the right side of the mount. Use a sharp trimming knife and metal ruler to cut the opening: make light strokes to score the card, working first from one corner, and

then in the opposite direction from the corner at the other end of the ruler. Gradually increase the pressure until you have cut through the card. Repeat down each side of the opening. Position the picture behind the opening and hold it in place with pieces of masking tape.

If you have a steady hand, you can outline the frame with a fine line, painted or drawn with a pen around the window. Strips of marbled paper, glued around the opening and mitred at the corners, provide a further embellishment: choose the colours carefully to suit the picture and the frame.

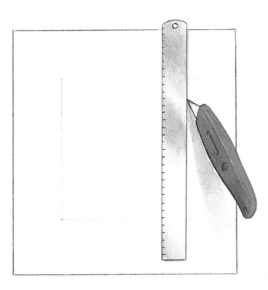

FITTING THE FRAME

The exact method of fitting a frame depends on the type of frame, but there are one or two hints to make the job easier. Use methylated spirits and a clean, dry, lint-free cloth to polish the glass thoroughly.

1 Position the frame on a padded surface (to stop it from slipping) and fit the glass into the frame, making sure you don't get any smears or fingerprints on the glass. Position the mounted picture inside the frame.

2 Fit the backing into the frame: the backing may be wood, hardboard or stiff card, depending on the type of frame. If the frame has lost its backing, cut a piece of hardboard or heavy card to size. Some frames have their own clips to hold the backing. If there are no clips, use headless tacks or sprigs to hold the backing in place.

3 Seal the back of the picture with gummed brown paper tape or masking tape. To hang the picture, fit a small screw eye to each side of the frame, about three quarters of the way up the frame.

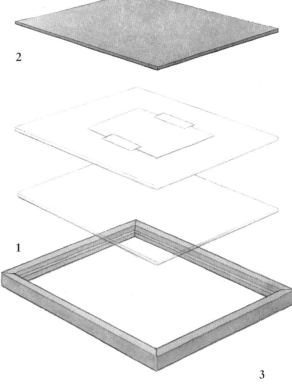

FABRIC FRAMES

There are various types of adhesive that can be used for sticking fabric to itself and to card or wood. Test the adhesive first to ensure it does not show through fabric and to check how long it takes to bond. You may need to weight the work, or hold it in place with clothes pegs if the adhesive does not bond on contact.

1 Cut a stiff card backing and a card frame to the desired measurements. Cut a second U-shaped card frame, leaving it open at one end, making it just 12 mm ($\frac{1}{2}$ in) wide. Cut fabric to size: you will need three panels 12 mm ($\frac{1}{2}$ in) larger all around than the finished frame; two backing panels the same size as the finished frame; and a piece of wadding the size of the finished frame.

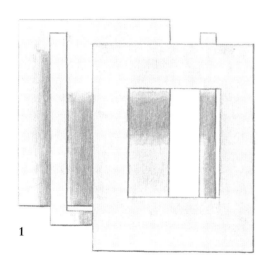

1

Trim the centre from the wadding and one of the smaller panels of fabric, so they match the card frame. Trim the centre from one of the larger panels of fabric to match the frame, allowing a 12 mm ($\frac{1}{2}$ in) turning all round. Lay out the larger fabric frame, wrong side up, and position the wadding and card frame on top. Clip into the turning and across the corners of the fabric, so that you can fold it neatly over the card, holding the wadding tightly. Glue in place. Trim the remaining panel of fabric so that it is 6 mm ($\frac{1}{4}$ in) smaller all round than the frame (including around the window opening) and glue to the back of the frame.

2 Trim the second large panel of fabric to make an open-ended frame 3 cm ($1\frac{1}{4}$ in) wide and wrap it around the narrow frame, gluing it in place.

Stitch a strip of ribbon to the back of the third large panel of fabric, about two thirds of the way up. Wrap the panel around the card backing and glue in place, then glue the last smaller panel of fabric over the inside.

3 Sandwich the three layers of fabric-covered card together and glue. Cut a wedge-shaped stand, two thirds of the height of the frame, and cover it in the same way. Glue the strip of ribbon down the back of the stand and add a restraining ribbon between the stand and the back of the frame if necessary.

2

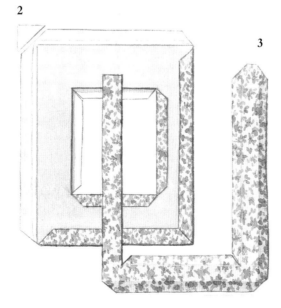

3

FINISHES FOR FRAMES

Frames made of wood or plaster, for example, can be decorated with a paint effect. Most of the paint techniques described on pages 62–65 can be applied to picture frames. Use finer brushes to suit the scale of the work.

To gild a frame, build up a suitable base. New wood and other porous surfaces should be given a base coat (known as fontenay) in a deep colour to provide an undertone. Red is normally used for gold finishes, and black for silver or pewter finishes.

If the frame is molded, it can be repaired with gesso (a type of prepared Plaster of Paris) or special wax gilt filler sticks, used mainly for small repairs, such as filling nail holes.

Gilt varnish is available in several tones to simulate metals of different ages. Apply it over the base coat, following the direction of the grain of the wood along each side of the frame.

For an antique effect, vary the thickness of the coat, or apply extra coats to highlight raised areas. Gilt cream can also be used to mellow the finish as well as to 'polish up' gilt frames which need a facelift.

To simulate natural ageing, use patina pencils to create variations in tone around the frame, mixing the colours to emphasize the shape of the molding.

Appendix

Sewing Techniques

Stitches

The following techniques provide the basis for all soft furnishings. Some people prefer to use hand sewing because of the control this allows.

Running Stitch

This stitch is used mainly for gathering up fabric or as a tacking stitch. Secure the thread with a backstitch (see below) and sew small, evenly spaced stitches. If you are gathering, work two parallel rows about 6 mm ($\frac{1}{4}$ in) apart and leave a length of thread at the end with which to gather up the fabric to the required length. Secure the threads to a pin in a figure of eight and adjust the gathers.

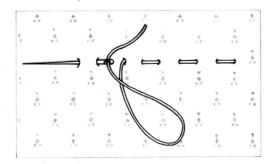

Backstitch

This hand stitch is firm and looks like machine stitches on the right side; on the wrong side the stitches will overlap. Working from right to left, insert the needle about 3 mm ($\frac{1}{8}$ in) behind the place where the thread came out and bring the needle out again the same distance in front of that point. Every time, insert the needle in the end of the last stitch.

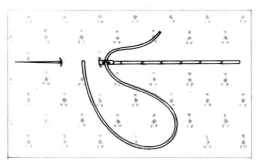

Prickstitch

This is similar to backstitch but is less obtrusive. Instead of inserting the needle in the end of the previous stitch, you should only pick up a couple of threads on the right side so that the finished seam looks rather like tiny running threads with the stitches like tiny prick holes on the fabric. This stitch can be used to secure seam allowances.

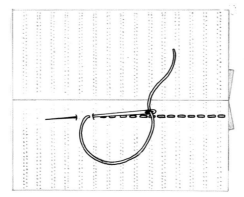

Slip-tacking

This tacking stitch invisibly secures two folded edges or a facing. It is the perfect way to match patterns at a seam line before machine stitching. Fasten the thread within one of the folds and take over to the other edge picking up a 6 mm ($\frac{1}{4}$ in) stitch. Cross over the opening again and continue, picking up fabric from just inside the fold.

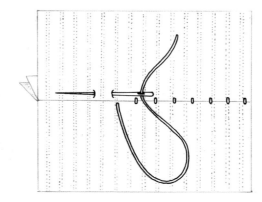

Lockstitch

This is rather like herringbone stitch, but the thread is left very loose because the main purpose of this stitch is to secure linings and interlinings to the curtain fabric and some give is necessary. Lay the fabric out flat and with wrong sides together, lay the lining or inter-lining in place over the curtain. Secure with pins at regular intervals down a straight line from the top to the bottom of the curtain. Fold back the lining along the line of pins. Secure the thread at the top, take a stitch through the folded lining and the curtain fabric **(1)**, picking up only a couple of threads with each stitch. Make the next stitch about 5 cm (2 in) further along and bring the needle out over the thread to produce a loop **(2)**. Keep the thread very loose. Work vertical rows of lockstitch about every 60 cm (24 in) so the lining doesn't sag.

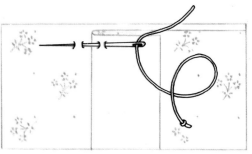

1

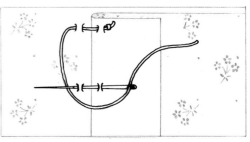

2

SLIPSTITCH

This is used to stitch any folded edge. Working from right to left, take a tiny stitch in the main fabric and insert the needle immediately into the fold as close as possible to the previous stitch. Pull the thread through. This should be one continuous movement.

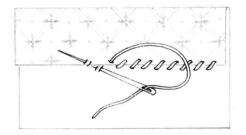

HERRINGBONE STITCH

This is a firm hemming stitch particularly appropriate for curtains; it doesn't need a folded hem because the raw edge is covered by the stitch. This is normally worked from left to right. Secure the thread and bring the needle up through the hem about 3 mm ($\frac{1}{8}$ in) from the edge, take the needle diagonally across to make a backwards stitch in the curtain fabric just above the hem edge. Bring the needle diagonally back to the hem again and take a backwards stitch in the hem. Keep the thread fairly loose as you work.

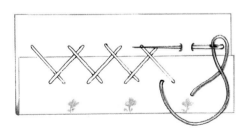

HEMMING STITCH

Hemming should be done delicately with similar coloured thread so that it is virtually invisible. Take a tiny stitch in the wrong side of the fabric and insert the needle diagonally under the folded hem about 6 mm ($\frac{1}{4}$ in) away. Continue along the hem, keeping the tension even so there is no puckering seen from the right side.

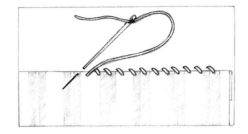

BLANKET STITCH

This stitch neatens raw edges on fabrics that don't fray, such as leather and felt. It can also be used as a decorative edge. Fasten the thread near to the fabric edge and, keeping the depth of stitch even, insert the needle at right angles to the edge of the fabric and bring it up and over the thread to form a loop stitch. Keeping the width of stitch constant, insert the needle into the fabric again so that the thread runs horizontally along the edge of the fabric.

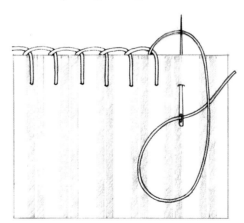

MACHINE STITCHING

When working on the machine, refer to your manual before you sew furnishing fabrics. The manual will recommend needle sizes, tension and the correct foot to use. Always select the thread according to the type of work and material, and the needle according to the thread.

A good tension is when the threads are locked together properly between the layers of fabric.

FINDING A STRAIGHT EDGE

To cut out any large piece of fabric, you need to start with a straight edge. This ensures that the fabric hangs true, on curtains, for example. For firmly woven fabrics, you can tear to get a straight edge. Cut into the selvedge and, grasping both sides, rip across the width. If the fabric is loose, pull out a crosswise thread right across the width and cut along this line.

Alternatively, lay the selvedge up against the edge of a table and check that the crosswise grain is level with the end of the table. To measure off the first length, use a set square or a large object with a right-angled corner. Draw across the width of fabric with dressmaker's chalk and cut along this line. Cut out the rest of the lengths in the same way.

SEAMS

A puckered or poorly finished seam will spoil the look of your soft furnishings. For example, the seams on full-length curtains need to be flat and tidy or the whole effect will be ruined.

Make sure the raw edges are together before you sew so that the allowances are the same width; most seams are about 1.5 cm ($\frac{5}{8}$ in) wide. Everyone has a favourite method of holding the fabric while sewing; either tack or pin at regular intervals. If you insert the pins across the seam you can sew straight over them and remove them at the end of the sewing. Reverse the stitch at either end of the seam to secure the threads. After stitching, press seams open or to one side, as directed.

OVERCAST SEAM

This can be worked on the machine with a zigzag stitch or more laboriously by hand by taking an even diagonal stitch over the raw edge along the seam. If the fabric is likely to fray, use pinking shears or make a line of machine stitching about 3 mm ($\frac{1}{8}$ in) in from the edge.

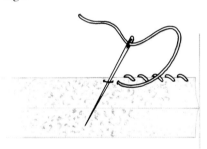

CURVED SEAM

Pin and stitch as usual but clip outward curves at intervals to ease the seam and cut V shapes along an inward curving seam. You can then press the seam open. This clipping also reduces bulk where the seam cannot be pressed open, as on a circular cushion.

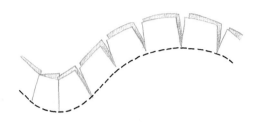

CORNERS

When sewing a regular corner, trim the seam allowance by cutting straight across the corner.

To get a clear point on sharp corners when using thick fabrics, make two or three stitches across the turning point (1). Trim the seam allowance parallel to the seam line.

To turn a corner on a welted or boxed cushion, clip into the welt at the corner point, reinforcing the corner with extra rows of stitching (2).

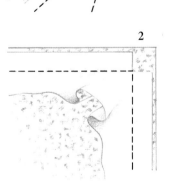

FLAT FELL SEAM

This is a very strong seam and perfect for home furnishings where wear and constant laundering could present problems. From the right side it looks like a topstitched seam. Sew an ordinary seam (1) and press the allowances to one side. Trim the underneath seam allowance to about 6 mm ($\frac{1}{4}$ in) (2) and fold the top allowance over it, turning under the raw edge to enclose the trimmed edge (3). Pin and press flat then sew through all layers close to the folded edge (4).

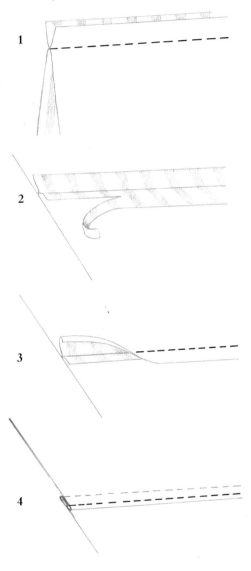

FRENCH SEAM

This encloses the raw edges but because it can be bulky it is best on lightweight fabrics. It is particularly appropriate for lace and voile because turnings are narrow and don't show through the fabric. With wrong sides together, sew a narrow seam **(1)**. Trim seam allowances **(2)**, even if fabric doesn't fray, and fold along the machined edge with right sides together **(3)**. Press. Stitch along this seam about 1 cm ($\frac{3}{8}$ in) from the seamed edge **(4)**.

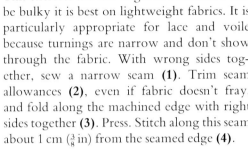

LAPPED SEAM

To match patterns from the right side of the fabric, turn under one edge of the fabric by 6 mm ($\frac{1}{4}$ in) and pin in place over the other piece to be joined, matching patterns if necessary **(1)**. On the right side of the fabric, pin and machine stitch along the fold **(2)** and then sew another seam parallel to the first to catch down the raw edge beneath **(3)**.

To join bulky widths of interlining, overlap the raw edges by about 6 mm ($\frac{1}{4}$ in) and machine stitch a line of zigzag down the length. Alternatively, butt the two raw edges together and hand sew down the length using a loose herringbone stitch (an abutted seam).

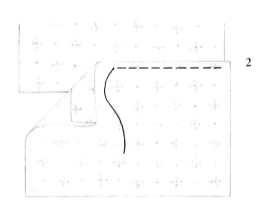

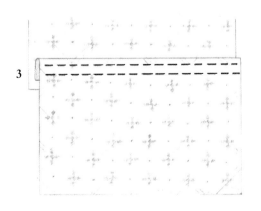

INTERLINED CURTAINS

For extra weight, lined curtains may be interlined. For interlining, you will need a panel of fabric for each curtain, the same size as the finished (ungathered) curtain, or slightly longer if you want to pad the hems for a fuller look. Calculate the total quantity by dividing the total width of the curtain by the width of the interlining fabric, and multiplying the number of drops required to make up the panel by the finished length of the curtains.

Interlining should be joined with a lapped or abutted seam.

Join interlining to the curtain fabric with lockstitch (p. 196), so that the interlining is centred on the panel of fabric for the curtain. Treat the curtain fabric and interlining as a single piece of fabric to finish the curtain.

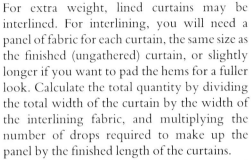

F*INISHES* & T*RIMMINGS*

There are many purchased finishes and trimmings used in home sewing. Ribbon, lace and braid are suitable for any seam which is straight but for curved seams and a truly professional finish, use bias-cut fabric.

C*UTTING* B*IAS* B*INDING*

To find the bias of the fabric, fold it so that the selvedge is parallel with the weft or crosswise grain **(1)**. Press this fold to give yourself the first cutting line. Now cut all the remaining bias strips parallel to this line to the desired width **(2)**. To join strips, position ends together as shown, right sides facing, so that the edges of the strips match at the stitching line **(3)**. Press seam open and trim away points of fabric after stitching.

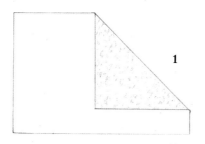

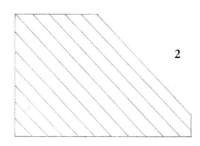

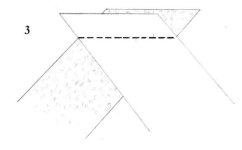

M*ITRING* C*ORNERS*

To turn up a hem at a corner, you need to mitre the corner. Turn up the hems along both edges of fabric to the same width and press **(1)**. Insert a pin at the edge of the fabric where the two hems intersect and open out again. Fold in the corner diagonally to meet the pins at both sides. Cut across the corner about 6 mm ($\frac{1}{4}$ in) from the folded edge **(2)** and turn in the hems again. Slipstitch the corner edges together and finish the other hems with your chosen method **(3)**. This works with hems of unequal width, for example, on curtains.

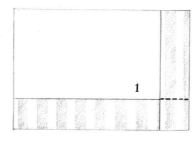

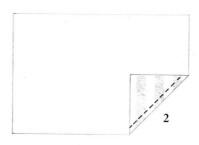

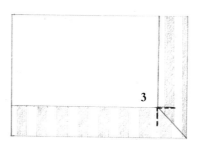

M*AKING* P*IPING*

Piping can be flat or corded, single or double. Cord for piping can be bought in many thicknesses, and you should choose your thickness carefully; a very heavy piping can look unwieldy on a light cotton cushion cover, for example. Join the strips of bias fabric together on the straight grain. The width of bias-cut fabric should be the circumference of your chosen cord plus two seam allowances.

Check when you buy that the cord is preshrunk. If not, wash it before use if it is to be sewn on something you intend to launder. If you need to join the cord, unravel a little from both raw ends and intertwine them for about 2.5 cm (1 in).

Press the length of bias strip and wrap it around the piping cord, raw edges together. Hold in place with pins. Using the zipper foot on the machine, sew close to the cord with a similar coloured thread. Lay the piping on the fabric, raw edges level. Pin and machine stitch close to the piping, covering the original seam line. Sew around corners as for welted borders.

To join raw ends of piping, trim away the cord and overlap the ends of the binding, curving them inwards. Sew through all thicknesses.

A quick method of applying piping to a square cushion is to fit the piping straight along each edge so that the ends cross at each corner. Sew through all the thicknesses and trim excess piping.

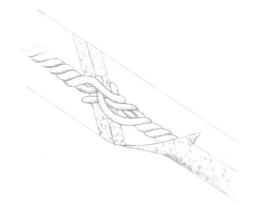

APPLYING CORD TRIM

Pin the cord in position, making sure the ends are not at a corner. Secure the thread in the fabric and sew through the cord and into the fabric with tiny stitches. Join the two ends of cord by unravelling a short length and intertwining the strands. Stitch the twisted ends to the fabric.

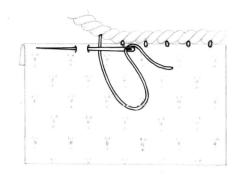

MITRING BORDERS OR RIBBON

Cut a length of ribbon or binding for each edge to be trimmed, allowing a good overlap at each end. Attach the trimming to the right side of the fabric with pins along one edge. Stitch up to the inside corner point where you intend to turn the corner (1). Fold the trimming so you can stitch a diagonal line between the inner and outer edges of trimming (2). Clip the seam, press the trimming flat or turn binding to wrong side (3), and continue down the next edges of the fabric.

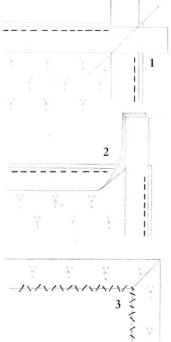

FRILLS

Ruffles or frills are used on cushions, curtains, bed drapes and loose covers. A single frill needs hemming or binding, whereas a double frill is a piece of fabric folded along its length and the right side of the fabric shows all the time. A single frill is preferable if you are using bulky fabrics.

Calculate the depth of frill and either add allowances for a double hem and the gathered edge seam or double the required depth and seam allowance for a double frill. Decide on the effect you want, then measure up for the length of the frill: one and a half to three times the length of the finished edge fullness. Sew two lines of gathering stitch and gather up the fullness to fit the edge. Pin and stitch in place – around the edge of a hem, for example, or inserted into a seam.

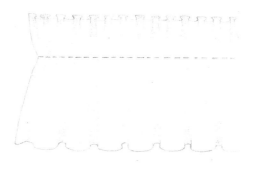

For a frilled edge to a round cushion, join the fabric strip into a circle, gather and distribute the gathers evenly around the cushion piece.

A double frill can be bound on the outside edge and the folded edge overlapped on to the cushion or curtain fabric. This frill can be applied after the rest of the sewing is completed.

A pleated frill gives a crisp finish. To calculate the fabric length needed for the frill, measure around the cushion piece or along the curtain edge and multiply by three for the frill length. Include seam allowances for any joins. The frill can be hemmed or double.

Mark the fabric length into 3 cm (1¼ in) sections along its length. Make 6 cm (2½ in) pleats and pin. Tack across the top of the pleats. Apply the frill as before.

ZIP INSERTION

For furnishing items, use metal zips where there will be considerable strain, on a loose cover, for example, and nylon ones on cushion covers. To centre the zip, as on the welt in a boxed cushion, tack the seam and press open. Pin the zip in place, face down over the centre of the seam, and machine or hand stitch. Unpick the tacking stitches. Turn to the right side and topstitch to secure and strengthen (1).

If the zip is enclosed, before inserting it, stitch the zip tapes at the top of the zip together by hand and sew across both ends by machine when the zip is in place.

INVISIBLE ZIP INSERTION

To insert a zip along a piped seam or where no stitching is to be seen on the finished article, open the zip and place the teeth right side down against the piping or away from the raw edge. Sew the zip tape to the seam allowance with the zipper foot about 3 mm (⅛ in) from the teeth. Close the zip and open out the seam allowance on the other piece of fabric. Place the folded edge against the teeth as before and pin. Sew 3 mm (⅛ in) from the fold and then sew across the end of the zip to the piping (2).

If you are inserting a zip in sheer fabrics or in a nap fabric such as velvet, sew it by hand, using a prickstitch.

For a lapped zip, use the same method, but adjust stitching position as shown (3).

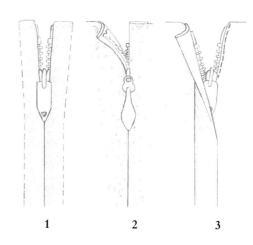

MACHINE QUILTING

Before you begin to quilt you must decide on the quilting design. There are many traditional designs; equally straight or wavy lines worked with a machine can be just as effective. Mark the design with dressmaker's chalk, or decide on the widths of the panels – for a traditional eiderdown, for example – or use the pattern on the fabric.

Quilting is always done on a sandwich of layers, varying in thickness, so the first thing to do is to join these layers with tacking stitches so all your quilting work isn't ruined because the layers drift and pucker. Press the fabric pieces (not the padding). The lines of tacking should run in a different direction to the lines of stitching: for diagonal quilting, tack the fabric in a grid along and across the grain of the fabric, spacing the lines of stitching about 10 cm (4 in) apart. Use the same technique for outline quilting. For striped fabric, tack across the strips.

If you are quilting by machine, mark the lines of quilting using dressmaker's chalk. Most machines have a quilting foot which holds the fabric flat as you sew. Always sew in the same direction to prevent puckering. Select the appropriate needle for the work. Use a loose, long machine stitch and reduce the pressure on the presser foot. Guide the fabric through the machine, keeping the layers together and taking care not to make any tucks where the lines of stitching cross. Roll up the fabric so that it will fit under the arm of the sewing machine as you work across the fabric.

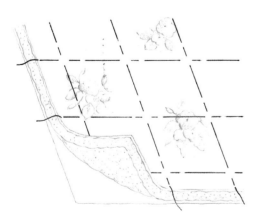

HAND QUILTING

To quilt by hand, use a sharp or crewel needle and a thread similar to the top fabric. The stitches should be about 2–3 mm ($\frac{1}{10}$–$\frac{1}{8}$ in) long and as even as possible. You can use different stitches; the most common are backstitch and running stitch. If the layers are thick and bulky, stab the needle through vertically, not at an angle. The stitches must be neither too close nor too far apart; the padded effect will be lost if the stitches are too close together, and the layers will not be held firmly if the stitches are too far apart.

If you prefer to work in small areas and join the work after the quilting has been done, butt the wadding layers together and secure with a herringbone stitch **(1)**. Fold back one edge of the main fabric by 2 cm ($\frac{3}{4}$ in) and cover the other raw edge. Pin down the length of the join. Turn the quilt over and do the same with the backing fabric. Join the seams invisibly **(2)** or machine stitch down the seam and continue the quilting design across the join.

For a reversible seam on ready-quilted fabric, unpick about 3 cm ($1\frac{1}{4}$ in) on either side of the edges to be joined. Join the fabric layers as described above. After sewing the seam, continue the quilting across the seam.

1

2

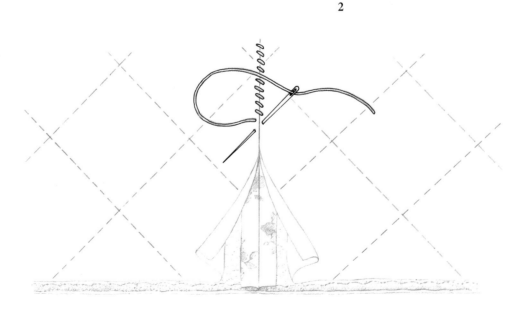

PATCHWORK

Patchwork is the perfect way to use up old remnants of fabric or to create a patterned fabric to use as a bedcover, cushion cover or draped tablecloth. All the seam allowances for patchwork must be the same. Decide from the start and cut out all the patches with exactly the same seam allowance. This means that when you sew the blocks or units of patches together, they will all align along the seams. Less regular shapes should be cut from templates. These can be bought as acetate or metal shapes, or made from stiff card.

The usual way to tackle a complex patchwork is to divide the whole into blocks. These are then constructed according to a pattern and sewn together. When enough are completed, the whole piece is assembled. This saves working on an enormous piece of cloth, although traditionally women would work together around a large patchwork, adding patches and then quilting the finished piece in a 'quilting bee'.

For hand-sewn patchwork, the method is slower and more precise. The patches are tacked on to paper templates to hold the patches rigid while they are sewn together (1). Commercial templates are usually sold in two parts – the window to cut the fabric (this includes the seam allowance) and the inner template to cut the paper shapes. Use quality cartridge paper or old envelopes for the papers. The fabric is cut using the window template and aligning at least two sides of the template with the straight grain of the fabric. The pieces are then tacked on to the paper, paying particular attention to the corners. With a diamond template, for example, you will need to trim one side of the seam allowance so that the point fits the paper exactly (2).

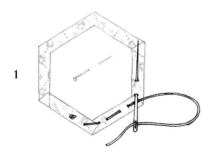

1

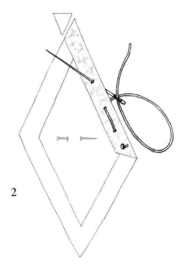

2

To join the patches by hand, oversew along one side with tiny close stitches (3), making sure you do not sew into the paper template. Join all the other patches in the block and then remove the papers and tacking thread.

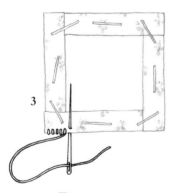

3

FINISHING OFF

Because the grain of the patchwork does not run in the same direction, it is usually necessary to line it. If you are making a bedspread, you might want to interline it with wadding first and quilt it (page 158). If you don't want a quilt, catch the wadding, patchwork and lining together through all layers from the lining side with strong knots.

If it is intended as a tablecloth, line the patchwork with a firmly woven fabric similar to that used in the patches. If it is large, catch the lining and patchwork together along the seams. A binding around the edge using a contrasting plain colour or one of the patchwork fabrics gives the tidiest finish.

APPLIQUE

Appliqué can be worked using shapes with the raw edges exposed or turned under. The shape can either be your own design, or a pattern cut from a piece of fabric. Pin and tack the motif in place and stitch around the outline first. Machine stitch around the edge, using a close zig-zag or satin stitch so that the fabric doesn't fray. Trim away any excess fabric close to the zig-zag edge.

Appliqué can be used as a border on pillowcases, roller blinds and unlined curtains. Plan the position of the motifs carefully, cutting them all out and rearranging them along the seam allowance line of the item to be edged. Choose a fabric that matches the weight of the main fabric. You may find the motifs easier to handle if you back them with Bondaweb (double-sided iron-on interfacing) first. Sew in place as described above and cut along the edge with sharp scissors to expose the decorative shaped edge.

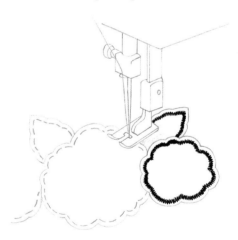

MEASURING UP

WINDOWS

Decide what sort of window dressing would best suit your windows – inside or outside the recess, floor length or to the sill. All these decisions have to be made before you can go any further.

To calculate the amount of fabric, use a retractable metal rule and measure up the area, depending on the type of curtain and the length you want it (pages 94–123). Before making the curtains, however, you should fix the curtain track or pole. There are a number of other details you need to consider too. Do you want a headed curtain to project above the curtain track? How deep will the rings be if the curtains are hanging from a pole? Do you want the sill to be covered or the curtain to rest level with the bottom of the sill? Do you want the curtain to trail on the floor, or sit just above the carpet?

Decide on the length of the curtain and add the appropriate turning allowances at the top and bottom. You can always make a deeper hem if you have cut the fabric lengths too long, but too short an allowance could change the window dressing radically.

Calculation of the width depends on the type of heading tape and the track or pole. Multiply the length of the curtain track or pole by the degree of fullness – usually one and a half, twice or three times the width of the window. Divide by the number of curtains you plan to make up for the window and add turning allowances for all sides. Any half widths should be joined on at the side edges.

When calculating the width of a roller or other type of blind, you should take into account any architrave around the window. The stiffened fabric of the roller blind could catch on a prominent architrave. The Roman blind may hang better if it is fitted outside the window frame to cover the entire frame when let down.

To work out the amount of fabric, multiply the total length of the curtain or blind by the number of fabric widths: most furnishing fabrics are 120 cm (47 in), 122 cm (48 in), 137 cm (54 in), 140 cm (55 in), or 150 cm (59 in) wide. Matching patterns and allowing for shrinkage are other considerations.

For windows that are not regular shapes, you need to design the appropriate window dressing and then measure up accordingly. A semi-circular top, for example, has to have a static heading with the fabric held back out of the way with a tie-back. For a shaped window, you can use screw eyes to hang the curtain hooks. Whatever the shape of your window, be generous with your allowances.

Lining and interlining quantities will be the same as for the main curtain fabric, without allowing for matching patterns.

When measuring up for hand-made curtains, such as draped swags and tails, you will need to make a toile to check on the degree of drape. Lace-edged curtains also need careful calculation because you will want to make sure that the lace edging rests just above the floor or sill.

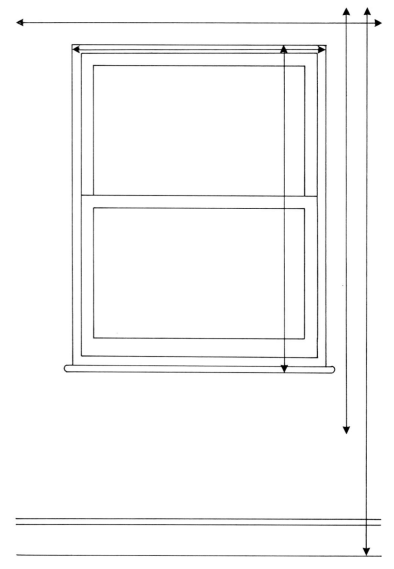

Measuring up for standard curtains or blinds

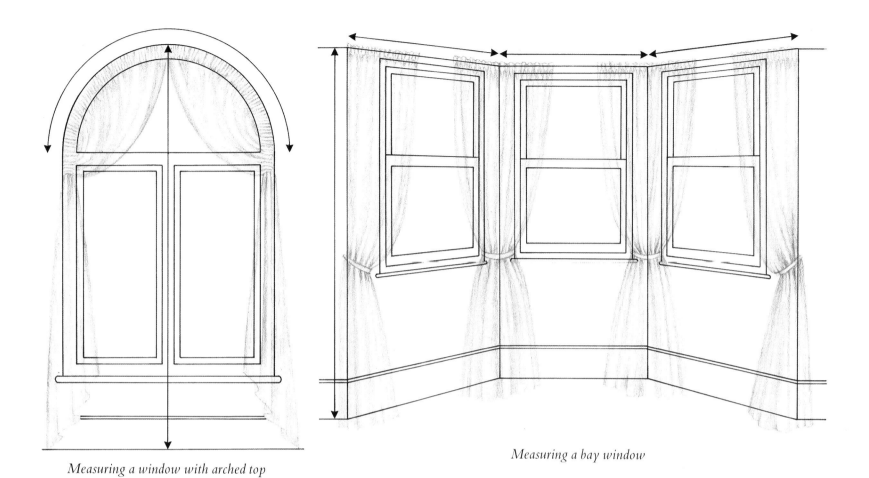

Measuring a window with arched top

Measuring a bay window

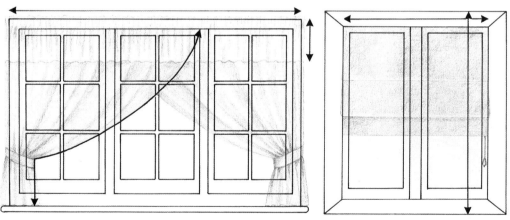

LEFT *Measuring up for draped curtains with blind*

ABOVE *Measuring up for cross-over curtains with cased heading and pelmet (valance)*

ABOVE RIGHT *Measuring up for a recessed blind*

BEDS

For a fitted divan cover, measure with the usual bedclothes in place excluding the pillows. Divan covers usually have a welt the same depth as the mattress and a skirt hanging below this. Measure the length and width of the bed, plus seam allowances. Measure the depth of the mattress (still with bedcovers) and the two sides and the foot widthways. The welt should be cut in three pieces, two long and one short, so the finished seams are at the corners of the cover. Measure the depth of the skirt from the base of the welt to the floor, allowing for gathers or pleats. Add on allowances for the seam and for the hem.

When measuring up for bedcovers, you may want to allow for a more generous effect – for example, the throwover could drape loosely on the floor at the corners. To curve the corners, see page 156.

To measure up for a throwover, leave the usual bedclothes in position. Measure the length and width including the pillows, and decide on the length of the overhang. Add a seam allowance of 15 mm ($\frac{5}{8}$ in) all round for a lined throwover, or 5 cm (2 in) for a double hem on an unlined cover. No seam allowance is necessary if the throwover is to be bound. If more than one width of fabric is necessary, add allowances for the seams. Try to position the seams down the edges of the bed, not down the middle. If you want the cover to tuck in under the pillow, or to wrap right around it, add on to the length for this too.

To measure up for a valance, take off the mattress and measure the length and width of the bed base. Add a seam allowance of 15 mm ($\frac{5}{8}$ in) all round. Measure from the edge of the bed to the floor and add a seam allowance at the top and a hem allowance at the bottom. The width of the skirt will depend on whether it is generously gathered, pleated along its length, or fitted with box pleats at the corners. Measure around the foot and two sides of the bed to get the basic width first.

CUSHIONS

Measure the top of the cushion pad and add seam allowances all round. For a welted or box cushion, the welt is usually made up of four pieces. Because the zip is inserted across the centre of the back part of the welt and around two corners, cut one piece to extend around two corners by about 8 cm (3 in) each side; this should be 3 cm ($1\frac{1}{4}$ in) wider than the depth of the welt to allow for the zip.

The front piece should be the depth and width of the front of the welt plus allowances and the two side pieces should be the depth of the welt plus allowances and 8 cm (3 in) shorter than the sides, plus seam allowances.

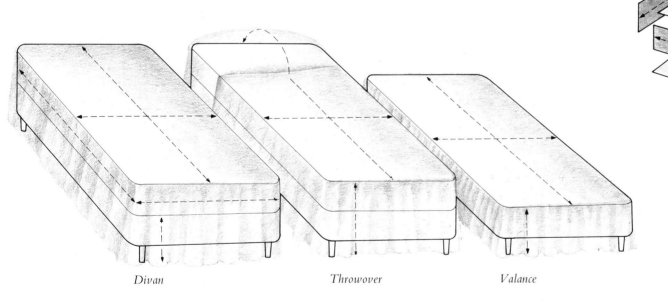

Divan   *Throwover*   *Valance*

SOFAS AND CHAIRS

To measure up for loose covers, whatever the shape of the chair or sofa, measure each panel of the piece of furniture to be covered at the widest point in each direction. Make a list, giving the dimensions of each named section.

Measure the height and the width and calculate the amount of fullness required for a gathered or pleated skirt. Add an allowance for a tuck-in along the lower edge of the back and the back of the seat, and a suitable seam allowance all round. This should be about 5 cm (2 in) except for the tuck-in areas around the seat which should have a 15 cm (6 in) allowance.

Draw the pattern pieces on graph paper to scale. Label each piece and mark which way the straight grain should go. Cut the pieces out. Mark out the width of the chosen fabric on another piece of graph paper and lay the scale pattern pieces on it, paying attention to the direction of the straight grain. If you have chosen plain fabric, the scale pieces can be economically laid out but for patterned fabric

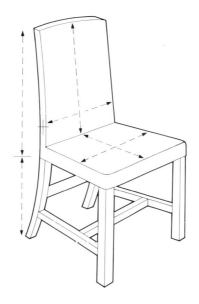

you will need to note the pattern repeats and where the motifs fall.

Use the scale pieces to measure and estimate the piping requirements and convert all the amounts to full scale to decide how much fabric you will need.

TABLES

Measure the width and length of the table and to these two measurements add twice the overhang. Decide if the cloth is to drape on the floor, reach knee length or just clear the floor. Add on a 5 cm (2 in) hem allowance or leave without any allowances if you are binding around the edge.

If the table is large, you will probably have to join lengths of fabric. Try to position the seams down the sides to avoid a centre seam. Centre the full width of the fabric over the table and join the seams equidistant from the sides. Allow extra fabric for seams.

For round tables measure the diameter and then add twice the overhang. The seams on circular cloths are also better positioned on either side of the centre of the table.

For oval tables measure the width and length and add twice the overhang as before.

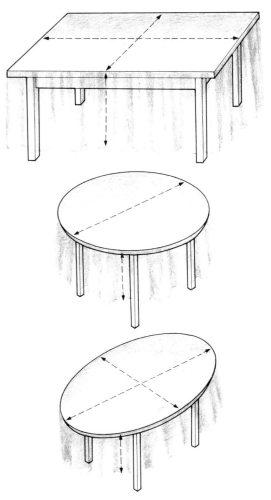

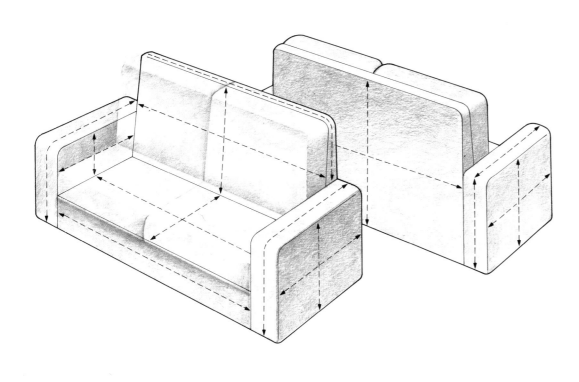

PREPARATION OF SURFACES

Before applying any decoration to walls, ceiling or woodwork, you must ensure the surface is dry, sound and clean. A dusty surface, for example, should be washed down and treated with a primer or the paper or paint won't adhere to it. Although it is time consuming and you may seem to be making slow progress, it is always worth preparing surfaces well before decorating.

PAINTED WOODWORK

If painted woodwork is in good condition and the paint has not been applied too thickly in the past, just wash it and rub down lightly with abrasive paper to provide a key. If the paint is flaking, loose or has been built up so much that windows or doors can't be opened, it should be stripped off. The stripping job must be thorough if you plan to leave the wood in its natural state.

Paint can be stripped from woodwork using heat or chemicals. A hot air gun **(1)** or blowtorch is used with a scraper. The heat softens the paint and the scraper (either a shavehook or broad blade scraper) strips it from the surface. Safety is important when using these methods. Wear gloves, don't put newspapers down to catch the old paint as this represents a fire hazard and keep the heat well away from plastic and glass. The heat source should be moved backwards and forwards to prevent the wood being scorched. The heat

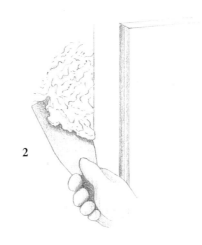

softens paint in a matter of seconds, so proceed slowly at first until you are used to the technique.

A chemical stripper, either paste or liquid, is the best method to use if you aren't going to repaint the wood. It is ideal for areas near glass and for intricate beading and architraves. Use a flat scraper for large, flat areas **(2)**, and a shave hook for intricate moldings **(3)**. However, it is more expensive and takes longer because you may need to re-apply the chemical if there are many layers of paint. Always follow the manufacturer's instructions carefully; wear gloves and some protection for your eyes. If the chemical comes into contact with your skin, wash it off immediately with water. Work in a well-ventilated area.

When you have finished the stripping, wash the surface with clean water and sand it, or rub with steel wool, and then wipe with white spirit. Difficult items, such as shutters or large doors, can be stripped professionally.

All untreated wood should be primed to reduce the absorbency of the material and to provide a key for the paint. Fill any holes in woodwork with flexible wood stopper. After this, apply the undercoat. Undercoats prevent any previous paint colour from showing through and should be in an appropriate colour for the top coat.

If you want to retain the wood look, you can stain it to change or standardize the colour. Stained wood can be sealed with polish or varnish. Alternatively you can use a coloured polyurethane varnish. Apply a coat of clear varnish first to seal the wood so that the coloured varnish can be applied evenly. It is advisable to thin the first coat of varnish with white spirit to accommodate the absorbency of the wood. Stains and varnishes are often very different on different woods so check the colour on a spare piece of timber first. To give the varnish a natural sheen, burnish with fine wire wool dipped in wax polish. Beeswax polish or linseed oil can be rubbed well into wood to give a more natural look, though these finishes are not so durable.

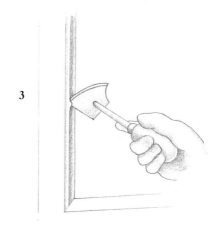

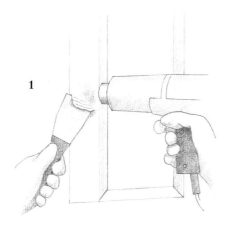

PREPARING WALLS

Wash down painted walls (working down the wall) and lightly rub down gloss-painted walls to provide a key. Scrape off and rub down flaking paint and wash off powdery distemper and apply stabilizing primer.

WALLPAPER

Regular wallpaper can be removed by soaking the wall with water and detergent. The paper needs to be thoroughly soaked and left long enough for the paste to soften. Score the surface (1), then try scraping off a small area (2); if the paper is still difficult to remove, wait longer.

Washable wallpapers are impervious to water, so you need to scratch the surface with a serrated scraper or abrasive paper first to allow the water to penetrate. Vinyl wallpapers have a backing which, if you remove only the top vinyl layer, can act as a lining paper if it is undamaged. You merely lift the top paper away from its backing and, keeping the paper as close as possible to the wall, pull the top layer off (3). If you then wish to remove the backing paper, follow the procedure for regular wallpaper.

The best method for large areas is to hire a steam stripper. This uses steam to dampen the paper so it peels off the wall (4). Take care when using a steam stripper if the surface beneath is plasterboard. this will also soften and you may dent it as you scrape off the paper.

Don't worry about any flecks of paper left after scraping; these can be removed with a scrubbing brush or glasspaper. Always allow the wall to dry out thoroughly before decorating.

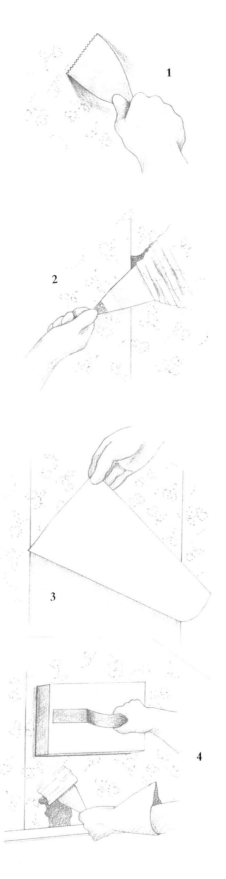

TEXTURED COATINGS

These are difficult to remove. You will need to clear the room as this is a messy job. Check with the manufacturer's recommendations; different textures require different removal methods, usually with either textured paint stripper or a steam wallpaper stripper.

TILES

If you decide to remove tiles from any surface, you will inevitably have to make good the surface as the tile cement or adhesive may pull plaster off a wall, or be difficult to remove from a wooden floor. A masonry chisel and hammer will help to prise ceramic tiles away from a wall.

FILLING HOLES & CRACKS IN WALLS

Hairline cracks, dents made by furniture, or holes should be filled flush with the surrounding walls. Fillers come ready mixed in paste form or in a powder to be mixed with water.

For filling cracks in plaster, use a filling knife to scrape out any loose material **(1)**. Dust with a brush and dampen the area. Apply the filler to the crack, and level off with the knife blade. When the filler is completely dry, sand the surface and the surrounding area with a fine sandpaper.

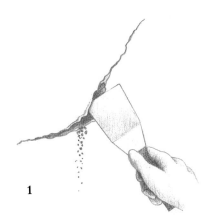

To fill a hole, chip away loose plaster with a cold chisel and hammer, dust the area and dampen as before. Mixing a little of the plaster filler at a time, fill the hole in layers about 12 mm ($\frac{1}{2}$ in) thick **(2)**. Allow the filler to dry before applying the next layer. Level off the last layer with a piece of wood or the blade of a trowel.

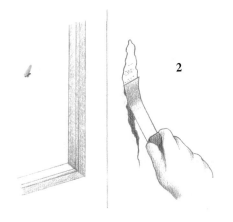

Large holes can be covered with a self-adhesive meshed tape and then covered with one layer of filler. Clean out the hole, leaving a slight ridge around the edges **(3)**. Sand the surrounding area and cut the mesh to fit the hole. Apply the edges of the mesh to the ridge with a little filler so that the mesh covers the hole completely **(4)**. Apply the filler as before, covering the edges of the hole and beyond **(5)**. Allow to dry and sand flush with the surrounding surface.

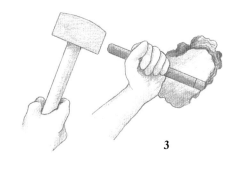

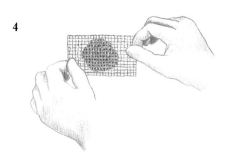

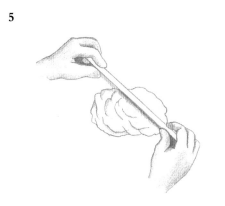

FLOORS

Floors, like all other surfaces, have to be clean, sound and dry. They should also be flat and have no protrusions to damage the new covering. This includes nail heads and uneven floorboards.

Concrete floors and other impervious floors can be levelled using a floor levelling compound. Check that there is no damp before levelling and fitting new flooring. Clean the floor of all grease and dirt, fill any holes with a suitable filler and allow to dry. Spread the compound, following the manufacturer's instructions carefully. Don't worry about any marks as the compound levels out on its own.

SUSPENDED FLOORS

If you have a wooden floor, you will need to fill in gaps, punch in nail heads or replace floor boards. If you are laying a vinyl or tiled surface, the floor must be completely even without any bulges or uneven floorboards. This is most successful if you lay an overlay of hardboard, chipboard or plywood to keep out draughts and provide a good surface for the new flooring to adhere to. Modern homes may have chipboard rather than floor boards. This saves the need for an overlay.

The sheets of overlay should be staggered rather like bricks, and the nails (for hardboard) or screws (for chipboard or plywood) made flush with the surface so as not to damage the new flooring.

Hardboard should be left in the room where it is to be laid for at least 48 hours so that it adjusts to the humidity in that room. Lay the sheets with the shiny surface downwards. The rough side provides the key for the adhesive.

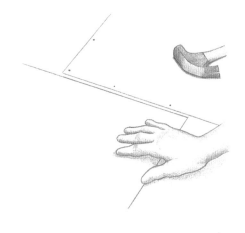

FIXING TO WALLS

You need to apply a framework before cladding a wall with wood or applying a fabric lining. For positioning battens for fabric lining, see page 72. If you intend to cover the wall with tongue-and-groove boards, the battens should be spaced about 50 cm (20 in) apart, either vertically or horizontally, at right angles to the way the boards are to be placed, and should provide support at the top and bottom and in the middle of the lengths **(1)**.

To attach moldings, such as a dado or picture rail, or to replace a skirting board, you need to find the timber studs or battens **(2)**. Note where the wood is by listening for a difference in sound as you tap on the wall. Plan the position of the moldings or panelling carefully to exploit their traditional effect. Check that the horizontal lines are level using a spirit level. Plan the lengths so that joins only occur at corners and use a mitre box to cut accurate mitres or scribe ends to fit **(3)**.

Prime the wood before offering it up to the wall. Countersink the masonry screws or knock in the nail heads with a nail punch when you attach the molding to the wall. Fill with wood filler before painting.

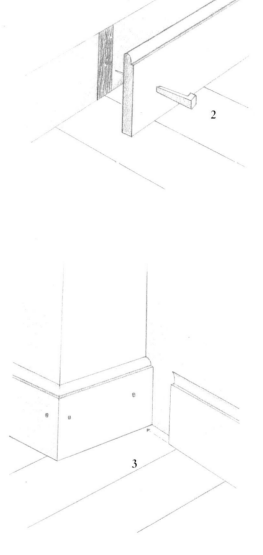

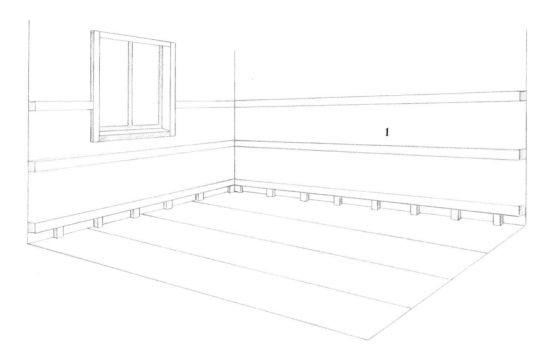

PAINTS

Paint can be broadly divided into oil-based and water-based categories. Oil-based paints include primers and gloss for woodwork and metal, and eggshell for walls and woodwork. Oil-based paints provide the best surface for areas where durability and washability are important – areas such as floors, skirting boards, rooms subject to condensation and so on. They can be thinned with white spirit and brushes usually need to be cleaned in white spirit too. Check the instructions; some brushes used with oil-based paints can be washed out with hot water and detergent. Scumble glaze, which is used for paint effects, and special lacquers are also oil-based.

Water-based paints are generally easier to handle and are commonly used on walls and ceilings; they include all finishes such as vinyl and matt, but they aren't as hard wearing as oil-based paints. Water-based paints are thinned with water and the brushes are easily washed out with soap and water.

Before starting to paint, you need to decide what equipment you will need. Generally, you should paint ceilings and walls, then woodwork. If you are using a roller, these tend to spray a light film of paint over everything so either cover up finished surfaces, or do the roller painting first.

○ If you are wallpapering, paint the woodwork which the wallpaper will butt up to first.
○ Prime all new wood and metal first and then apply the undercoat.
○ Don't mix paints: woodwork to be painted with an oil-based paint should have an oil-based undercoat.
○ Allow the undercoat to dry completely before applying the top coat.

HOW MUCH PAINT?

The amount of paint you need will depend on the area to be covered and on the surface. Porous surfaces use more paint and the amount of top coat will depend on the number of undercoats.

ESTIMATE THE NUMBER OF TILES

The number of tiles needed to cover an area of a square metre or yard on either the floor or a wall will be stated on the packet. Measure up the room and determine the square measure-ment. On the floor, don't subtract the area taken up by a chimney breast, for example; this will provide the extra allowance needed in case of breakages or for cutting.

You may need to be more specific if you are buying tiles in different sizes and want to be more economical. For example, if one design in vinyl tiles is being laid in the centre of the room with a different border around the edge, measure up and plan the laying area carefully. Divide the room into small areas and deter-mine the tile needs for each part, then add up the total.

WALLPAPER

Measure the total length around the room, excluding major obstacles such as picture windows and built-in cupboards, but includ-ing doors and windows. Measure the height of the wall from skirting board to picture rail or cornice. If there is a large pattern repeat on your wallpaper, add an extra allowance for pattern matching to give the length of each drop of paper. Divide the length of the drop into the length of the roll to find out how many drops you can cut from each roll. Divide the perimeter of the room by the width of the roll to find out how many drops you will need for the room. Then divide this number by the number of drops per roll to give the number of rolls. If there are a lot of irregularities add an extra allowance. The chart below gives a guide to quantities.

Decide where any borders are to go and measure the line they will follow. Check the manufacturer's label as borders don't always come in standard lengths.

METRIC WALLPAPER CALCULATOR (No. of rolls needed for walls)

Wall height from skirting in metres	Measurement around room in metres (including doors and windows)												
	10	11	12	13	14	15	16	17	18	19	20	21	22
2.0 m to 2.2m	5	5	5	6	6	7	7	7	8	8	9	9	10
2.2 m to 2.4m	5	5	6	6	7	7	8	8	9	9	10	10	10
2.4 m to 2.6m	5	6	6	7	7	8	8	9	9	10	10	11	11
2.6 m to 2.8m	6	6	7	7	8	8	9	9	10	11	11	12	12
2.8 m to 3.0m	6	7	7	8	8	9	9	10	11	11	12	12	13
3.0 m to 3.2m	6	7	8	8	9	10	10	11	11	12	13	13	14
3.2 m to 3.4m	7	7	8	9	9	10	11	11	12	13	13	14	15

IMPERIAL WALLPAPER CALCULATOR (No. of rolls needed for walls)

Wall height from skirting in feet	Measurement around room in feet (including doors and windows)												
	33	36	39	43	46	49	52	56	59	62	66	69	72
6' 6" to 7' 2"	5	5	5	6	6	7	7	7	8	8	9	9	10
7' 2" to 7' 10"	5	5	6	6	7	7	8	8	9	9	10	10	10
7' 10" to 8' 6"	5	6	6	7	7	8	8	9	9	10	10	11	11
8' 6" to 9' 2"	6	6	7	7	8	8	9	9	10	11	11	12	12
9' 2" to 9' 10"	6	7	7	8	8	9	9	10	11	11	12	12	13
9' 10" to 10' 6"	6	7	8	8	9	10	10	11	11	12	13	13	14
10' 6" to 11' 2"	7	7	8	9	9	10	11	11	12	13	13	14	15

Glossary

Baluster Plain or turned support for the handrail on a staircase.

Batten A narrow piece of wood, often used as fixing for tiles, fabric etc. Also known as furring strip (US).

Beading Timber or other material used as decoration.

Bracket A projecting right-angled support for strengthening or holding up a shelf or pelmet (valance).

Butt To join edge to edge but not to overlap.

Casement window A window that opens on a side hinge.

Chair rail Another name for dado rail.

Chalk line Another name for a plumb line made by snapping a taut piece of string that is covered with coloured chalk against a wall to get the true vertical.

Chipboard Board made from lots of wooden particles bonded together. Also known as particle board (US).

Cold chisel A chisel specially designed to chip away masonry.

Colourwash A base colour with several coats of thinned paint or glaze applied on top with loose brush strokes.

Cornice The plaster or wooden band at the junction of the ceiling and the wall. It can be shallow or deep, highly decorated or plain. Also known as crown molding (US).

Countersink A drill hole that allows the nail or screw to lie flush with the surface.

Coving Like a cornice but concave and not highly decorative.

Cross lining A preparation for walls when the lining paper is hung horizontally before painting or wallpapering.

Dado The lower portion of the wall when treated differently or separated from the rest of the wall by the dado rail.

Dado rail A horizontal rail applied to the wall at the height where traditionally the back of a chair would rest. A dado rail can be simulated by a wallpaper border.

Dormer window A vertical window built into the slope of the roof.

Dragging A paint effect where a brush is dragged across the wet glaze to reveal the base colour.

Eggshell An oil-based paint that has a slight sheen finish.

Emulsion A water-based paint that is quick drying. Also known as latex (US).

Glasspaper An abrasive paper, available in different grades, that is used to sand down surfaces as preparation or between coats of paint.

Glaze Commercial (scumble) or prepared transparent or semi-transparent colour used in paint effects to enrich the base coat.

Grain Direction of the straight weave of fabric or the growth of timber.

Grout A filler used between tiles to seal and make a level surface.

Hardboard Board made from compressed fibre. One side is rough to provide a key for adhesive making it a good surface for tiles.

Jamb The vertical sides of a door or window.

Key A roughened surface to which adhesive, paint or stain can adhere.

Laying off Finishing light brush strokes of paint or stain to give a smooth surface.

Louvre Horizontal slats that make up a door, window or shutters.

Marbling Paint effect used to give the effect of marble.

Mask To cover an area while an adjacent area is being decorated, for example when using a multi-coloured stencil.

Mitre To match the angles where two materials meet at a corner.

Molding A shaped trim of wood or plaster to give a decorative finish. Sometimes referred to as beading.

Mural A picture or pattern painted directly on to a wall.

Open plan A living area without partition walls.

Pelmet (valance) Wood or fabric (which may be stiffened and shaped or gathered) used to disguise the top of a window or four poster bed.

Picture rail A molded wooden rail set down from the ceiling from which to hang pictures.

Pile The raised surface on carpet or certain fabrics, such as velvet.

Polyurethane A synthetic resin used in varnishes, now the common name for a clear wood varnish.

Primer The first coat that seals and protects new wood or metal and prevents subsequent coats being absorbed.

Ragging A paint effect where rags or plastic bags are dipped in glaze or thinned paint and used to make a pattern on the base colour.

Relief decoration Wallcovering or plasterwork where the design stands out against the background.

Rose Decorated or plain central ceiling fitting, usually where the light is connected.

Scribe To make a mark parallel to a wall to show the cutting line.

Skirting board Wood, plaster or other trim around the edge where floor meets wall. Also known as baseboard (US).

Sponging Paint effect that uses a sponge to apply colour in a random way on a base coat.

Subfloor The floor on to which the main floor is laid.

Template A cutting guide used like a paper pattern.

Tongue-and-groove boards Wood panels used for cladding walls and ceilings with a tongue down one side which fits into the groove. Also available as a finish for flooring grade softwood or chipboard.

Trompe l'oeil Literally 'to deceive the eye'. A painted picture or pattern that seems three dimensional but is not.

Undercoat Coat of paint between the primer and the top coat to provide a good key and to blank out any darker colours beneath that might show through the top coat.

Universal Ceramic tile glazed on the chamfered edges to give a decorative finish.

Valance A frill of fabric used to cover the base of a bed or chair legs. Often used to describe a fabric pelmet above a window.

Wainscot Panelling applied to internal walls.

Fabric Chart

Fabric	Uses	Durability	Cleaning	Ease of handling	Available widths
CALICO (Unbleached cotton)	Tight upholstery (beneath loose covers/slipcovers), cushion pads	Several weights available, so check with shop assistant. Some types of calico also contain synthetic fibres	Natural cotton calico may shrink up to 10 per cent, so wash before sewing	Easy to sew	90–150 cm/36–60 in
CAMBRIC (Downproof)	This and other downproof fabrics such as ticking are used for making cushion pads, pillow pads and duvets	Firm weave makes the fabric durable, but various weights are available	Because of the feathers in items made of cambric, specialist cleaning is necessary	Easy to sew	140 cm/55 in
CHINTZ (Glazed or polished cotton, in plain colours or prints)	Curtains, pelmets (valances), blinds, bedspreads and drapes, cushions, loose covers (slipcovers), eiderdowns and upholstery (heavier weight only)	Varies according to quality; glazed finish helps to shed dust; avoid plain colours for covers and upholstery in family living rooms	May be washed (allow for up to 3 per cent shrinkage). Dry clean to retain glaze	Easy to handle, but work carefully as unpicked seams will show	120–150 cm/47–60 in
CORDUROY	Upholstery, cushions	Depending on the weight can be very durable; check when buying	Dry clean to avoid crushed pile	Moderately easy to sew; a thick pile can cause problems on heavy seams	120–150 cm/48–60 in
DOBBY (Plain fabric with texture and small woven motif)	Loose covers (slipcovers), upholstery	Hardwearing	Dry cleaning recommended, although some dobby weaves, with synthetic fibre content, may be washed	Extra bulk may make sewing a little more difficult	140 cm/55 in
FURNISHING COTTON (Plain weave cotton in prints or plain colours)	Curtains, pelmets (valances), blinds, bedspreads, cushions, loose covers (slipcovers); heavier upholstery weight furnishing cotton also available	Varies according to weight; fade resistant	Light to medium weights may be washed, but allow for up to 3 per cent shrinkage (40°F, hot iron); upholstery weight should be dry cleaned	Easy to sew, although heavier weights may be bulky	120–150 cm/47–60 in
INTERLINING (Soft, bulky fabric, normally white or off white, known as bump or domette)	Adds bulk and gives a soft drape to curtains, pelmets (valances), swags and tails, bedspreads and decorative table cloths	Tends to crush if used for items which are frequently handled	Dry clean only	Should be sewn by hand	120–130 cm/47–52 in

Fabric Chart

Fabric	Uses	Durability	Cleaning	Ease of handling	Available widths
LACE AND VOILE (Patterned and plain sheer fabrics)	Curtains, pelmets (valances), gathered blinds, throwover bedspreads, bed drapes, tablecloths, cushion covers	Delicate, small polyester content may help to improve wear	Hand or machine wash in pure soap solution, 40°F, cool iron	Tack carefully before sewing	140–150 cm/56–60 in; lace for pelmets (valances), 30–37.5 cm/12–15 in
LINEN UNION (Plain, textured weave and prints)	Curtains, pelmets (valances), drapes, simple blinds, cushions, loose covers (slipcovers) and upholstery	Hardwearing, due to fibre content: normally 60 per cent linen, 40 per cent cotton	Dry clean only	Fairly easy to handle, although it tends to fray, and may be bulky	140 cm/55 in
LINING (Plain cotton, with a slight satin weave, often white or off white)	Lining curtains, pelmets (valances), drapes, bedspreads, decorative table cloths	Good; improves the durability of curtains, bedspreads etc	Clean as for the main fabric. If main fabric is to be washed, wash both before sewing to prevent uneven shrinkage	Easy to sew	120–136 cm/47–52 in
OTTOMAN (Cotton fabric with a slightly ribbed weave, plain or lightly patterned)	Loose covers (slipcovers) and upholstery	Hardwearing	Dry clean only	Fairly easy to sew	140 cm/55 in
PLASTIC COATED FABRIC (Plastic covered cotton plain weave fabric)	Table cloths, aprons, covers for kitchen appliances. Not suitable for blinds or shower curtains	Very hard wearing, but tends to yellow with age	Wipe with a damp cloth. Do not wash or dry clean.	Easy to cut, but may be stiff to sew. Sandwich work between layers of tissue paper to help prevent sticking	140 cm/55 in
SATIN WEAVE (Cotton fabric, often with traditional print, woven to give a sheen finish)	Curtains, pelmets (valances), blinds, drapes, bedspreads, eiderdowns, loose covers (slipcovers) and upholstery	Wide range of qualities available, so check with shop assistant	Wash (40°F, medium hot iron) or dry clean	Fairly easy to sew, but make sure you have plenty of room to handle large items	122–135 cm/48–54 in
VELVET (Cotton, synthetic or mixed fibres)	Curtains, drapes, cushions, upholstery, decorative tablecloths	Hardwearing, but quality may vary; check when buying	Must be dry cleaned	Difficult to handle. Make sure the pile runs in the same direction on all sections. Mark fabric on the wrong side when cutting out. Sew in the direction of the pile.	120–140 cm/48–54 in

LAURA ASHLEY SHOPS

AUSTRALIA
The Gallerie,
Gawler Place,
ADELAIDE,
South Australia 5000

1036 High Street,
ARMADALE,
Victoria 3134

Shop 84,
Wintergarden,
171 Queen Street,
BRISBANE,
Queensland 4000

Shop 58,
The Gallery,
Lemon Grove,
Victoria Avenue,
CHATSWOOD,
N.S.W. 2067

3 Transvaal Avenue,
DOUBLE BAY,
N.S.W. 2028

Shop 49,
Market Square,
Moorabool Street,
GEELONG,
Victoria 3220

Centrepoint,
209 Murray Street,
HOBART,
Tasmania 7000

Shop 36,
State Bank Centre,
385 Bourke Street,
MELBOURNE,
Victoria 3000

Shop 6,
30 Collins Street,
MELBOURNE,
Victoria 3000

179 Collins Street,
MELBOURNE,
Victoria 3000

City Arcade,
Hay Street Level,
PERTH,
Western Australia 6000

Mezzanine Level –
Centrepoint,
Castlereagh Street,
SYDNEY,
N.S.W.

AUSTRIA
Judengasse 11,
SALZBURG

Weihburggasse 5,
1010 VIENNA

BELGIUM
Frankrijklei 27,
2000 ANTWERP

32 Rue de Namur,
1000 BRUSSELS
(Home Furnishings only)

81/83 Rue de Namur,
1000 BRUSSELS
(Garments only)

32 Le Sablon
1000 BRUSSELS
(Decorator Showroom)

CANADA
2110 Crescent Street,
MONTREAL,
Quebec,
H3G 2B8

136 Bank Street,
OTTAWA,
Ontario,
K1P 5N8

2452 Wilfred Laurier Bld,
STE-FOY,
Quebec,
G1V 2L1

18 Hazelton Avenue,
TORONTO,
Ontario,
M5R 2E2

1171 Robson Street,
VANCOUVER,
British Columbia,
V6E 1B5

Bayview Village Shopping
Center,
2901 Bayview Avenue,
WILLOWDALE,
Ontario,
M2K 1E6

FRANCE
4 Rue Joseph Cabassol,
13100 AIX EN PROVENCE

2 Place du Palais,
Porte Cailhau,
33000 BORDEAUX

Centre Commercial
'Grand Var',
Avenue de l'Université,
83160 LA VALETTE
(Au Printemps)

Niveau 1,
Centre Commercial Parly 2,
Avenue Charles de Gaulle,
78150 LE CHESNAY
(Au Printemps)

Rez de Chaussée,
39–45 Rue Nationale,
59800 LILLE
(Au Printemps)

98 Rue Président Edouard
Herriot,
69002 LYON

Galeries Lafayette,
6 Avenue Jean Medicin,
0600 NICE

Galeries Lafayette,
40 Bld Haussmann,
75009 PARIS

Nouveau Magasin,
2 ième Etage,
64 Bld Haussmann,
75009 PARIS
(Au Printemps)

Le Printemps de la Mason,
7 ième Etage,
64 Bld Haussmann,
75009 PARIS

95 Avenue Raymond Poincaré,
75016 PARIS

94 Rue de Rennes,
75006 PARIS

261 Rue Saint Honoré,
75001 PARIS

34 Rue de Grenelle,
75007 PARIS
(Decorator Showroom)

5 ième Etage,
1–5 Rue de la Haute Montée,
67004 STRASBOURG CEDEX
(Au Printemps)

2 Rue du Temple Neuf,
67000 STRASBOURG

50 Rue Boulbonne,
31000 TOULOUSE

Niveau 3,
Avenue de l'Europe,
Centre Commercial Velizy II,
78140 VELIZY VILLACOUBLAY
(Au Printemps)

ITALY
Via Brera 4,
20121 MILAN

IRELAND
9–10 Merchants Quay,
CORK

7 Dawson Street,
DUBLIN 2

60–61 Grafton Street
DUBLIN 2

JAPAN
14–15 3-Chome Sakae,
Naka-ku 460,
NAGOYA-SHI

10–12 6-Chome Ginza,
Chuo-ku 104,
TOKYO

NETHERLANDS
Leidsestraat 7,
1017 NS AMSTERDAM

Bakkerstraat 17,
6811 EG ARNHEM

Demer 24A,
5611 AS EINDHOVEN

Papestraat 17,
2513 AV S-GRAVENHAGE

M. Smedenstraat 9,
6211 GK MAASTRICHT

Lijnbaan 63,
3012 EL ROTTERDAM

Oude Gracht 141,
3511 AJ UTRECHT

SWITZERLAND
Stadthausgasse 18,
4051 BASEL

8 Rue Verdaine,
1204 GENEVA

Augustinergasse 21,
8001 ZURICH

WEST GERMANY
Am Holzgraben 1–3,
AACHEN

Karlstrasse 15,
8900 AUGSBURG

Im Kadewe,
Tauentzienstr 21–24,
1000 BERLIN 30

Niedernstrasse 14,
4800 BIELEFELD

Sögestrasse 54,
2800 BREMEN 4

Hohestrasse 160–168,
5000 COLOGNE

Hunsrückenstrasse 43,
4000 DUSSELDORF

Goethestrasse 3,
6000 FRANKFURT AM MAIN

Neuer Wall 73–75,
2000 HAMBURG

Georgstrasse 36,
3000 HANOVER

Kaiserstrasse 187,
7500 KARLSRUHE

Ludgeriestrasse 79,
4400 MUENSTER

Sendlingerstrasse 37,
8000 MUNICH

Ludwigplatz 7,
3500 NUERNBERG

Breite Strasse 2,
7000 STUTTGART

Langgasse 30,
6200 WIESBADEN

UNITED KINGDOM
191–197 Union Street,
ABERDEEN

10 Hale Leys,
AYLESBURY

43 Market Place,
BANBURY

56A Eastgate Centre,
BASILDON

Winchester Road,
BASINGSTOKE
(Sainsbury's Homebase)

The Old Red House,
8–9 New Bond Street,
BATH

Pines Way,
BATH
(Sainsbury's Homebase)

75 High Street,
BEDFORD

38/40 Toll Gavel,
BEVERLEY

Unit 28,
The Pavilions,
38 High Street,
BIRMINGHAM

17 South Street,
BISHOP'S STORTFORD

1 Parkinson Way,
BLACKPOOL
(Sainsbury's Homebase)

80 Old Christchurch Road,
BOURNEMOUTH
(Home Furnishings)

58 Commercial Road,
BOURNEMOUTH
(Garments only)

762 Harrogate Road,
BRADFORD
(Sainsbury's Homebase)

Redlands,
Parkstone,
BRANKSOME,
Poole
(Sainsbury's Homebase)

45 East Street,
BRIGHTON
(Garments only)

The Square,
Brighton Marina Village,
BRIGHTON
(LA Home & Garments)

62 Queens Road,
Clifton,
BRISTOL

39 Broadmead,
BRISTOL

56–58 Cornhill,
BURY ST EDMUNDS

14 Trinity Street,
CAMBRIDGE

41–42 Burgate,
CANTERBURY

11 Queen Street,
CARDIFF

Colchester Avenue,
off Newport Road,
Roath,
CARDIFF
(Sainsbury's Homebase)

3–4 Grapes Lane,
CARLISLE

10–13 Grays Brewery Yard,
Springfield Road,
CHELMSFORD

100 The Promenade,
CHELTENHAM

17–19 Watergate Row,
CHESTER
(Home Furnishings)

50 Eastgate Row,
CHESTER
(Garments only)

4 Portfield Retail Park,
Westhampnet Way,
CHICHESTER
(Sainsbury's Homebase)

32 North Street,
CHICHESTER

4–5 Trinity Square,
COLCHESTER

St Andrews Avenue,
COLCHESTER
(Sainsbury's Homebase)

Junction Fletchampstead
Highway & Sir Henry
Parks Road,
COVENTRY
(Sainsbury's Homebase)

Stadium Way,
CRAYFORD
(Sainsbury's Homebase)

6–10 Albert Street,
DERBY

Kingsway,
DERBY
(Sainsbury's Homebase)

129–131 Terminus Road,
EASTBOURNE

90 George Street,
EDINBURGH
(Home Furnishings)

137 George Street,
EDINBURGH
(Decorator Showroom)

126 Princes Street,
EDINBURGH
(Garments only)

41–42 High Street,
EXETER

The Barn,
Lion & Lamb Yard,
FARNHAM

Metro Centre,
GATESHEAD

84–90 Buchanan Street,
GLASGOW

215 Sauchiehall Street,
GLASGOW

St Oswalds Road,
GLOUCESTER
(Sainsbury's Homebase)

Old Cloth Hall,
North Street,
GUILDFORD

3–5 James Street,
HARROGATE

Oldings Corner,
Comet Way,
HATFIELD
(Sainsbury's Homebase)

7 Commercial Street,
HEREFORD

30 White Hart Street,
HIGH WYCOMBE

121–123 Bancroft,
HITCHIN

3–4 Middle Street,
HORSHAM

Priory Sidings,
Sainsbury Way,
Hesle Road,
Hessle,
HULL
(Sainsbury's Homebase)

714–720 High Road,
7 Kings,
ILFORD
(Sainsbury's Homebase)

Felixstowe Road,
IPSWICH
(Sainsbury's Homebase)

17 Buttermarket,
IPSWICH

48–49 High Street,
KING'S LYNN

108 The Parade,
LEAMINGTON SPA

Church Institute,
9 Lands Lane,
LEEDS

King Lane,
Moortown,
LEEDS
(Sainsbury's Homebase)

37 Putney Road,
LEICESTER
(Sainsbury's Homebase)

310 High Street,
LINCOLN

Unit 16,
Clayton Square,
LIVERPOOL

30 Great Oak Street,
LLANIDLOES

LONDON:

256–258 Regent Street,
Oxford Circus,
LONDON W1

449–451 Oxford Street,
LONDON W1

96B Kensington High Street,
LONDON W8

Warwick Road,
LONDON W8
(Sainsbury's Homebase)

35–36 Bow Street,
LONDON WC2

7–9 Harriet Street,
LONDON SW1

71–73 Lower Sloane Street,
LONDON SW1
(Decorator Collection)

47–49 Brompton Road,
LONDON SW3
(Garments only)

120 Kings Road,
LONDON SW3
(Garments only)

157 Fulham Road,
LONDON SW3

Unit 22,
The Spires,
BARNET

D6/V13 Brent Cross Shopping
Centre,
BRENT CROSS,
London NW4
(Garments only)

62 High Street,
BROMLEY

10 Beckenham Hills Road,
CATFORD,
London SE6
(Sainsbury's Homebase)

11–12 Drummond Place,
CROYDON
(LA Home & Garments)

50 Purley Way,
CROYDON
(Sainsbury's Homebase)

5 The Broadway,
EALING,
London W5

36–37 High Street,
HAMPSTEAD,
London NW3

Rookery Way,
The Hyde,
HENDON,
London NW9
(Sainsbury's Homebase)

714–720 High Road,
Seven Kings,
ILFORD
(Sainsbury's Homebase)

The Griffin,
Market Place,
KINGSTON–UPON–THAMES
(Home Furnishings)

32–33 Market Place,
KINGSTON–UPON–THAMES
(Garments only)

229–253 Kingston Road,
NEW MALDEN
(Sainsbury's Homebase)

3 Station Road,
NEW SOUTHGATE,
London W8
(Sainsbury's Homebase)

45 Oakfield Road,
off Penge High Street,
PENGE,
London SE20
(Sainsbury's Homebase)

68–70 George Street,
RICHMOND

3–4 Times Square,
SUTTON

2c Fulborne Road,
WALTHAMSTOW,
London E17
(Sainsbury's Homebase)

473 High Street,
WILLESDEN,
London NW10
(Sainsbury's Homebase)

Weir Road,
WIMBLEDON
(Sainsbury's Homebase)

Enterprise Way,
LUTON
(Sainsbury's Homebase)

8–10 King Street,
MAIDSTONE

28 King Street,
MANCHESTER

48 Linthorpe Road,
MIDDLESBROUGH

40–42 Midsummer Arcade,
MILTON KEYNES

45 High Street,
NEWCASTLE–UNDER–LYME

33 Brook Lane,
NEWCASTLE–UNDER–LYME
(Sainsbury's Homebase)

Unit 3,
Eldon Square,
NEWCASTLE–UPON–TYNE

36 High Street,
NEWPORT

Unit 3B,
Peacock Place,
NORTHAMPTON
(Garments only)

Victoria Promenade,
NORTHAMPTON
(Sainsbury's Homebase)

19 London Street,
NORWICH

Mousehold Lane,
Roundtree Way,
NORWICH
(Sainsbury's Homebase)

58 Bridlesmith Gate,
NOTTINGHAM

Castle Marina Park,
Castle Boulevard,
NOTTINGHAM
(Sainsbury's Homebase)

50 Halesowen Street,
OLDBURY
(Sainsbury's Homebase)

26–27 Cornmarket,
OXFORD
(Decorator Showroom)

26–27 Little Clarendon Street,
OXFORD
(Garments only)

10 High Street,
OXFORD
(Home Furnishings)

189–191 High Street,
PERTH

Unit 90,
Queensgate Centre,
PETERBOROUGH

The Armada Centre,
PLYMOUTH

1 Western Approach,
PLYMOUTH
(Sainsbury's Homebase)

32 Fishergate,
PRESTON

Claydon's Lane,
RAYLEIGH WEIR
(Sainsbury's Homebase)

75–76 Broad Street,
READING

50 Kenavon Drive,
READING
(Sainsbury's Homebase)

Rom Valley Way,
ROMFORD
(Sainsbury's Homebase)

13 Market Place,
ST ALBANS

49–51 New Canal,
SALISBURY

87 Pinstone Street,
SHEFFIELD

401 Chesterfield Road,
Woodseats,
SHEFFIELD
(Sainsbury's Homebase)

65 Wyle Cop,
SHREWSBURY

Unit 13,
Craven Court,
SKIPTON

124 High Street,
SOLIHULL

2 Above Bar Church,
High Street,
SOUTHAMPTON

Lordshill Shopping Centre,
SOUTHAMPTON
(Sainsbury's Homebase)

107 High Street,
SOUTHEND

465–467 Lord Street,
SOUTHPORT

4 Great Portwood Street,
STOCKPORT
(Sainsbury's Homebase)

Unit 1A,
The Warren Bulkeley,
Warren Road,
STOCKPORT

41–42 Henley Street,
STRATFORD-UPON-AVON

Unit 4, 164 The Parade,
Grace Church Centre,
SUTTON COLDFIELD

Quay Parade,
SWANSEA
(Sainsbury's Homebase)

19E Regent Street,
SWINDON

2–4 High Street,
TAUNTON

19–21 High Street,
TENTERDEN

Units 5 & 24,
Fleet Walk,
TORQUAY

7 Pydar Street,
TRURO

61 Calverley Road,
TUNBRIDGE WELLS

Ing's Road,
WAKEFIELD
(Sainsbury's Homebase)

1 Bradford Place,
WALSALL
(Sainsbury's Homebase)

Sturlas Way,
WALTHAM CROSS
(Sainsbury's Homebase)

50 Halesowen Street,
WARLEY
West Midlands

Unit 3,
1–7 The Parade,
High Street,
WATFORD

114 St Albans Road,
WATFORD
(Sainsbury's Homebase)

North Wall District Centre,
Queensway,
Worle,
WESTON-SUPER-MARE
(Sainsbury's Homebase)

17 Grove Street,
WILMSLOW

126 High Street,
WINCHESTER

32 Peascod Street,
WINDSOR
(Garments only)

99–101 Peascod Street,
WINDSOR
(LA Home)

54–55 Dudley Street,
WOLVERHAMPTON

Crown Passage,
Broad Street,
WORCESTER

Hylton Road,
WORCESTER
(Sainsbury's Homebase)

Unit 28,
Vicarage Walk,
Quedam Centre,
YEOVIL

7 Daveygate,
YORK

Junction Monkgate/Foss Bank,
YORK
(Sainsbury's Homebase)

UNITED STATES
Crossgates Mall,
120 Washington Avenue
Extension,
ALBANY, NY 12203

139 Main Street,
ANNAPOLIS, MD 21401

514 East Washington Street,
ANN ARBOR, MI 48104

29 Surburban Square,
ARDMORE, PA 19003

Lenox Square,
3393 Peachtree Road,
ATLANTA, GA 30326

Perimeter Mall,
4400 Ashford-Dunwoody
Road,
ATLANTA, GA 30346

Highland Mall 1224,
6001 Airport Boulevard,
AUSTIN, TX 78752

Pratt Street Pavilion,
Harborplace,
BALTIMORE, MD 21202

203 Beachwood Place,
26300 Cedar Road,
BEACHWOOD, OH 44122

200–219 Riverchase
Galleria Mall,
BIRMINGHAM, AL 35244

180 Town Center Mall,
BOCA RATON, FL 33431

83 Newbury Street,
BOSTON, MA 02116

23 Church Street,
BURLINGTON, VT 05401

Charles Square,
5 Bennett Street,
CAMBRIDGE, MA 02138

Charleston Place,
130 Market Street,
CHARLESTON, SC 29401

The Mall at Chesnut Hill,
199 Boylston Street,
CHESNUT HILL, MA 02167

Watertower Place,
835 N. Michigan Avenue,
CHICAGO, IL 60611

The Citadel,
750 Citadel Drive E. 2008,
COLORADO SPRINGS,
CO 80909

The Village,
CORTE MADERA,
CA 94925

3333 Bristol Street,
South Coast Plaza,
COSTA MESA, CA 92629

Galleria 13350 Dallas Parkway,
Suite 1585,
DALLAS, TX 75240

423 North Park Center,
DALLAS, TX 75225

Danbury Fair Mall C-118,
7 Backus Avenue,
DANBURY,
CT 06810

1439 Larimer Street,
DENVER, CO 80202

The Kaleidoscope at the Hub,
555 Walnut Street,
Suite 218,
DES MOINES, IA 50309

Twelve Oaks Mall,
27498 Novi Road,
Suite A,
DETROIT, MI 48056

Galleria Shopping Center,
3505 West 69th Street,
EDINA, MN 55435

11822 Fair Oaks Mall,
FAIRFAX, VA 22033

West Farms Mall,
FARMINGTON, CT 06032

2492 E. Sunrise Boulevard,
Galleria Mall,
FORT LAUDERDALE,
FL 33304

213 Hulen Mall,
FORT WORTH, TX 76132

321 Greenwich Avenue,
GREENWICH, CT 06830

Riverside Square Mall,
HACKENSACK, NJ 07601

Ala Moana Center 2246,
HONOLULU, HI 96814

The Galleria,
5015 Westheimer,
Suite 2120,
HOUSTON, TX 77056

1000 West Oaks Mall,
Suite 124,
HOUSTON, TX 77082

Fashion Mall,
8702 Keystone Crossing,
INDIANAPOLIS, IN 46240

Country Club Plaza,
308 W. 47th Street,
KANSAS CITY,
MO 64112

The Esplanade,
1401 W. Esplanade,
KENNER, LA 70065

White Flint Shopping Mall,
11301 Rockville Pike,
KENSINGSTON, MD 20895

7852 Girard Avenue,
LA JOLLA, CA 92037

Pavilion in the Park,
8201 Cantrell Road,
LITTLE ROCK, AR 72207

10250 Santa Monica Boulevard,
LOS ANGELES, CA 90067

Beverly Center,
121 N. La Cienaga Boulevard,
Suite 739,
LOS ANGELES, CA 90048

Louisville Galleria 109,
LOUISVILLE, KY 40202

2042 Northern Boulevard,
Americana Shopping Center,
MANHASSET, NY 11030

The Falls,
Space 373,
8888 Howard Drive,
MIAMI, FL 33176

The Grand Avenue,
275 W. Wisconsin Avenue 5,
MILWAUKEE, WI 53203

208 City Center,
40 South 7th Street,
MINNEAPOLIS, MN 55402

The Mall at Green Hills,
2148 Abbot Martin Road,
NASHVILLE, TN 37215

260–262 College Street,
NEW HAVEN, CT 06510

333 Canal Street,
151 Canal Place,
NEW ORLEANS,
LA 70130

714 Madison Avenue,
NEW YORK,
NY 10021
(Home Furnishings)

398 Columbus Avenue,
NEW YORK,
NY 10024

21 East 57th Street,
NEW YORK, NY 10021
(Garments only)

2164 Northbrook Court,
NORTHBROOK, IL 60062

224 Oakbrook Center,
OAKBROOK, IL 60521

Owings Mills Town Center,
10300 Mill Run Circle 1062,
OWINGS MILLS,
MD 21117

320 Worth Avenue,
PALM BEACH,
FL 33480

469 Desert Fashion Plaza,
123 North Palm Canyon Drive,
PALM SPRINGS, CA 92262

12 Stanford Shopping Center,
PALO ALTO, CA 94304

221 Paramus Park,
Route 17,
PARAMUS, NJ 07652

401 South Lake Avenue,
PASADENA, CA 91101

1721 Walnut Street,
PHILADELPHIA,
PA 19103

Biltmore Fashion Park,
2478 E. Camelback Road,
PHOENIX, AZ 85016

20 Commerce Court,
Station Square,
PITTSBURGH, PA 15219

1000 Ross Park Mall,
PITTSBURGH,
PA 15237

2100 Collin Creek Mall,
811 No. Central Expressway,
PLANO, TX 75075

419 S.W. Morrison Street,
PORTLAND, OR 97204

46 Nassau Street,
Palmer Square,
PRINCETON,
NJ 08544

2 Davol Square Mall,
Point & Eddy Street,
PROVIDENCE,
RI 02903

Crabtree Valley Mall,
4325 Glenwood Avenue,
RALEIGH,
NC 27612

South Bay Galleria,
1815 Hawthorne Boulevard,
Space 172,
REDONDO BEACH,
CA 90278

Commercial Block,
1217 E. Cary Street,
RICHMOND,
VA 23219

Regency Square Mall,
1404 Parham Road,
RICHMOND, VA 23229

531 Pavilions Lane,
SACRAMENTO, CA 95825

74 Plaza Frontenac,
ST LOUIS, MO 63131

St Louis Center C-330
515 N. 6th Street,
ST LOUIS, MO 63101

247 Horton Plaza,
Space 265,
SAN DIEGO, CA 92101

1827 Union Street,
SAN FRANCISCO, CA 94123

563 Sutter Street,
SAN FRANCISCO, CA 94102
(Decorator Showroom)

Suite 1224,
North Star Mall,
7400 SAN PEDRO,
San Antonio, TX 78216

La Cumbre Galleria,
3891 State Street 109,
SANTA BARBARA, CA 93105

Valley Fair Mall,
Suite 1031,
2855 Stevens Creek Boulevard,
SAN JOSE, CA 95050

696 White Plains Road,
SCARSDALE,
NY 10583

F-331 Woodfield Mall,
SCHAUMBURG, IL 60173

405 University Street,
SEATTLE, DC 98101

The Mall at Short Hills,
SHORT HILLS, NJ 07078

20 Old Orchard Shopping
Centre,
SKOKIE, IL 60077

Stamford Town Center,
100 Greyrock Place,
STAMFORD, CT 06902

139 Main Street,
STONY BROOK, NY 11790

Old Hyde Park Village,
718 S. Village Circle,
TAMPA, FL 33606

2845 Somerset Mall,
TROY, MI 48084

Utica Square,
1846 21 Street,
TULSA, OK 74114

1171 Broadway Plaza,
WALNUT CREEK, CA 94596

3213 M. Street NW,
Georgetown,
WASHINGTON, DC 20007

85 Main Street,
WESTPORT, CT 06880

Bullocks Westwood Shops,
10861 Weyburn Avenue,
WESTWOOD, CA 90025

422 Duke of Gloucester Street,
WILLIAMSBURG, VA 23185

740 Hanes Mall,
WINSTON-SALEM, NC 27103

279 Promenade Mall,
WOODLANDS HILLS, CA 91367

108 Worthington Square Mall,
WORTHINGTON, OH 43085

OTHER STOCKISTS
18 Ioannou Metaxa Street,
Glyfada,
ATHENS,
Greece

28 Herodotou Street,
10673 Kolonaki,
ATHENS,
Greece

Engen 51,
5000 BERGEN,
Norway

Via Val d'Aposa 30E,
40121 BOLOGNA,
Italy

Via Dante 69,
09100 CAGLIARI,
Sardinia

Via Senna 58,
50019 FLORENCE,
Italy

O. Hamngat 46–48,
41107 GOTHENBURG,
Sweden

Unioninkatu 32,
HELSINKI 10,
Finland

29 Wyndham Street,
Central,
HONG KONG

F26–28,
Yow Chuan Plaza,
Jalan Tun Razal,
KUALA LUMPUR
Malaysia

Via Rampe,
Brancaccio N5,
80132 NAPLES,
Italy

Riddervoldsgate 10B,
OSLO 2,
Norway

Steinwall,
Rua Formosa 340,
PORTO,
Portugal

Via Danta 19,
90139 PALERMO,
Sicily

Laugavegi 99,
REYKJAVIK,
Iceland

Piazza S. Lorenzo in
Lucina 2,
01886 ROME,
Italy

PO Box 477,
SEOUL,
South Korea

6–8 Scotts Road,
03–06/7 Scotts Shopping Centre,
SINGAPORE

Jakobsbergsgat 6,
11144 STOCKHOLM,
Sweden

Via Andrea Doria 21,
10123 TURIN,
Italy

MAIL ORDER
Frankrijklei 27,
2000 ANTWERP,
Belgium

Lerzenstrasse 14,
8953 DIETIKON,
Switzerland

7 Dawson Street,
DUBLIN 2,
Ireland

Monschaustrasse 1,
4000 DUSSELDORF,
West Germany

Postbus 128,
5700 AC HELMOND,
Netherlands

PO Box 891,
MAHWAH,
NJ 07430,
United States

Via Brera 4,
20121 MILAN,
Italy

Box 19 Mail Order Dept.,
NEWTOWN POWYS,
Wales

27 BP 93212 La Plaine,
SAINT-DENIS,
France

3442 Griffith Street,
ST. LAURENT,
Quebec,
Canada

Weihburggasse 5,
1010 VIENNA,
Austria

INDEX

Page numbers in *italic* refer to illustrations

Acknowledgements

Photographs are reproduced courtesy of the following photographers, agencies and magazines (abbreviations: LA = Laura Ashley; W & N = Weidenfeld & Nicolson; EWA = Elizabeth Whiting & Associates; WPN = World Press Network). Figures refer to page numbers.

1 Andrew Twort © LA; **2–3** David Garcia © LA/W&N; **4** left & right David Garcia © LA; **5** left & right David Garcia © LA; centre Andreas von Einseidel © LA; **8–9** Andrew Twort © LA; **10** above © Fritz von der Schulenburg (Peter Farlow, Mimi O'Connell); below David Garcia © LA; **11** David Garcia © LA/W&N; **12** above David Davidson © W&N; below left © Fritz von der Schulenburg (John Stefanidis); below right David Garcia © LA/W&N; **13** © Fritz von der Schulenburg, *Country Homes and Interiors*/WPN; **14** left © Fritz von der Schulenburg; above right Arabella Ashley © LA/W&N; below right © Tom Leighton/EWA; **15** above LA Archives; below left © Fritz von der Schulenburg; below right Arabella Ashley © LA/W&N; **16** left Arabella Ashley © LA; above right © Rodney Hyett/EWA; below right © Tom Leighton/EWA; **17** above left © Fritz von der Schulenburg; above right Arabella Ashley © LA/W&N; below David Garcia © LA; **18** left David Garcia © LA/W&N; above right Arabella Ashley © LA/W&N; below right © Fritz von der Schulenburg (Peter Westenholz); **19** above left, above right & below left David Garcia © LA; below right © Rodney Hyett/EWA; **20** above left & above right © Fritz von der Schulenburg; below right LA Archives; **21** above © Spike Powell/EWA; below © Tim Beddow, *Country Homes and Interiors*/WPN; **22** left & above right © Fritz von der Schulenburg; below right LA Archives; **23** above right & below left © Fritz von der Schulenburg; above left Fritz von der Schulenburg © W&N; below right LA Archives; **24** left © Fritz von der Schulenburg; above right John Mason © LA; below right *The World of Interiors*; **25** above left David Garcia © LA; above right David Garcia © LA/W&N; below left *The World of Interiors*; below right © Fritz von der Schulenburg (Judy Falcon); **26** © Fritz von der Schulenburg; **27** David Garcia © LA; **28** above Arabella Ashley © LA/W&N; below David Garcia © LA/W&N; **29** Andreas von Einseidel © LA; **30** left © Andreas von Einseidel/EWA; right © Fritz von der Schulenburg; **31** © Fritz von der Schulenburg; **32** David Garcia © LA/W&N; **33** © Richard Bryant/ARCAID; **34** left © Fritz von der Schulenburg (Mimi O'Connell); right David Garcia © LA/W&N; **35** © Fritz von der Schulenburg

(Anne Griggs); **36** left Andrew Twort © LA; right Chris Drake, *Country Homes and Interiors*/WPN; **37** David Garcia © LA; **38** left David Garcia © LA; right Andreas von Einseidel © LA; **39** David Garcia © LA; **40** David Garcia © LA/W&N; **41** above © Richard Bryant/ARCAID; below © Rodney Hyett/EWA; **42** David Garcia © LA/W&N; **43** left David Garcia © LA; right David Garcia © LA/W&N; **44** Andreas von Einseidel © LA; **45** Andrew Twort © LA; **46** David Garcia © LA; **47** David Garcia © LA; **48** above Andrew Twort © LA; below Peter Woloszynski, *Country Homes and Interiors*/WPN; **49** above left & below David Garcia © LA; above right David Garcia © LA/W&N; **54** above © Michael Dunne/EWA; below © Andreas von Einseidel/EWA; **55** left © Spike Powell/EWA; above © John Donat/EWA; below © Fritz von der Schulenburg; **58** above & below © Fritz von der Schulenburg (Peter Farlow, Mimi O'Connell); **59** above © Fritz von der Schulenburg (Peter Farlow, Mimi O'Connell); below © Fritz von der Schulenburg (Verona Stencilling); below left David Garcia © LA/W&N; **68** above © Gary Chowanetz/EWA; below © Kate Zari; **69** above David Garcia © LA/W&N; below David Garcia © LA; **72** © Fritz von der Schulenburg (Peter Farlow, Mimi O'Connell); **78** below left Arabella Ashley © LA; below right Andreas von Einseidel © LA; **79** Simon Brown © LA; **84** above & below David Garcia © LA; **85** above Andrew Twort © LA; below Shona Wood/Robert & Colleen Bery Designs; **88** above David Garcia © LA; below © Fritz von der Schulenburg (Peter Farlow, Mimi O'Connell); **89** above left David Garcia © LA; above right Trevor Richard © LA; below David Garcia © LA/W&N; **92–3** David Garcia © LA; **94** above © Spike Powell/EWA; below LA Archives; **95** left © Andreas von Einseidel/EWA; right © Spike Powell/EWA; **96** David Garcia © LA; **97** above left Andreas von Einseidel © LA; above right David Garcia © LA/W&N; below left, right & centre LA Archives; **98–9** Richard Green (A. C. Cooper Ltd) © W&N; **106** above Keith Scott Morton © LA/W&N; below David Garcia © LA; **107** left David Garcia © LA/W&N; above © Fritz von der Schulenburg (B. Thornhill); below David Garcia © LA; **112** left © Fritz von der Schulenburg; right Keith Scott-Morton © LA/W&N; **113** David Garcia © LA/W&N; **116** left Andrew Twort © LA; right David Garcia © LA/W&N; **117** above Jan Baldwin, *Homes and Gardens*/WPN; below left © Jerry Tubby/EWA; below right Andrew Twort © LA; **122** left David Garcia © LA/W&N; right David Garcia © LA/W&N; **123** above left © Di Lewis/EWA; above right © Fritz von der

Schulenburg (Peter Farlow, Mimi O'Connell); below Simon Brown © LA; **126–7** David Garcia © LA; **128** above Fritz von der Schulenburg © LA/W&N; below Trevor Richards © LA; below right David Garcia © LA; **129** Andrew Twort © LA; **130** left Andrew Twort © LA; right David Garcia © LA; **131** above David Garcia © LA; below left Trevor Richards © LA; below right David Garcia © LA; **134** left & right Trevor Richards © LA; **135** above & below David Garcia © LA/W&N; **140** © Fritz von der Schulenburg; **141** above left, above right, below centre David Garcia © LA; below right John Mason © LA; below left David Garcia © LA/W&N; **146** above Peter Andersen, *Country Homes and Interiors*/WPN; below Trevor Richards © LA; **147** above Simon Brown © LA; below left © Fritz von der Schulenburg; below right Arabella Ashley © LA; **150–1** Simon Brown © LA; **152** above © Michael Dunne/EWA; below David Garcia © LA; **153** Peter Andersen, *Country Homes and Interiors*/WPN; **154** © Fritz von der Schulenburg (Peter Westenholz); **155** above Bill Batten © LA; below © Richard Bryant/ARCAID; **160** Andrew Twort © LA; **161** above, below right & below left LA Archives; **166** David Garcia © LA/ELLE; **167** above left © Jerry Tubby/EWA; above right David Garcia © LA/ELLE; below David Garcia © LA; **168** above & below David Garcia © LA; **169** John Mason © LA; **174–5** LA Archives; **176** Trevor Richards © LA; **177** above Andreas von Einseidel © LA; below left David Garcia © LA/W&N; below right LA Archives; **178** above left David Garcia © LA/W&N; above right © Richard Bryant/ARCAID; below left Trevor Richards © LA; below right Andrew Twort © LA; **179** above left David Garcia © LA/W&N; above right © Richard Bryant/ARCAID; below left Trevor Richards © LA; below right Andrew Twort © LA; **180** left Andrew Twort © LA; right LA Archives; **181** above © Fritz von der Schulenburg; below left & below right David Garcia © LA/W&N; **182** above left LA Archives; above right © Jan Baldwin; below left & below right © Fritz von der Schulenburg (John Stefanidis/below right); **183** © Clive Helm/EWA; **186** left David Garcia © LA; right David Garcia © LA/W&N; **187** left David Garcia © LA; above right Trevor Richards © LA; below right © Andreas von Einseidel; **190** above and below © Fritz von der Schulenburg (Brian Junos/below); **191** above © Neil Lorimer/EWA; below left David Garcia © LA; below right © Fritz von der Schulenburg (Anne Griggs).

Appendix illustrations: Antony Duke and Nicki Kemball.